Thomas Daniel
of
Colonial Virginia
and Eight Generations
of His Descendants

Kevin W. Daniel

HERITAGE BOOKS
2019

HERITAGE BOOKS

AN IMPRINT OF HERITAGE BOOKS, INC.

Books, Cds, and more—Worldwide

For our listing of thousands of titles see our website
at
www.HeritageBooks.com

Published 2019 by
HERITAGE BOOKS, INC.
Publishing Division
5810 Ruatan Street
Berwyn Heights, Md. 20740

Copyright © 1995 Kevin W. Daniel

International Standard Book Numbers
Paperbound: 978-0-7884-0235-7
Clothbound: 978-0-7884-6932-9

TABLE OF CONTENTS

CHAPTER	PAGE NUMBER

TABLE OF CONTENTS

CHAPTER	PAGE NUMBER

INTRODUCTION

This book has two main goals. The first goal is to preserve information, pictures and family traditions that I feared were being lost while I was spending time in researching the origins of our Daniel family. Several people, kinfolk and family friends, with unique information and artifacts concerning our family have passed on in the seven years I have been engaged in research. Most of the pictures are included in this book with the hope of ensuring their survival and the knowledge of the identity of those portrayed in them. My second goal is to aid other Daniel family researchers in determining if there is a connection to our family. If this book also entertains the reader in some fashion that is an extra dividend.

Facts about the life and ancestry of our earliest identifiable ancestor, Thomas Daniel, are obscure. Several other researchers have undertaken exhaustive examinations of the various Daniel families in Colonial Virginia, so if the ancestry of our family there was readily apparent it would surely have been set forth by one of these other authors. I spent some time in reviewing their works and conducting my own research in the records of various likely counties in Kentucky and Virginia but have so far been unsuccessful in discovering proof as to the ancestry of Thomas Daniel or even clear proof of the names of his wife(s) or children.

One of the researchers that I referred to in the previous paragraph was Charles Brunk Heineman. His Daniel ancestors lived in Clark and Montgomery counties, Kentucky at the same time and near where ours did. His research in Kentucky and Virginia was meticulous. He was also aware of the work of all of the other credible Daniel researchers up to the time that he published his book in 1949. His book is available on microfilm through local LDS Family History Centers. He comes closer than any other author in distinguishing between the various

Daniel families in Colonial Virginia. I do feel, though, that he did not thoroughly examine the Daniel families in north eastern Virginia. This may be the area where our line resided for many years. I have loosely based the structure of this book on his work as I feel it is a good compromise between the various styles I have examined.

I welcome any contact with others interested in Daniel surname research and will accept any contributions of information for future books. I am interested in stories and copies of pictures, documents, bibles, diaries, etc. I intend to include more copies of pictures and other documents in a later book. While I hope that I have not made any major errors I do not doubt that I have made many small ones and welcome correction, as well.

Kevin W. Daniel
14 May 1995

Kevin W. Daniel
2010 W. Alice Ave.
W. Peoria, Il 61604

ABBREVIATIONS

b.	born
m.	married
d.	died
aft	after
bef	before
abt	about
*	indicates there is biographical information about this person later in the book.

DESCENT CHART

ANCESTOR	ID NUMBER	PAGE NUMBER
THOMAS DANIEL	1	1

1. THOMAS DANIEL b. abt 1735 d. abt 1805.
Thomas Daniel was listed in Kentucky tax
records[1] from 1789 to 1805. The Clark County,
Ky tax list for 1794 shows he had moved there
from Madison County, Ky. He settled in the
part of Clark County, Ky that was later cut off
into Montgomery County. This is shown by
tracing him in these tax lists for several
years and noting the watercourse on which his
neighbors owned land. This watercourse was
Slate Creek, where one of his sons owned land
for many years. When his sons came of age they
appeared in tax lists on the same days as he
did. Thomas Daniel was taxed for horses and
cattle but no slaves or land until 1804 when he
was taxed for land on Slate Creek. I have found
no record of him purchasing this land. That he
was from Virginia is shown by the birthplaces
of his sons as shown in census and other
records.

There were seven men named Thomas Daniel
in the 1787 tax lists[2] of Virginia. I have
read claims that these lists contain the names
of 95% of the males 21 years of age and over
living in Virginia at this time. I believe our
ancestor is the Thomas Daniel appearing in
Fairfax County, Va tax lists[3] from 1783 to
1791, but I have no proof of this. The type and
amount of personal property shown for this man
over the period covered by these lists more
closely matches what I know of our ancestor
than that shown for any of the other six men.

---

1. Family History Center (FHC) Films
#0008126, Kentucky, Madison County, Tax Books,
1782-1795. #0007930, Kentucky, Clark County,
Tax Books, 1799-1809. #0008168, Kentucky,
Montgomery County, Tax Books, 1797, 1799-1812.
2. The 1787 Census of Virginia, compiled
by Nettie Schreiner-Yantis, Genealogical Books
in Print, Springfield, Va, 1988.
3. Virginia, Fairfax County, Tax Books,
1782-1795. Also FHC Film #0029294.

Thomas Daniel was exempted from taxes[4] "hereafter" in 1783 in Fairfax County, Va and appeared that way in later lists. Tax records there indicate that he may have had brothers named James and John. He may have moved to Kentucky in 1789, when Thomas Daniel first appears in Madison County tax lists, but had property and family in Fairfax County until 1791 when his name last appears in tax lists there. His sons appear to have been fairly well educated so Thomas may have been an educated man as well. Thomas Daniel appointed a Mr. Beamwell constable[5] in Madison County in 1791. I have found few records for Thomas Daniel and there are no records for the administration of his estate in Montgomery County, Ky. His last appearance in records there is in the 1805 or 1806 tax list which may indicate when he died. I have estimated his dates of birth and death based upon the birth dates and life spans of his sons so it is possible that I am off by several years on either date.

An examination of tax lists for Madison, Clarke and Montgomery Counties, Kentucky on days when Thomas, William, John and Thomas Daniel Jr. were taxed did not show any clear relationship between the Daniels and their neighbors. There were several men taxed on the same days as them in more than one year. Some of these men's surnames were Clarke, Tipton, Patton, Owley or Owsley, Brown, Loveless, Lock, Turner, McNeely and Stephens. Several of these families were closely associated with the Daniel family in later years.

There was another Thomas Daniel associated with both Madison and Montgomery Counties in Kentucky. He received a grant of one thousand acres in Kentucky. He gave power of attorney to Reuben Guthrie in 1796 in Madison County and

---

4. Virginia, Fairfax County, Index to Court Records, 1748-1801. Also FHC Fiche #6330XXX, 206 Fiche.
5. Kentucky, Madison County, Order Books 1786-1800. Also FHC Film #0183274.

Enoch Smith in 1809 in Montgomery County to
manage this land for him. He was residing in
Green County, Georgia in 1809. He is reportedly
the man who died intestate in Wilkes County, Ga
in 1825 where a suit names his heirs. I mention
him because of his association with both
counties and the fact that the dates when he
granted power of attorney for his land roughly
coincide with periods when the location of our
Thomas is in doubt. There was another Thomas
Daniel who died testate in Green County, Ga in
1813. His will names his children. Both of
these men are mentioned in the book[6] of
Charles Brunk Heinemann.

While it seems likely that Thomas Daniel
of Montgomery County, Ky was father to the sons
listed for him, there is no clear indication of
his wife's name. Her first name may have been
Malinda, Narcissa or Elizabeth as these were
names frequently used by her descendents. Her
maiden name may have been Estridge, Tipton,
Davis, Stephens, Fox or Patton. Except for
Estridge, these were all families known to be
associated with her children.

The tradition has been passed down by the
descendents of Thomas' son, John, that their
ancestors migrated to Kentucky via the
Wilderness Trail[7]. Thomas Daniel was probably
not the immigrant but was more likely a
grandson or great grandson of the first of this
line in America according to the tradition told
in the biography of his grandson, Perry Daniel
(#20). Thomas Daniel Sr. and his wife had:

2. William Davis Daniel* b. 1766 d. aft
   1800
3. Francis Daniel* b. 1770 d. aft 1792

---

6. Daniel Families of the Southern States
by Charles Brunk Heinemann, 1949, Volume One,
page 211, #93, and page 252, #44. Also FHC Film
#0908840.
7. Letter of Hazel Daniels Singleton,
Landing, N.J., dated May 30, 1994. She is a
descendant of John Daniel (#3).

3

4. John Daniel* b. 26 May 1773 d. 11 May
   1849
5. Thomas Daniel* b. 2 Feb 1777 d. 29 Mar
   1843
6. Estridge Daniel* b. 15 May 1782 d. 6
   Nov 1852
7. James Daniel* b. 1783 d. aft 1860

2. William Davis Daniel b. 1766 d. aft 1800. I
include this man because Thomas Daniel was
charged with William Daniel's tax in 1787 in
Fairfax County, Va and William was taxed on the
same days as Thomas in later lists. There was
also a William Daniel taxed in Kentucky on or
near the same days as Thomas Daniel in 1794 and
1800. William Daniel was in Madison County tax
lists for one year after Thomas disappeared
from these lists. He was taxed on the same day
as men who had been taxed on the same days as
Thomas Daniel in previous tax lists. His middle
name was given as Davis in Fairfax County tax
lists. He may have been the Davis Daniel in
Ohio tax and census lists in 1820 and 1830.
    William may have had a son named Amstance
M. Daniel b. 1789 who married Julia A., both
of whom were born in Virginia, and who were in
the 1850 census of Concord Twp, Champaign
County, Ohio near members of our family.
Amstance and Julia had children named William,
Malinda and Sarah born in Ohio. A James M.
Daniel and family living nearby were probably
also related. Lots of guesses here.

3. Francis Daniel b. 1770 d. aft 1792. This man
was taxed in Fairfax County in 1791 and 1792.
There were a few men named Francis or Francis
Marion Daniel in the descendents of Thomas
Daniel. This is a guess. He is probably of this
family but may have been a cousin to these men,
possibly a son of James Daniel.

4. John Daniel b. 26 May 1773, probably in
Fairfax County, Va, d. 7 May 1849, aged 75
years 11 months and 11 days, in Champaign
County, Oh. He is buried in the Johnson

Cemetery[8] in Concord Twp, Champaign Co., Oh near where he had resided from about 1808 until his death. I found that his stone was nearly unreadable in 1993 and it is likely that it could only be read now by doing a rubbing. Fortunately, the information was taken from this stone by the Urbana DAR Chapter in 1955 or it may have been lost to us. John was in Kentucky tax lists from 1795 to 1806.

John and his brother, Thomas, moved to Ohio about 1806 and were in tax lists[9] in Fairfield County in that year. John Daniel was elected the first township clerk[10] of Concord Twp, Champaign County in 1818. He bought land[11] there in 1814, if not earlier. He may have been a soldier in the War of 1812 but a search of bounty land files showed none for him or his wife. Unfortunately both probably died shortly before legislation was passed that would have enabled them to receive bounty land. He appears in Champaign County censuses from 1820 through 1840. His will[12] is in Champaign County will books.

John married Rebecca Tipton[13] about 1800, probably in Montgomery County, Ky. According to the 1850 census she was born in 1783 in Kentucky and probably died about 1855 in Champaign County. She was the daughter of Thomas Tipton who enlisted as a soldier in the Continental Army in Fairfax County, Va in 1776.

---

8. Ohio, Champaign County, Concord Township, Johnson Cemetery, Tombstone. Also FHC Film #1763587, Ohio, Champaign County, Cemetery Records, Three Volumes, Compiled by Urbana Chapter DAR, 1955. Volume 1, page 22.
9. Early Ohio Tax Payers, page 103, Seattle, Wa Public Library, R929.3771 P871E.
10. History of Champaign County, Ohio, Beers, 1881, page 493. Also FHC Film #0907117.
11. History of Champaign County, Ohio, Beers, page 487. Also FHC Film #0907117.
12. Ohio, Champaign County, Will Book C, page 126. Also FHC Film #0295235.
13. Ohio, Champaign County, Deed Book D, page 75.

Tipton received a pension[14] for his service. John and Thomas Daniel witnessed his pension application in 1837, signing an affidavit attesting that they had known him "well on to fifty years". Thomas Tipton appears in Madison County, Ky tax lists from 1787 and later in Clark and then Montgomery County lists. His pension file gives his last residence in Kentucky in Montgomery County. Tipton left a will[15] in Champaign County naming a daughter, Rebecca "Dannels". He is buried near John Daniel in the Johnson Cemetery. Also buried in this cemetery is Richard Stanhope, valet to General George Washington, who lived to the age of 114 years. Thomas Tipton lived to the age of 111 years and his death was reported in newspapers as far away as Lebanon, Ky. John Daniel's will follows:

I, John Daniel, of the County of Champaign in the State of Ohio do make and publish this my last will and testament in manner and form following, that is to say. First it is my will that my funeral expenses and all my just debts be paid. Second. I give and devise and bequeath to my beloved wife Rebecca Daniel her natural lifetime all of the land lying between what I have deeded to Shelby Daniel and Eastridge Daniel in the south east corner of Section No 17 in Township No 4 of Range No 12 lying between the Miami Rivers supposed to be about thirty acres more or less and at the death of my said wife all the hereby devised or bequeathed to her as aforesaid to my son Thomas Daniel and to his heirs and assigns forever. Third. I give and bequeath to my son Eastridge Daniel all of the livestock, horses, cows, sheep, hogs, etc. by me owned. Also all of the farming utensils, household and kitchen

14. National Archives, Washington, D.C., Revolutionary War Pension File #S16274 Rev, Tipton, Thomas.
15. Ohio, Champaign County, Will Book B., pp. 280-282. Also FHC Film #0295235.

furniture by me owned after selling enough to pay my just debts and funeral expenses.

In testimony whereof I have hereunto set my hand and seal this 20th day of March in the year of our Lord one thousand eight hundred and fortynine.   John Daniel seal

This will was witnessed by Perry Daniel and Benjamin Davis and proved 1 Apr 1854. John and Rebecca's son, Thomas, disposed of the land left to his mother on 22 May 1855. John and Rebecca may have had a daughter named Huldah, who married James Miller in 1827, in addition to those listed below. John and Rebecca had:

8. Elizabeth Daniel* b. 1802 d. bef 1850
9. Nancy Daniel* b. 1807 d. aft 1870
10. Elihu Daniel* b. 26 Dec 1808 d. 26 Feb 1858
11. Pelina Daniel* b. 28 Nov 1810 d. 28 Jun 1837
12. Shelby Daniel* b. 27 May 1814 d. 22 Jan 1879
13. Thomas Tipton Daniel* b. 1817 d. bef 1879
14. Lucretia Daniel* b. 1819 d. bef 1860
15. Eastridge Daniel* b. 21 Apr 1824 d. 1904

Thomas Daniel

5. Thomas Daniel b. 2 Feb 1777, probably in Fairfax County, Va, d. 29 Mar 1843 in Harrison Township, Champaign County, Oh. He was in Montgomery County, Ky tax lists after 1799. He moved to Ohio with his brother John about 1806 and was living in Fairfield County, Ohio in 1809 when he purchased land[16] in Champaign

---

16. Ohio, Columbus, Office of the Auditor of State, Tract Book, Entries for Lands West of the Miami River and Between the Miamis, 8 Ranges East, Fractional Ranges 1 and 2 and Ranges 1-15.

County from the government. He is mentioned in two Champaign County histories[17] that contain biographies of his son, Perry. Beer's 1881 History of Champaign County says that Thomas' great great grandfather was a Welshman who was in love with a noblewoman and had to smuggle her out of that country in order to marry her. Though this story is probably romanticized it may be an indication of approximately when our family came to America and their nationality. I have included this biography in its entirety in the biography of Perry Daniel (#20).

Thomas built houses for the father-in-law of Henry Clay in Kentucky and taught school in Ohio as well as farmed. He was a member of the Whig party and belonged to the Methodist Episcopal Church. He was a private in the company[18] of Capt. Benjamin Schooler in the War of 1812. His tombstone denotes his service. He married Sarah Cainbell or Cambell about 1802 in Kentucky. She was born 29 Mar 1785 in Bourbon County, Ky and died about 1837. Thomas and Sarah are both buried and have tombstones[19] in the Calland Cemetery in Harrison Township, Champaign County, Ohio where they resided after about 1809. This cemetery was abandoned when I visited there in 1993 and in poor condition. The stones for Thomas and his wife were standing but hard to read as they were made of a reddish colored stone and the lettering was not deeply cut. Thomas left a lengthy will[20] in Champaign County. The body of this will follows:

---

17. A Centennial Biographical History of Champaign County, Ohio, Lewis Pub. Co, New York, 1902, pp. 657-659. Also Beers, page 475.

18. Roster of Soldiers in the War of 1812, Clearfield Co., Baltimore, Md., 1989, page 72, Peoria, Illinois Public Library.

19. Ohio, Champaign County, Harrison Township, Calland Cemetery, Tombstone. Also FHC Film #1763587.

20. Ohio, Champaign County, Will Book B, pp. #311-313. Also FHC Film #0295235.

I Thomas Daniel of the County of Champaign
in the State of Ohio do make and publish this
my last will and testament in manner and form
following that is to say.
First it is my will that my funeral
expenses and all my just debts be fully paid.
Second. I give and devise to my eldest son
George Daniel and my daughter Miriam Daniel the
Farm now rented to William Watkins situate in
Champaign County State of Ohio. To wit the
South West quarter of Section fifteen in
Township four of Range thirteen between the
Miami Rivers in the District of land subject to
sale at Cincinnati Ohio containing one hundred
and fiftyseven acres and eight hundredths of an
acre to them the said George Daniel and Miriam
Daniel their heirs and assigns forever.
Third. I give and devise to my two sons,
To wit Perry Daniel and Andrew Jackson Daniel
the farm I now Reside on Situate in the County
of Champaign in the State of Ohio, To wit the
South West Quarter of Section nineteen of
Township four in Range Thirteen lying between
the Miami Rivers of the land divided to be sold
at Cincinnati Ohio containing one hundred and
sixty acres more or less to them the said Perry
Daniel and Andrew Jackson Daniel and to their
heirs and assigns forever.
Fourth. I give and devise to my daughter
Miriam Daniel the Cooking Stove which I have
now in use together with all the utensils
belonging to said Stove, also one young gray
horse two years old this Spring and two hundred
dollars in money which I bind my three sons, To
wit, George Daniel, Perry Daniel and Andrew
Jackson Daniel to pay each one his
proportionable part of said two hundred dollars
within eighteen months after my death to my
daughter Miriam Daniel. Fifth. I give and
devise to my grand daughter Etna McIntire one
hundred dollars which I bind my three sons Viz:
George Daniel, Perry Daniel and Andrew Jackson
Daniel each one to pay his proportionable part
to my said grand daughter Etna McIntire when
she arrives at the age of eighteen years old.

10

Sixth. I give and devise to my grand son Samuel McIntire fifty dollars which I bind my three sons viz: George Daniel, Perry Daniel and Andrew Jackson Daniel each one to pay his proportionable part to my grand son Samuel McIntire when he arrives at the age of twentyone years old. Seventh. I give and devise to my grand son Joseph Near Travis one hundred dollars which I bind my three sons viz. George Daniel, Perry Daniel and Andrew Jackson Daniel each one to pay his proportionable part to my said grand son Joseph Near Travis when he arrives at the age of twentyone years old.

Eighth. I give and devise to my son-in-law John J. Patton one hundred dollars which I bind my three sons viz. George Daniel, Perry Daniel and Andrew Jackson Daniel each one to pay his proportionable part to my son-in-law John J. Patton within two years after my death.

Ninth I give and devise to my three sons To wit: George Daniel, Perry Daniel and Andrew Jackson Daniel and my daughter Miriam Daniel and Etna McIntire my grand daughter all the rest of my personal property after my just debts and funeral expenses are paid out of it.

And lastly I hereby Constitute and appoint my two sons, viz Perry Daniel and Andrew Jackson Daniel, to be the executors of this my last will and testament revoking and annulling all former wills by me made and ratifying and confirming this and no other to be my last will and Testament. In testimony whereof I have hereunto set my hand and Seal this 23rd day of March A.D. 1843.

                              Thomas Daniel seal

Thomas' will was witnessed by Benjamin Davis and Elihu Daniel and proved 12 Apr 1843. Thomas and Sarah had:

    16. America Daniel* b. abt 1803 d. aft
        1830
    17. Narcissa Daniel* b. 1805 d. 12 Jul
        1838

11

18. George Daniel* b. 8 Nov 1809 d. 20
    May 1856
19. Malinda Daniel* b. 1813 d. aft 1840
20. Perry Daniel* b. 8 Jan 1814 d. 15 Dec
    1887
21. Lurana Daniel* b. 5 Mar 1816 d. 16
    May 1841
22. Andrew Jackson Daniel* b. 1820 d. bef
    1860
23. Milton Daniel b. aft 1820 d. bef 1843
24. Etna Daniel b. aft 1820 d. aft 1850
25. Gatch Daniel b. aft 1820
26. Miriam Daniel* b. 22 Apr 1822 d. 31
    May 1893
27. Thomas Daniel* b. 1827 d. Feb 1843

Estridge Daniel [SEAL]

6. Estridge Daniel b. 15 May 1782, probably in
Fairfax County, Va, d. 6 Nov 1852 in Montgomery
County, Ky. He is buried in the Daniel Cemetery
near Lucky Stop, Camargo Township, Montgomery
County, Ky, 8.8 miles southeast of Mt. Sterling
on Route 460. This cemetery was abandoned many
years ago and when I was there in 1989 was
overgrown. It lies on a bluff overlooking Slate
Creek. I found only two stones there that were
finished stones, one of these belonging to
Estridge. There are many field stone markers in
this cemetery and I suspect several of my
ancestors are buried there. I ordered and
received a marble grave marker from the U.S
Veterans' Administration denoting Estridge's
service in the War of 1812 and intend to place
it on his grave at some point in the future.

Estridge Daniel remained in Montgomery
County, Kentucky after his brothers had moved
on. He married[21] Mary Samantha "Polly" Fox 1
Jan 1805 in Montgomery County, Ky. Their
marriage date comes to us from Estridge's War

---

21. Washington, D.C., National Archives,
Bounty Land Warrant File, BWT 82300-120-55,
Eastridge, Daniel.

of 1812 Bounty Land File, since records for marriages before 1864 in Montgomery County were lost in a courthouse fire. Estridge and Polly were married by Daniel Williams, a Separate Baptist minister, but I am reasonably certain that Estridge was a member of the Methodist Episcopal Church.

Mary was born about 1783 in Va and d. Sep 1863 in Audrain County, Mo where she is buried[22] on the farm her son, James Quincy Daniel, purchased there. She was probably the daughter of James Fox of Loudoun County, Va and Clark and Montgomery Counties, Ky. Her mother may have been Mrs. Hannah Scott[23] who was James Fox's second wife. The name of James' first wife is not proven but she may have been Mary Bartleson. James Fox purchased 995 acres of land in Kentucky using two Virginia Treasury Warrants[24] dated 1779 and 1782. James Fox sold part of this land to Estridge Daniel in 1807 and deeded the rest of his property to Estridge in 1814 in exchange for lifetime care for his wife and himself[25].

As I mentioned earlier, Estridge was a soldier in the War of 1812, for which service he and his wife received bounty land. His military service records were misfiled under the name Daniel Eastridge. He enlisted as a private in the 17th Kentucky Militia and was promoted to corporal within a few days. He would probably have attained higher rank had the war not ended. His regiment was marching to Detroit to relieve the garrison there but was

---

22. Missouri, DeKalb County Historical Society, The Daniel Family by Alicia Pearl Mayer.

23. Fox Cousins by the Dozens by Nellie Fox Adams and Bertha Fox Walton, 1976, page 117. FHC Film #1036250.

24. Virginia, Richmond, Virginia State Library and Archives, Land Office (Old) Treasury Warrants; Reel #333, Warrant 704, Reel #334, Warrant 13722.

25. Kentucky, Montgomery County, Deed Book 4, pp. 111-112 and Deed Book 7, page 77.

disbanded at Urbana, Ohio when news of the end of the War reached them. This was near where his brothers, John and Thomas Daniel, and several other Montgomery County, Ky families had settled, so it seems likely that the discharged soldiers visited with kinfolk there before returning home.

Estridge Daniel was a large land owner and slaveholder in Montgomery County where he farmed all of his adult life. He may have speculated in land as well. He appears in tax and census records there from 1804 until his death. He was apparently well educated and left a sizeable estate, including a large sum of cash and cash notes. Charles Brunk Heinemann mentions[26] Estridge as a certain descendent of Capt. William Daniel, an early colonial settler of Middlesex County, Va. Heineman's Daniel ancestors were long time residents of Montgomery County, Kentucky. Estridge was appointed commissioner[27] for several estates in Montgomery County and was referred to as Capt. Estridge Daniel[28] in the records of the administration of his estate. His will[29] is in Montgomery County will books.

Tradition has it that he was a large man, well over six feet tall, and a wrestler, and Mary was a petite red head[30]. According to

26. Daniel Families of the Southern States by Charles Brunk Heinemann, 1949, Volume 2, Family #60. Also FHC Film #0908840.

27. Kentucky, Montgomery County, Will Book B, pp. 2-3, 64-65, Book C, pp. 28-29. Also FHC Film #0252360.

28. Kentucky, Montgomery County, Record Book C, pp. 64-67, and 224-225, Appraisement Bill of Estridge Daniel.

29. Kentucky, Montgomery County, Will Book E, pp. 163-164. Also FHC Film #0252361.

30. Letter of Mrs. Mary McComas Roitman, North Kansas City, Mo, as related to her by her grandmother whose parents were both grandchildren of Estridge and Mary Fox Daniel. Mr. Leo Daniel, Jeffersonville, Ky, a great grandson.

another tradition[31] Estridge was a wrestler
and defeated a visiting opponent named John
Myres by coating himself with lard and wearing
as few clothes as possible to make himself
slippery and hard to hold on to. Estridge won
this match and John Myres married a neighbor
girl, settled near Estridge and they became
lifelong friends. Estridge's will follows:

Whereas I, Estridge Daniel, of the County
of Montgomery and State of Kentucky am of sound
and composed state of mind but taking into
consideration that though now in health I may
soon be called unto death, I do make this my
last will and Testament.

First I will that all my debts should be
paid. Second, I give and bequeath to my wife
Mary, a certain negro woman named Manerva with
her offspring if she should have any after this
date and also the household and kitchen
furniture to have and to hold the same so long
as she may live and at her death the same is to
be divided equally between Malinda Hon, Shelby
Daniel, Harvey Daniel, Isom Daniel, Jane
Alexander, James Q. Daniel. The Indian Creek
tract of land containing one hundred acres and
the Sand Mountain tract containing two hundred
acres is also to be equally divided between the
above named children.

Of my cash and cash notes I will and
bequeath to Santford Estridge Stephens and
William Stephens sons of Narsissa Stephens and
Estridge son of Elizabeth Stephens and Pelina
Daniel fifty dollars cash. Pelina's is to come
out of her mother's part. The said children
shall not have this portion until they are
twentyone.

The balance of the cash and cash notes
together with what other property I may have at
my death shall be equally divided between
Malinda Hon, Shelby Daniel, Harvey Daniel, Isom
Daniel, Jane Alexander and James Q. Daniel. The
farm on which I now live is to be James Q.

---

31. Mr. Leo Daniel, Jeffersonville,
Montgomery County, Ky.

Daniel's at my death. And I acknowledge this to
be my last will and testament all others being
null and void in witness whereof I hereunto set
my hand and seal in this 1st day of Feb. one
thousand eight hundred and fiftyone.
                              Estridge Daniel seal
Attest R.C. Porter, Estridge D. Hon

                         Codicil
     In addition to what has been named in the
foregoing, my last will and Testament I request
that Shelby Daniel and James Q. Daniel should
be the executors to settle my estate. In
witness whereof I set my hand and seal on this
second day of Feb 1851. Estridge Daniel seal
Attest R.C. Porter

     Estridge's will was proved in December
1852 and the codicil in January 1853. I believe
that Estridge wrote his own will since it was
necessary to add a codicil to name his
executors. This is not something that would be
omitted by one who was accustomed to making
wills. I believe that the Pelina Daniel
mentioned in Estridge's will was the daughter
of Malinda or Arminta Jane Daniel and a
grandchild of Estridge and Mary. Estridge and
Mary had:

     28. Malinda Daniel* b. 17 Sep 1805 d. 22
         Sep 1890
     29. Shelby Daniel* b. 20 Feb 1808 d. 10
         Dec 1862
     30. Harvey Daniel* b. 27 Jul 1813 d. 24
         Mar 1895
     31. Narcissa Daniel* b. 1815 d. bef 1853
     32. Isom Daniel* b. 1817 d. aft 1854
     33. Elizabeth Daniel* b. 1819 d. aft 1854
     34. Arminta Jane Daniel* b. 1823 d. aft
         1880
     35. James Quincy Daniel* b. 17 Dec 1824
         d. 5 Oct 1901

7. James Daniel b. 1783, probably in Fairfax
County, Va, d. aft 1860 probably in or near
Hardin County, Tx. James Daniel moved to the

Mississippi Territory around 1810 and was drafted into service[32] during the War of 1812 in Clarke County, Mississippi Territory in 1814. This area later fell in the Alabama Territory and then, eventually, the state of Alabama. James received awards of bounty land for this service in 1850 and 1855, applying while a resident of De Soto Parish, La. James married[33] Sarah Robinson about 1806. She was born in Georgia or North Carolina in 1783.

James Daniel

James' place of birth was given as Kentucky in the 1850 census[34] and Virginia in the 1860 census[35], which ties him to both states. This, along with the names of his children, Estridge, Francis Marion, Narcissa and Elizabeth, is enough circumstantial evidence to include him as a child of Thomas Daniel. A cousin, Alicia Daniel Mayer, spoke[36] with elderly cousins in Kentucky in the early part of this century and was told that some of the family had moved south about the time two of the brothers moved to Ohio but she was never able to locate them. It was probably James they were referring to.

James was a planter and slaveholder and resided with his family in Clarke County, Al for many years. From a Clarke County, Alabama

---

32. Washington, D.C., National Archives, Bounty Land Warrant File, 1855 Rejected 182814, James Daniel.

33. Louisiana, De Soto Parish, Deed Book F, pp. 36-38.

34. Louisiana, De Soto Parish, 1850 census, page 186A, Family #398.

35. Texas, Hardin County, 1860 census, page 335A, Family #20.

36. Telephone conversation with Maria Daniel Hunton Halford, San Diego Genealogical Society, friend of Alicia Daniel Mayer, 14 May 1989.

history[37]; "The last three years of this decade, from 1837 to 1841, are mentioned by some of the older citizens as a period of emigration. The new lands of the regions lying west were beginning to attract settlers from what was now becoming 'Old Clarke.' some thirty families, forming a single party, are said to have met near Clarksville and started together in their wagons for Louisiana and Texas. Among these were members of old families bearing the names of Chapman, Pugh, Cox, Daniels and Calhoun."

James and Sarah moved with some of their children and their families to Caddo Parish, Louisiana about 1838 and they were in the 1840 census there. This area was later cut off into De Soto Parish, La where they were enumerated in the 1850 census. Two of their sons moved to Arkansas briefly and were in the 1840 census there but later rejoined their relatives in Louisiana. James, and most of his family, moved on to Jefferson and Hardin County, Texas by 1860. He owned property in Alabama, Louisiana and Hardin County, Texas. James and Sarah were living with or very near their son Estridge and his family in 1850 and 1860. They may have built their homes close together or lived in the same home. The 1860 census shows that James owned a modest amount of real estate but the value of his personal estate was significant. His occupation was listed as farmer in 1860 so he was apparently still active then. I have found no record of James or Sarah after the 1860 census. There is a large family cemetery in Kountze, Hardin County, Tx but the earliest marker there dates from 1885. If James and Sarah are buried there no marker is visible. James and Sarah had:

36. Carna Daniel* b. 1807 d. bef 1850
37. Elizabeth Daniel* b. 1810 d. aft 1850
38. Aaron Kinsey Daniel* b. 1813 d. 1859

---

37. History of Clarke County, Alabama by John Simpson Graham, 1923, Reprinted by Heritage Books, Inc., 1991.

39. Narcissa Daniel* b. 1815 d. bef 1850
40. Estridge Daniel* b. 1816 d. 1 Oct 1866
41. Francis Marion Daniel* b. 1821 d. aft 1870
42. Mahala Daniel* b. 29 Sep 1822 d. 2 Mar 1897
43. James Daniel* b. 24 May 1826 d. 8 Nov 1862

8. Elizabeth Daniel b. 1805 in Montgomery County, Ky d. bef 1850 in Champaign or Logan County, Ohio. She married Francis Patton who was b. 1797 in Va d. 1853 in Logan County, Oh. They were married[38] in Champaign Co. 28 Feb 1822. There is some doubt about this marriage as the record reads Francis Potter not Patton, but this was also the case with the marriage of her cousin Lurana Daniel who married John J. Patton. Since two of her cousins married Pattons and I have found no record of any men named Potter in any records of Logan or Champaign counties I attribute this to the handwriting of the clerk who recorded these marriages. She died before 1850 and Francis was living with several children in Miami Twp. Logan Co., Ohio in 1850. I have not been able to determine when she died or if all of these were her children. They had four children in their home in 1830. The record of these children comes from the 1850 census but should be accepted with caution. Francis and Elizabeth had:

44. Martha A. Patton b. 1827 d. aft 1850
45. Benjamin Patton b. 1828 d. aft 1850
46. Sylvester Patton b. 1832 d. aft 1850
47. Robert F. Patton b. 1834 d. aft 1850
48. Booth B. Patton b. 1838 d. aft 1850
49. Joseph T. Patton b. 1841 d. aft 1850
50. Elizabeth B. Patton b. 1845 d. aft 1850
51. Mary Patton B. 1848 d. aft 1850

9. Nancy Daniel b. 1807 in Ohio, probably Fairfield County, d. aft 1870. She married[39] Benjamin Cox 2 Dec 1830 in Champaign County, Ohio. He died before 1850 when she and her

38. Ohio, Champaign County, Marriage Book B, page 331.
39. Ohio, Champaign County, Marriage Book C, page 57.

children appear in the census there. She next married[40] Abraham Coffee 23 Oct 1851 in Champaign County and was with him in the 1860 census of Miami Township, Logan County, Ohio. Several of her siblings and cousins moved to Illinois and Indiana between 1840 and 1860 and she was in the 1870 census of Butler Township, Vermilion County, Il with her son Jacob and nephew Thomas Tipton Daniel, son of Elihu Daniel. Abraham Coffee apparently died before 1870. Benjamin and Nancy Daniel Cox had:

   52. Lucretia Cox b. 1834 d. aft 1850
   53. Jacob Cox b. 1843 d. aft 1870
   54. Edward Cox b. 1845 d. aft 1860

Elihu Daniel

10. Elihu Daniel b. 26 Dec 1808 in Fairfield County, Ohio d. 26 Feb 1858 of spotted fever[41] in Champaign County, Il. His name was pronounced Elli-hue. He owned land in Logan County, Ohio where he was reported in the 1840 census. He and his family moved to Illinois about 1844. He is buried in the Pleasant Grove Cemetery in Button Township, Ford County, Il and, though his stone is down and broken into several pieces, it is easily read. This intricately carved stone gives his name, his age at death as 49 years 2 months and his date of death. He died intestate and his estate was administered in Champaign County, Il and files[42] there contain copies of his and some

---

        40. Ohio, Champaign County, Marriage Book E.
        41. History of Ford County, Il by E.A. Gardner, S.J. Clarke Pub., Chicago, 1908, pp. 141-142.
        42. Illinois, Champaign County, Urbana, Urbana Free Library, Archives Room, Chancery Court Records, 1861-Packet 341, 1862-Packet 449. Final Probate Papers, Packet 219, Daniel, Elihu.

of his children's signatures. His estate was administered by David Patton with John and Solomon Wilson as his securities.

Elihu married[43] Margaret Travis 18 Apr 1832 in Champaign County, Ohio. He witnessed the will of his uncle, Thomas Daniel, in Champaign County, Oh. He is not mentioned in his father's will, probably because he had moved to Illinois before it was made, but when he came of age in 1831 was listed next to his father in tax lists[44]. He is mentioned with high regard in the History of Ford County, Illinois. He was a farmer. He owned land in Champaign County, Il which was divided between his children and spouse when his estate was settled. After his death his widow next married Argalus B. Lucas 30 Jul 1859 in Champaign County, Il. Argalus and Margaret were raising Elihu's grandson, John Charles Galloway, in 1870 and later Argalus appeared in Kansas census records with his stepchildren. Elihu and Margaret had:

55. John Daniel* b. 26 Sep 1832 d. 14 Nov 1930
56. Colwell Travis Daniel* b. 4 Apr 1836 d. 12 Dec 1897
57. Thomas Tipton Daniel* b. 2 Feb 1839 d. 4 Jul 1916
58. Rachel Ann Daniel* b. 1841 d. 1861
59. Hiram Daniel* b. 3 Aug 1843 d. 30 Nov 1874
60. Miriam Daniel* b. 1845 d. aft 1870
61. Elizabeth Daniel b. 5 Feb 1847 d. 28 Feb 1847
62. Marion Francis Daniel* b. 5 Feb 1847 d. 3 Jan 1921
63. Sarah Ann Daniel* b. 12 Aug 1850 d. 5 Aug 1929

---

43. Ohio, Champaign County, Marriage Book C, page 97.
44. Ohio, Champaign County, Concord Township, Tax List, 1831. Also FHC Film #0559343.

64. Sylvester W. Daniel b. 1852 d. 22 Feb 1856
65. Margaret Lucretia Daniel b. 1855 d. 1861

11. Pelina Daniel b. 28 Nov 1810 in Champaign County, Oh and d. there 28 Jun 1837. She is buried in the Johnson Cemetery in Concord Township, near her father. She married[45] James Bowen 1 May 1834 in Champaign County. After her death her husband married her sister Lucretia. Pelina's son, Horace, was a Lieutenant in the 76th Ill Infantry during the Civil War. Horace Bowen's Union pension file[46] gives his place of birth as Urbana, Ohio. Horace married but had no children according to this file. He joined the 76th as a private in Iroquois County, Il where his father and family had relocated before 1840. James and Pelina Daniel Bowen had:

66. Horace M. Bowen b. 18 May 1836 d. 23 Mar 1916

12. Shelby Daniel b. 27 May 1814 in Concord Township, Champaign County, Oh d. intestate[47] 22 Jan 1879 in Barkley Township, Jasper County, Indiana. He married[48] Mary Ann English 26 May 1837 in Champaign County, Ohio. She was the daughter of Abel B. English and Mary Wolfe. She died 3 Jun 1866 and is buried near her husband and mother in the Smith Cemetery in Barkley Twp, Jasper County, Indiana. Shelby married[49] second Mary Jane Jenkins 5 Dec 1867. She was

---

45. Ohio Champaign County, Marriage Book C, page 163.
46. Washington, D.C., National Archives, Union Pension File SC267.988, Bowen, Horace M.
47. Indiana, Jasper County, Rensselaer, County Court House, Box 215, Probate Folder #250.
48. Ohio, Champaign County, Marriage Book C, page 364.
49. Indiana, Jasper County, Marriage Book 1, page 101.

the widow of James E. Burns, a Union soldier,
and a daughter of Truman Jenkins and Rebecca
Sattle, Shelby's neighbors. She was b. 27 May
1835 in Vermont d. 2 Oct 1906 at Rensselaer, In
and is reportedly buried at Remington, Indiana.
I have a photocopy of the original copy of her
will. Shelby was appointed guardian of her
children by her previous marriage.

SHELBY AND MARY ANN ENGLISH DANIEL

Shelby was apparently illiterate, which is
unusual as the other males in his family could
read and write and several of his female
cousins were educated as well. He was a
successful farmer in Jasper County and the home
he built is standing in 1994. He may have seen
militia service during the Civil War as a
biography of his son, George, mentions that he
carried an heirloom rifle when rumors of rebel
activity were reported in their area. I have a
photograph of a charcoal or pencil sketch of
Shelby and his first wife. A short notice of
his death appeared on the front page of the
Rensselaer Union on 30 Jan 1879:

25

Shelby Daniels, an old resident of Barkley township, died last Thursday, 23d instant. He was a man possessed of many excellent qualities, and held in high esteem.

Shelby and Mary Ann had:

67. Martha Jane Daniel* b. 12 Apr 1842 d. 5 May 1893
68. William H. Daniel* b. 18 Dec 1843 d. 22 Dec 1911
69. Margaret Daniel b. 28 Jul 1845 d. 5 Nov 1848
70. Mary Ellen Daniel* b. 15 Jan 1847 d. 2 Jun 1874
71. George Daniel* b. 16 Feb 1850 d. 16 Jan 1917
72. Infant b. 1854 d. 1854
73. Rhoda Jane Daniel* b. 23 Jun 1856 d. 11 Dec 1889
74. John Charles Daniel* b. 26 Jul 1858 d. 1933
75. Thomas Tipton Daniel* b. 1 Nov 1861 d. Aug 1929
76. Horace Greely Daniel* b. 28 Aug 1865 d. 23 Sep 1943

Shelby Daniel and Mary Jane had:

77. Aurilla Daniel* b. 1869 d. aft 1900

13. Thomas Tipton Daniel b. 1817 in Concord Township, Champaign County, Oh d. bef 1879. He was listed in the home of his cousin Andrew Jackson Daniel in the 1850 census of Quincy, Miami Township, Logan County, Ohio. He married[50] Alcinda Elizabeth Yost 13 Apr 1856 in Logan County, Ohio. She was born 28 Dec 1830 in Morgan County, Virginia and d. 7 Feb 1919 at Decatur, Macon County, Il and is buried in the Bement Cemetery, Bement, Piatt County, Il. She was the daughter of Rev. John and Susanne Ambrose Yost of Morgan County, Va. Much of the

---

50. Ohio, Logan County, Marriage Book C, page 49.

information about Alcinda comes from her death
certificate on file at the Macon County, Il
courthouse. Since Thomas may have died during
the Civil War or his wife may have drawn a
pension, pension records and veteran's records
of Piatt and Macon County, Il should be
searched.

In 1860 Thomas and Alcinda were in Van
Wert County, Ohio when the census was taken.
They may have moved to Illinois with his
brothers for a time as their daughter Alice was
born in that state 1857. Thomas was occupied as
a carpenter in 1850 and 1860. I have not found
his middle name listed, just the initial "T.",
but I am guessing his middle name was Tipton
after his famous grandfather. I have not found
him in records after 1860.

A cousin[51] in Oakwood, Il told me that
Eastridge Daniel, Thomas' brother, had a
falling out with one of his brothers which was
caused when he was security for a three hundred
dollar loan. The brother defaulted on the loan
and Eastridge had to pay the full amount. It
could be that it was Thomas that defaulted on
the loan and moved back to Ohio since the
remaining two brothers, Elihu and Shelby, were
apparently successful farmers.

Alcinda moved to Monticello, Il in 1875
and later to Bement, Il where she worked as a
tailoress and owned property. She has a brief
biography in an 1883 history[52] of Piatt
County. I do not know if Thomas died in Ohio or
Illinois or in between. A biography of one of
their daughters seems to indicate that he died
about 1879. After Alcinda retired she lived
with her daughter, Gertrude, in Decatur, Il
where she was living when she died. She was
listed in the 1917 Decatur City Directory[53]

---

51. Conversation with John Henry Atwood,
10 May 1993, Oakwood Illinois.
52. History of Piatt County, Il, Emma C.
Piatt, 1883, page 366.
53. Illinois, Decatur Genealogical and
Historical Society, Decatur City Directory For
1917, pp. 173, 236.

as the widow of Thomas Daniels and was living at the same address as her daughter, Mrs. Gertrude (Sidney) Grant. Alcinda has brief obituaries in newspapers in Bement and Decatur, Il. Thomas and Alcinda had:

78. Alice Daniel* b. 1857 d. bef 1900
79. Emo May Daniel* b. Aug 1859 d. 13 Oct 1902
80. Frances Gertrude Daniel* b. Jun 1861 d. aft 1925
81. Dell Libbie Daniel* b. 6 Aug 1863 d. 12 Mar 1922

14. Lucretia Daniel b. 1819 in Champaign County, Oh d. bef 1860 in Iroquois County, Il. She married[54] James Bowen 20 Sep 1838 in Champaign County, Ohio after the death of her sister, Pelina, his previous wife. James was b. 1811 in Ohio d. Dec 1865 in Iroquois Co., Il where his estate[55] is administered.

They moved to Iroquois County, Il around 1840 and were in censuses there up to 1860. James enlisted[56] in Co. C, 51st Illinois Infantry 20 Sep 1861 and was mustered out 25 Sep 1865. Several of his sons also served, his son James died in the line of duty in 1864 and his son Horace was a Lieutenant of Co. A, 76th Illinois Infantry. James Bowen was taxed for land in Middleport Twp in 1866. Though both James and his wife died in Iroquois County there is no mention of tombstones for them in what appears to be a thorough census of the tombstones of that county I found at the historical society in Watseka.

I found scattered records for various people named Bowen in records of this county who may have been related to James Bowen and

---

54. Ohio, Champaign County, Marriage Book C, page 337.
55. Illinois, Iroquois County, Old County Courthouse Museum, Watseka, Probate Box 5.
56. Past and Present of Iroquois County, Il, S.J. Clarke Pub., Chicago, 1907, pp. 695-699.

his two wives. The last descendent I found named Bowen that definitely belonged to this family, Charles E. Bowen, died there 5 Jun 1936. He was a son of John and Susan Crozier Bowen. There are descendents of female lines living in Sheldon, Iroquois County in 1994. The Union pension file of Horace M. Bowen, James's son by Lucretia's sister, indicates that some of the Bowen's moved to Livingston County, Mo and Rice County, Ks. James and Lucretia had:

82. John Bowen b. 1840 d. 1869
83. James Bowen b. 1843 d. 1864
84. William Bowen b. 1845 d. aft 1891
85. Melissa Bowen b. 1847 d. aft 1883
86. Samantha Bowen b. 1848 d. aft 1860
87. Jane Bowen b. 1850 d. aft 1860
88. Harriet Bowen b. 1853 d. aft 1866

Eastridge Daniel

15. Eastridge Daniel born[57] 21 Apr 1824 in Concord Township, Champaign County, Oh d. abt 1904. He married[58] Caroline R. Kiser, daughter of Jacob and Catherine Kiser, 19 Apr 1849 in Champaign County, Ohio. Her middle name is thought to have been Rankin.

They moved to Champaign County, Illinois about 1855 and settled next to his brother Elihu in Kerr Township. He sold his land and moved to Blount Twp, Vermilion County, Il before 1860. According to his descendents[59] this was because of lack of wood on the prairie. Eastridge was a farmer and, according to the 1860 Agricultural Census of Vermilion County, he owned 160 acres of land, of which 60

57. Eastridge Daniel Family Bible, a photocopy in the possession of the author.
58. Ohio, Champaign County, Marriage Book E, page 1.
59. Conversation with John Henry Atwood, Oakwood, Il, 10 May 1993, Eastridge and Caroline's grandson, aged 88.

acres were improved. He was primarily engaged
in raising Indian corn but other crops and
livestock were listed as well. Sometime in the
late 1890s he became senile, probably from
Alzheimer's disease, and was later
institutionalized[60] at the mental hospital at
Kankakee, Il after 1900. Eastridge and Caroline
had been living with family in their old age
and he would wander from the house into the
woods and fall down. Being an extremely large
man, the womenfolk could not manage him and the
men would have to be called in from the fields
to get him back to the house, so the family
felt they had little choice but to commit him.
He was later moved without his family's consent
to another facility but died on the train
before getting there. The family thinks he is
buried in either Iowa or Indiana in a potter's
field.

His family bible gives the birth and death
dates of all of their children. This bible also
gives Eastridge and Caroline's birth dates,
year of his death and full date of her death.
The location of the bible is unknown at this
time, but I have photocopies of the pages from
the bible containing family information which
were given to me by a family member.

Eastridge died intestate. There appears to
be no administration of his estate in Vermilion
County records, probably because he had already
deeded all of his property to his children.
Caroline Kiser was born 11 Dec 1833 in
Pennsylvania and died near Danville, Il 29 Jan
1929 where she was living with a daughter. Her
obituary appears in the Danville Commercial
News. She is buried in the Fairchild Cemetery
in Vermilion County with several of her
children. I have pictures of her.

Eastridge was left-handed according to
descendents. A son of Louisa Matilda Daniel
told me that Eastridge owned a St. Bernard dog
that did not like having his dog house "patted

---

60. Conversation with John Henry Atwood,
grandson, Viola Cundiff, great granddaughter,
Oakwood, Il May 1993.

on". Eastridge warned his children not to do this but being children they did so anyway and the dog bit them. Eastridge took the dog into the woods and hanged it. Eastridge and Caroline had:

89. Luvena Daniel b. 12 Dec 1849 d. 16 May 1855
90. Miriam Daniel* b 21 Dec 1850 d. 17 Aug 1929
91. Mary Jane Daniel* b. 11 Dec 1852 d. 9 Dec 1885
92. Infant son b. 27 Dec 1854 d. 6 Mar 1855
93. Harriet Rebecca Daniel* b. 18 May 1856 d. 9 May 1895
94. Napoleon Daniel* b. 10 May 1858 d. 24 Nov 1939
95. Etna Daniel* b. 24 Sep 1860 d. 9 Sep 1882
96. Capitola Daniel b. 18 Nov 1862 d. 16 May 1876
97. Nancy Ann Daniel* b. 4 Oct 1863 d. 7 Nov 1958
98. Louisa Matilda Daniel* b. 25 Nov 1866 d. 29 Jan 1949
99. Frank Daniel* b. 27 Aug 1869 d. 22 Aug 1898

16. America Daniel b. 1803, probably in Montgomery County, Ky, d. aft 1830. She married[61] Thomas McIntire 27 Sep 1827 in Champaign County, Ohio. I have not located her or her husband in census records but she may have died before 1843 when her father mentioned two grandchildren named McIntire in his will. She is named in a county history[62] as his child. Thomas and America had:

---

61. Ohio, Champaign County, Marriage Book B, page 296.
62. A Centennial and Biographical History of Champaign County, Ohio. Lewis Pub. Co., New York, 1902, pp. 657-659.

        100. Samuel McIntire b. aft 1827 d. aft
        1843
        101. Etna McIntire b. aft 1827 d. aft 1843

17. Narcissa Daniel b. 1805, probably in
Montgomery County, Ky, d. 12 Jul 1838. She is
buried in the Calland Cemetery in Champaign
County, Ohio near her parents. She apparently
did not marry and her tombstone gives her age
as 33 at her death. Narcissa was a family name
and used for several generations in all
branches of the family.

18. George Daniel b. 8 Nov 1809 in Fairfield
County, Ohio died[63] 20 May 1856 in Barkley
Township, Jasper County, Indiana. He is buried
in the Smith Cemetery, Barkley Township, Jasper
County next to the wife of his first cousin
Shelby Daniel. When I first visited this
cemetery about 1989 I found his stone broken
across the date of his death and age but was
able to get his dates by holding the broken
stone together. A few years later when I
returned to this cemetery the stone was in
worse condition and I do not think it would now
be possible to decipher this information. He
purchased government land in Jasper County
about 1840 and later purchased land there from
his brother Andrew Jackson also. At one time he
was a large landholder in Jasper County. He was
living in the home of a Williams family in
1850. By 1856, when he died, he had sold all of
his land. I have found no record of his
marriage or settlement of his estate. I have a
copy of his signature from the estate records
of his father.

---

        63. Indiana, Jasper County, Smith
Cemetery, Tombstone.

19. Malinda Daniel b. 1813 in Champaign County,
Oh d. aft 1840. She married[64] Miles W.
(Wilson?) Travis 21 Feb 1833 in Champaign
County, Ohio. She and her husband were in the
1840 census of Hancock County, Ohio. They both
may have died by 1843 when her father made his
will. Thomas mentioned his grandson, Joseph
Neer Travis, in his will and a Joseph Travis
was living with Perry Daniel, Malinda's
brother, in Harrison Twp, Champaign County in
1850 during the census. Malinda and Miles had:

   102. Joseph Neer Travis b. 1833 d aft 1850

20. Perry Daniel b. 8 Jan 1814 in Harrison
Township, Champaign County, Ohio d. 15 Dec 1887
in Champaign County, Ohio. He married[65] Mary
E. Barkshire daughter of Henry and Sarah Morris
Barkshire. She was b. at Dayton, Ohio 6 Nov
1825 and d. 10 Apr 1903 in Champaign County,
Ohio. They retired to Spring Hills, Ohio and
are buried[66] in the Oakdale Cemetery in
Urbana, Ohio. I have a picture of her. The
record of her estate[67] contains signatures of
all of her living children and the children of
her son Allen. I have copies of Perry's
signature from the estate records of his
father. He became the owner of his father's
farm after his death and became a prominent
farmer in Champaign County. He was a Mason, a

---

      64. Ohio, Champaign County, Marriage Book
C, page 127.
      65. Ohio, Champaign County, Marriage Book
E, page 31.
      66. Ohio, Champaign County, Urbana,
Oakdale Cemetery, Tombstone. Also FHC Film
#1763587, Champaign County, Ohio Cemetery
Records, Volume 3, page 43.
      67. Ohio, Champaign County, County
Courthouse, Urbana, Estate records of Mary E.
Daniels.

well known member of the Republican party and a
constable for a number of years. He was a
trustee of Harrison Township in 1862. He has
biographies[68] in two Histories of Champaign
County, Ohio. He was apparently a well known
and popular man. His biography from Beers' 1881
History of Champaign County in which he is
mentioned as a contributor follows:

PERRY DANIEL, retired farmer; P.O. Spring
Hills, born in Harrison Township, Champaign
Co., Ohio, Jan. 8, 1814; is a son of Thomas and
Sarah Daniel. She was born in Bourbon Co., Ky.,
March 29, 1785, and he in Virginia Feb. 2,
1777, but was taken to Kentucky while quite
young. In 1808, he moved to Ohio and settled in
Pickaway Co., Ohio, then went to Champaign Co.
in 1810. To depart from what is truly
biographical, his great-great-grandfather was a
native of Wales, and a carpenter. His great-
great-grandmother belonged to the nobility of
Wales. Her maiden name is not known. It was
contrary to the laws of the country for any of
the nobles to marry among the common people. He
loved this lady, and as love is not to be
defeated, he made a chest, in which he carried
her out of the country, and married her. In
early life, Thomas "picked up" the carpenter
trade and built several houses for the father-
in-law of Henry Clay. For several winters
following his settlement here, he engaged in
teaching. His principle occupation, however,
was farming. He owned 317 acres of land.
   The subject of this sketch has been a
life-long farmer, but has retired from active
farm labor within the last year. He owns 157
acres of good land under good cultivation. In
1849, Nov. 5, he married Mary E. Barkshire. She
was born in Montgomery Co., Ohio, Nov. 6, 1825.
Her ancestors on both sides of the house were
of Irish and Welsh blood, the latter
predominating. Eight Children are the fruits of

---

   68. A Centennial and Biographical History
of Champaign County, Ohio. Lewis Pub. Co., New
York, 1902, pp. 657-659.

their marriage - Allen G., Sarah Alice,
Margery, Adelia, William T., Maggie R., Minnie
E. and Anna May. Mrs. Daniel and one daughter
are members of the Methodist Episcopal Church.
Five of the children are members of the
Presbyterian Church. Allen G. is a minister of
the latter, and is officiating in the State of
New York.

MARY E. BARKSHIRE DANIEL

Perry Daniel's biography from A Centennial
Biographical History of Champaign County, Ohio:

PERRY DANIELS

Perry Daniels was one of the pioneers who
aided in laying the foundation on which to
erect the superstructure of Champaign county's

35

present prosperity and progress, and through
the period of early development he was an
important factor in the improvement and
advancement of this section of the state. His
father, Thomas Daniels, was born, reared and
educated in the famous old Blue Grass state,
but in 1813, after his marriage he left his
southern home for Ohio, locating on the present
Daniels homestead in Champaign county, The land
was then in its primitive condition, but as the
years passed by he cleared a portion of this
farm, and here his death occurred in 1841. He
was married in his native state to Sarah
Cainbell, and she too, was born and reared in
Kentucky. This union was blessed with ten
children, four sons and six daughters, as
follows: America, Narcissa, George, Malinda,
Perry, Laniana, Andrew Jackson, Milton, Etna
and Gatch. All but four of the children were
born in Champaign county, and here all were
reared. The father gave his political support
to the Whig party and religiously was a member
of the Methodist Episcopal church.

Perry Daniels, the immediate subject of
this review, was born in this locality on the
8th of January, 1814, and throughout his youth
and early manhood he assisted his father in
clearing and improving his Ohio home. The
educational privileges which he received were
those afforded by the district schools of the
neighborhood. In early life he also studied the
art of surveying, but never followed that
profession, preferring to give his energies to
the tilling of the soil. After his father's
death he became owner of the old home place of
one hundred and fifty seven and a half acres.
He performed his part in the arduous task of
clearing new land, plowing and planting the
crops and throughout his entire life he was
engaged in agricultural pursuits on the old
homestead in Harrison township. He was
prominently identified with the Republican
party, and for a number of years held the
office of constable. His social relations
connected him with the Masonic fraternity,

holding membership with the lodge at West Liberty.

As a companion on the journey of life Mr. Daniels chose Miss Mary Barckshire, who was born in Dayton, Ohio, and she there remained until within a few years of her marriage. Her father, Henry Barckshire, was a native of the northern part of Ohio. In an early day he moved to Dayton, making the journey by boat, and during the trip a fire was kept burning in kettle until it was discovered by the Indians. In that city he was married to Miss Sarah Morris, a native of Virginia, but when an infant she was brought to this state and was reared in Clark county, This worthy couple became the parents of six children, of whom Mrs. Daniels was the oldest in order of birth. By her marriage with our subject she became the mother of eight children, namely: Allen, deceased; Sarah, at home; Margery, the wife of L.J. Baker, who is engaged in the implement business in Urbana; Adelia, the wife of J. H. Wilson, who is engaged in business in Corning, California; Margueritte, who also makes her home in that state; Minnie, the wife of Don Wilson, of California; Anna, who is unmarried and resides in that state. All of the children were born in the old home farm in Champaign county. Mr. Daniels was called to his final rest on the 8th of December, 1887. His was a long active, useful and honorable life, and his name is indelibly inscribed on the pages of Champaign county's history.

Perry and Mary had:

103. Allen G. Daniel* b. 9 Aug 1850 d. 30 Mar 1893
104. Sarah Alice Daniel* b. 1852 d. aft 1904
105. Margery Daniel* b. Dec 1853 d. aft 1904
106. Mary Adelia Daniel* b. 1855 d. aft 1904
107. William Thomas Daniel* b. 15 Jul 1858 d. 23 Mar 1944

37

108. Margaret R. Daniel* b. May 1860 d.
aft 1904
109. Minnie E. Daniel* 23 Jan 1863 d. 30
Oct 1938
110. Anna May Daniel* b. 1865 d. 1943/5

21. Lurana Daniel b. 5 Mar 1816 in Harrison
Township, Champaign County, Oh and died there
16 May 1841. She married John J. Patton and his
name is inscribed on her tombstone. The name of
her husband on the record of their marriage
reads John J. Potter but her father's will and
her tombstone prove that this is not correct.
She is buried next to her parents in the
Calland Cemetery, Harrison Twp, Champaign
County, Ohio.

Andrew J Daniel

22. Andrew Jackson Daniel b. 1820 in Harrison
Township, Champaign County, Oh d. aft 1857. He
is mentioned in his father's will. He purchased
government land[69] near his brother George and
cousin Shelby in Jasper County, Indiana in
1841. He sold this land to his brother George
before 1850 while he was living in Clark
County, Oh. He and his wife were living in
Logan County, Oh in 1850. His occupation was
school teacher. One descendent says he was a
doctor. A Logan County, Ohio history[70] says
that he was the first recorder at Quincy, Ohio.
He married[71] Margery Patton 8 Sep 1844 in
Logan County, Ohio. She was b. 19 Dec 1823 in
Ohio and was living in Russellville, Putnam
County, Indiana in 1880. She died there 21 Apr
1893 and is buried in the Russellville Cemetery
with her daughter Almira. They share a large

---

69. Indiana, Jasper County, Deed Book 39,
page 46.
70. Baskin's History of Logan County,
Ohio, 1880.
71. IGI, Ohio, Logan County, Marriage
Records.

red marble tombstone that gives their dates and
also names A. J. Daniels as husband and father.
Margery's portion says MOTHER so it was
probably erected by her daughter, Miriam
Daniels Couchman, who lived nearby. Andrew
Jackson apparently died before 1860 when his
children were divided between various relatives
and his wife. There is no record of his death
in any of the counties I found him associated
with. His estate was settled in 1879 in Logan
County, Ohio when deed[72] records show final
division of his land was made among his
children. I have copies of his signature from
the estate records of his father. Andrew and
Margery had:

111. Miriam Daniel* b. 1844 d. aft 1884
112. Almira Daniel* b. 9 Aug 1845 d. 11
     Apr 1898
113. Robert Francis Daniel* b. 1849 d. aft
     1880
114. Nancy Jane Daniel* b. 1855 d. 1906
115. Dora E. Daniel* b. 1857 d. aft 1879

Miriam Daniel

26. Miriam Daniel b. 22 Apr 1822 in Harrison
Township, Champaign County, Oh d. 31 May 1893
and is buried[73] in the Oakdale Cemetery. She
apparently lived her whole life in Champaign
County, Ohio. She is mentioned in her father's
will. She married[74] John Taylor 19 Dec 1845
in Champaign County. He was b. in Scotland in
1818 and d. after 1880. He became a large
landowner in Champaign County and purchased

---

72. Ohio, Logan County, Deed Book 58, page
407 and Deed Book 59, page 17.
73. Ohio, Champaign County, Urbana,
Oakdale Cemetery, Tombstone. Also FHC Film
#1763587, Champaign County, Ohio Cemetery
Records, Volume 3, page 109.
74. Ohio, Champaign County, Marriage Book
D, page 209.

land from several of Miriam's cousins, sons of
John Daniel, including John's home farm. There
is probably more information available on this
family. They had:

116. Albert Taylor b. 1848 d. aft 1880
117. Zachariah Taylor b. Mar 1849 d. aft
     1880
118. Samuel M. Taylor b. 1857 d. aft 1880
119. Etna F. Taylor b. 1863 d. aft 1880

27. Thomas Daniel b. 1827 in Harrison Township,
Champaign County, Oh d. there Feb 1843. He died
about the same time as his father. They may
have died as a result of a shared injury or
illness. He is buried near his parents in the
Calland Cemetery.

28. Malinda Daniel b. 17 Sep 1805 in Montgomery
County, Ky and d. 22 Sep 1890 in Platte County,
Mo. She is buried in the Riverview Cemetery
there. She m. Moses Hon, son of Joseph Hon, 19
Nov 1829. She was Moses' second wife. Moses b.
30 Nov 1803 in Kentucky d. 21 Apr 1858 and is
buried near Springfield, Il. Joseph Hon has
been mistakenly reported as a Revolutionary War
soldier. All of their children were born in
Kentucky. Malinda and her family are
mentioned[75] in The Annals of Platte County,
Mo. This short biography gives her birth and
death dates and names their children. Malinda
and Moses had:

120. Almanza Hon b. 1 Sep 1830 d. 2 Dec
     1913
121. Estridge Daniel Hon b. 12 Apr 1832 d.
     14 Jun 1859
122. Mary Ellen Hon b. 18 May 1834
123. John J. Hon b. 9 Sep 1836
124. Amanda Jane Hon b. 27 Feb 1831 d. 13
     May 1931
125. Cynthia Ann Hon b. 15 Apr 1841 d.
     1926

---

75. The Annals of Platte County, Missouri
by W.M. Paxton, 1897, pp. 927-928.

126. Elizabeth C. Hon b. 25 Feb 1843 d. 4
     Jan 1925
127. Armanda Jane Hon b. 8 Nov 1845
128. Isaac Hon b. 23 Apr 1848 d. aft 1920

29. Shelby   Daniel b. 20 Feb 1808 in Montgomery
County, Ky d. 10 Dec 1862 in Platte County, Mo.
He married Cynthia Ann Gordon abt 1832 in
Montgomery County. She was the daughter of
William and Lucretia Muir Gordon. She b. 1815
d. Sep 1886. Shelby moved his family to Platte
County, Mo in 1854. There is a brief mention of
him and his family in The Annals of Platte
County, Mo. by Paxton. He is buried in the
Brown Cemetery in Platte Co. He was a farmer
and slaveholder. He died intestate. Members of
his family were southern sympathizers and were
persecuted during the Civil War. His brother-
in-law, Si Gordon, was an infamous confederate
guerilla who operated in western Missouri.
There was a photo of Shelby with a party of
hunters in existence as late as the early part
of this century, the 20th, but it has since
been lost. I have not personally examined all
of the records available in Platte County. His
biography from the Annals of Platte County:

    Feb 9.-   Shelby Daniel   having died,
Cynthia, his widow administers. Bond $6,000. He
came from Kentucky in 1854, and settled four
miles west of Platte City. He married Cynthia
A. Gordon, died in September 1886. She was an
aunt of Si. Gordon, an suffered severely during
the war. Mr. Daniel was social gentleman and
highly respected.

This short biography goes on to name his
children.

    Shelby and Cynthia had:

129. William Estridge Daniel* b. 18 Apr
     1834 d. 11 Jun 1928
130. James Harvey Daniel* b. 7 Dec 1835 d.
     24 Jan 1920

41

131. Armilda Jane Daniel* b. 18 Oct 1838
     d. 24 Feb 1900
132. Randall Richardson Daniel* b. 23 Mar
     1839 d. 6 Dec 1917
133. Mary Lucretia Daniel* 20 Feb 1847 d.
     9 Jul 1933

30. Harvey Daniel b. 27 Jul 1813 in Montgomery
County, Ky d. there 24 Mar 1895. He m. Mary
Frances Jameson 12 Jun 1839, probably in
Montgomery County. She was the daughter of
William O. and Anna Orear Jameson who are
buried on the old Pleasant Jameson Daniel farm.
Mary was b. 12 Jul 1817 in Montgomery County,
Ky d. 23 Jan 1907 in Montgomery County. Much of
this information comes from the family bible in
the possession of descendents still living in
Montgomery County in 1994. Mary was
crippled[76] in later years due to a fall from
a horse and was living near Beaver Pond, Powell
County, Ky in 1889. Harvey was a farmer and
slaveholder and lived his whole life in
Montgomery Co. in the area where he was born.
He was a member of the Methodist Church. The
cemetery where they are buried was apparently
bulldozed over. No pictures of them have
survived. Harvey had a brief obituary[77] in a
Kentucky newspaper:

Mr. Harvey Daniel, one of the oldest and
most highly respected citizens of this county,
aged 84 years, died at his home of pneumonia
last Sunday.

Harvey and Mary had:

134. William Jameson Daniel* b. 20 Mar
     1841 d. 14 Oct 1907
135. James Estridge Jameson Daniel* b. 11
     Mar 1843 d. 29 Jul 1858

----

76. Kentucky, Montgomery County, Mt.
Sterling Sentinel Democrat, "Aged & Venerable
in Montgomery Co., Ky.-1889".
77. Kentucky, Montgomery County, Mt.
Sterling Advocate, 26 Mar 1895.

136. Pleasant Jameson Daniel* b. 19 Aug
     1845 d. 15 Aug 1929
137. Armina Jameson Daniel* b. 4 Apr 1848
     d. 17 Jun 1921
138. Elizabeth Jameson Daniel b. 29 Jul
     1850 d. 21 Dec 1878.
139. Columbus Quincy Daniel* b. 14 Jul
     1852 d. 11 May 1910
140. Harvey Jameson Daniel* b. 18 Aug 1854
     d. 12 Jan 1930
141. Mary Jameson Daniel* b. 21 Jan 1857
     d. 1921
142. Anna Jameson Daniel b. 28 May 1859 d.
     27 Feb 1880

31. Narcissa Daniel b. 1815 in Montgomery
County, Ky died before 1853. Much of the
information about this woman is guesswork. I
believe she was a daughter of Estridge and Mary
as her sons were left money in Estridge's will.
Two of her uncles had daughters named Narcissa
and that name ran in the family for several
generations. I believe she m. Jesse Stephens
about 1832. I think she died about 1835 and
Jesse next married her sister, Elizabeth. Jesse
made a deed[78] in Montgomery County deeding
all of his property to his three sons. These
were probably the three Stephens boys mentioned
in Estridge Daniel's will. Information in the
Family Registry at my local FHC indicates that
their son Santford died in Missouri in 1914 and
married Francis Ficklin in Montgomery County,
Ky. Jesse and Narcissa had:

     143. Santford Estridge Stephens b. 1833 d.
          1914
     144. James William Stephens b. 1835 d. aft
          1854

32. Isom Daniel b. 1817 in Montgomery County,
Ky d. aft 1854. The notes of Alicia Pearl
Daniel (#422) indicate that he died in Missouri
but she gives no source for her information. He

---

     78. Kentucky, Montgomery County, Deed Book
21, page 432.

43

married[79] Mary Jane Pergram daughter of James and Emily Stephens Pergram abt 1840. The Pergrams were a feuding Kentucky family and their enemies were the Harris family. Several members of each family were killed during their feud and Mary's brother, Enoch, stood trial for murder. Emily Stephens Pergram was the daughter of John and Mary Stephens. John Stephens was a Revolutionary War soldier and received a large land grant in Kentucky in what was later Montgomery and Bath Counties.

Isom and Mary probably moved to Missouri with Isom's brother, Shelby. Family tradition has it that he was hung by Jesse James and his wife cut him down and saved him. I have not located him or his family in the 1860 census. There was an Isom Daniel, about the right age and born in Kentucky, who was working as an overseer for Thomas Gordon in 1860 in Platte County, Mo. Isom's brother, Shelby, married Cynthia Ann Gordon and they were residing in Platte County at this time. Isom and Mary's daughter, Narcissa, was married in Bath County, Ky in 1860. Members of Isom and Mary's family lived in Bath County up to the early 1900s. Mary Pergram Daniel was living with members of her family there in 1870 and 1880. She was b. abt 1817 and d. after 1880. Isom was a farmer and slaveholder. They had:

145. Narcissa Daniel* b. 1841 d. aft 1870
146. James H. Daniel b. 1842. d. aft 1850
147. John C. Daniel b. 1844 d. aft 1850
148. Joseph Daniel* b. 1845 d. aft 1880
149. Leroy Daniel* b. 1847 d. aft 1884
150. Mary L. Daniel* b. 1849 d. aft 1850
151. Emily Daniel* b. 1851 d. aft 1870
152. Luther C. Daniel* b. 11 Mar 1853 d. aft 1910

33. Elizabeth Daniel b. 1819 in Montgomery County, Ky d. aft 1854. She married Jesse

---

79. Kentucky, Montgomery County, Vital Statistics, Birth Records, 1853, Daniel, Luther C.

44

Stephens, the husband of her deceased sister
Narcissa, about 1836. She and her husband were
sold 200 acres of land[80] by her father for
the sum of one dollar. They were living in
Montgomery County in 1850 and in 1853 when her
father's estate was settled. Jesse and Estridge
Stevens were living in Jackson Township,
Livingston County, Missouri in 1860 and 1870.
Those censuses indicate that the Stephens lived
in Indiana between 1850 and 1870. Jesse and
Elizabeth's son was named in Estridge Daniel's
will. Jesse and Elizabeth had:

    153. Estridge M. Stephens b. 1837 d. aft
        1851

34. Arminta Jane Daniel b. 1823 in Montgomery
County, Ky d. aft 1880. She m. John Alexander
about 1849. John was b. 1823 in Ky and d. aft
1880. John was a farmer. They were in the 1850
and 1860 Montgomery County censuses and the
1870 census of Aaron's Run Precinct, Montgomery
County, Ky. John and Arminta, with most of
their children, were living in Mt. Sterling, Ky
in 1880. They are mentioned in several deeds
involving her father's estate. Both were
illiterate. Family tradition has it that they
moved to Lexington. Their son George lived near
them with his family in Mt. Sterling, Ky in
1880. Arminta and John had:

    154. James S. Alexander b. 1850 d. aft
        1880
    155. Paulina Alexander b. 1851 d. aft 1880
    156. William Shelton Alexander b. 23 Jun
        1852 d. aft 1870
    157. George W. Alexander b. 1854 d. aft
        1880
    158. John H. Alexander b. 1856 d. aft 1870
    159. Mary E. Alexander b. 1858 d. aft 1880
    160. Sarah Alexander b. Apr 1860 d. aft
        1880
    161. Louisa Alexander b. 1864 d. aft 1880

---

    80. Kentucky, Montgomery County, Deed Book
18, pp. 450-460.

45

James D. Daniel

35. James Quincy Daniel b. 17 Dec 1824 in
Montgomery County, Ky d. 5 Oct 1901 Fairport,
DeKalb County, Mo. He was known as Quincy
Daniel to many of his relatives. He m. Mariam
Boone Wright 15 Aug 1848. Their marriage date
comes to us from family tradition, probably
from a family bible that no longer exists.
Mariam was the daughter[81] of Meredith and
Sarah Calbraith Wright. Sarah was the daughter
of John and Eleanor Davis Calbraith. Mariam was
b. 25 Nov 1829 in Montgomery County d. 2 May
1911 near Shields, Ralls County, Mo. at the
home of her daughter Sarah. James and Mariam
are buried at the Fairport Cemetery, DeKalb
County, Mo. There is a brief mention of James'
death in the DeKalb County Union Star Herald
and she has an obituary in both the DeKalb
County Herald and Republican Pilot there.

These were my great grandparents. James
Quincy inherited his father's home farm,
probably because he stayed at home after he was
married to help his parents. He sold this farm
in 1857 and moved his family, including his
mother, to Audrain County, Mo where he settled
about 6 miles northwest of Mexico, Mo. He was a
farmer and slaveowner in Kentucky and Missouri.
He sympathized with the Confederate cause
during the Civil War. James and Mariam owned
several hundred acres of land in Audrain
County. About 1878 they sold the last of their
Audrain County property and moved to Clay
County, Mo, near Kansas City, where they were
reported in the 1880 census. Family tradition
says that James pursued the trade of
stockbroker there in partnership with Webster
Ringo, outfitting wagon trains.

---

81. Kentucky, Montgomery County, Deed Book
13, pp. 347-348. Deed Book 25, pp. 19-20, 614-
615.

46

JAMES QUINCY DANIEL

When James Quincy retired he moved to
DeKalb County, Mo and lived with or near his
son James Edwin Daniel at Fairport, Mo. He and
Mariam were living with their son, Charles, in
Ralls County, Mo in 1900 so probably stayed
with their children in other parts of Missouri
at various times. I have pictures of both James
and Mariam and copies of their signatures from
Estridge Daniel's bounty land file. A great
granddaughter told me that "Quincy was a good
horseman and a real go-getter, a pusher and
number one man, and Mariam was very easy
going". Mariam was a very tiny woman, under
five feet tall, with black hair and eyes. She

47

Mariam B Daniel (handwritten signature)

MARIAM BOONE WRIGHT DANIEL

was supposedly one quarter Cherokee. My dentist
corroborated this when he told me that my teeth
exhibit racial characteristics present only in
those of American Indian descent. One great
grandchild, Willie Mills Thompson, told me that
when they attended church Mariam, when an old
woman, sat in a booster seat so she could see
the minister. Willie also told me that Mariam
suffered greatly from asthma and when she lived
with them Mariam's son, Ed, would burn a powder
called Green Mountain in a lid and Mariam would
breath the vapor to relieve her symptoms. James

Quincy's obituary[82] from the Union Star Herald, DeKalb County, Mo. follows:

J.Q. Daniels an old resident of the vicinity of Fairport died at his home last Saturday. His demise was the result of a fever.

From the DeKalb County Herald, No. 39, Maysville, Mo., 11 May 1911:

OBITUARY: Mariam Boone Wright was born in Montgomery County, Kentucky. November 25, 1829 and was married to James Quincy Daniel at the age of twenty years. To this union nine children were born, five of whom are still living. She united with the Christian Church at an early age and lived a faithful Christian life, until death which occurred at her home near Hannibal, Mo., May 2, 1911. The body was brought to Fairport, where after a brief funeral service, conducted by the writer, May 6, the body was laid to rest in the Fairport cemetery by the side of her husband, who preceded her to the spirit world ten years. The deceased was the mother of Ed Daniel who lives six miles northeast of Maysville. The sympathy of the entire community is extended to the relatives in this bereavement. Wm Turnage.

James and Mariam had:

162. John Meredith Daniel* b. 22 Feb 1850 d. 26 Dec 1890
163. Sarah Eleanor Isabel Daniel* b. 15 Apr 1852 d. 5 May 1916
164. Estridge Shelby Daniel* b. 7 Nov 1854 d. 16 Apr 1857
165. James Edwin Daniel* b. 10 Jan 1858 d. 10 Mar 1952
166. Charles Daniel* b. 7 May 1861 d. 19 Dec 1936

---

82. Missouri, DeKalb County, Union Star Herald, 11 Oct 1901, Vol. IV, Number 21, page 1.

167. Elmyra Webster Daniel* b. 22 Feb 1864
     d. 5 Dec 1949
168. Albert Ringo Daniel* b. 31 Mar 1867
     d. 16 Jan 1896
169. George Martin Daniel* b. 18 Jul 1870
     d. 7 Apr 1897
170. Robert Quincy Daniel* b. 7 Sep 1874
     d. 15 Apr 1943

36. Carna "Carney" Daniel b. abt 1807 d. bef
1850, probably in Louisiana. He married[83]
Celia Chapman 25 Aug 1824. Their fathers gave
consent. She b. 20 Sep 1807 in the Newberry
District, South Carolina d. aft 1870. She was
the daughter of Elijah and Elizabeth Martin
Chapman. Carney was a planter and landowner in
Clarke County, Al.
     Carney and Celia moved to Sevier County,
Arkansas where they were enumerated in the 1840
census. There were five male and three female
children enumerated in that census. Carney died
between 1845, when his last child was born, and
1850, when Celia and her children were in the
1850 De Soto Parish, La census. She is probably
the Sally Daniel in the 1870 De Soto Parish
census. Carney purchased property from estate
sales in De Soto Parish in 1843 and 1844 which
shows he did live there. I have not been able
to locate records pertaining to the
administration of his estate. Their children
were born in Alabama, Arkansas and Louisiana.
Much of the information about Carney and
Celia's descendents comes from members of this
family I have contacted in Texas and Louisiana.
They have been very generous with their help
but have not always provided documentation or
complete information. In some cases I believe
the information is from personal knowledge and
in others it has been obtained from other
family members. I have not yet made a thorough
survey of the records available in these areas
so am using this information but wanted to

---

83. Alabama, Clarke County, Marriage Book
A, page 186.

explain the lack of footnotes for these people. Carney and Celia had:

171. Amos R. Daniel* b. 1825 d. aft 1850
172. Elizabeth Daniel* b. 1828 d. 1866
173. Sarah Daniel* b. 1833 d. aft 1850
174. James Daniel b. 1834 d. aft 1861
175. Thersa Daniel* b. 1836 d. aft 1850
176. Giles Daniel* b. 1838 d. abt 1875
177. Mahala Daniel b. 1840 d. aft 1850
178. Mary Daniel* b. 1842 d. aft 1850
179. Emily Daniel b. 1845 d. aft 1850.

37. Elizabeth Daniel b. 1810 d. aft 1850. Her birthplace was given as Alabama in the 1850 census. She married[84] Joshua Martin Chapman 13 Aug 1824 in Clarke County, Al. He was b. 27 Oct 1804 in the Newberry District, South Carolina d. aft 1869. Joshua was the son of Elijah and Elizabeth Martin Chapman and brother of Celia Chapman, wife of Carney Daniel. They moved to Caddo Parish, La with the families of her parents and siblings about 1838 and were in the 1840 census there and in De Soto Parish in 1850. Joshua made several deeds to his children between 1857 and 1869 in De Soto Parish. They had:

180. Axetto Chapman b. abt 1826 d. bef 1868
181. Rachael Chapman b. 1828 d. aft 1857
182. Paines Chapman b. 1830 d. aft 1850
183. Amanda Ann Chapman b. 1833 d. aft 1857
184. John G. Chapman b. 1839 d. aft 1850
185. Sarah Elizabeth Chapman b. 1848 d. aft 1869
186. M. Chapman (a daughter) b. 1850 d. aft 1850

38. Aaron Kinsey Daniel b. 1813 in Clarke County, Al d. 1859 in Jefferson County, Texas.

---

84. Alabama, Clarke County, Marriage Book A, page 184.

He married[85] Mary Ann Bumpas on or after 29
Jul 1835 in Clarke County, Alabama. She was b.
1819 in Alabama and d. 1863 in Texas. They
moved to Arkansas and were in the 1840 census
of Pike County there. They then moved to De
Soto Parish, La and purchased land. They next
moved to Jefferson County, Texas and were in
the 1850 census of that county. Aaron Kinsey
gave his father power of attorney to dispose of
his land in Louisiana in 1847. Aaron died in
Jefferson County, Tx and his estate was
administered in that county. A suit[86] brought
by their son Eastridge in 1901 named all of
their children and living heirs of deceased
children. They had:

    187. James Willis Daniel* b. 1838 d. 1863
    188. Marion E. Daniel b. 1840 d. 1864
    189. John C. Daniel b. 1842 d. 1894
    190. Aaron Kinsey Daniel* b. 1844 d. 1875
    191. Eastridge M. Daniel* b. 1846 d. aft
         1912
    192. Carna Polk Daniel b. 1849 d. 1877
    193. Mary E. E. Daniel b. 1852 d. aft 1910
    194. Benjamin F. Daniel* b. 1853 d. 1878
    195. Sarah C. Daniel* b. 1856 d. aft 1901

39. Narcissa Daniel b. 1815 in Clarke County,
Al d. between 1844 and 1847 in De Soto Parish,
La. Narcissa was a family name and two of her
uncles had daughters by that name. She
married[87] James Howell in Clarke County,
Alabama 9 Feb 1833. He b. 1802 South Carolina
d. about 1858. They moved to De Soto Parish
with her family. He is mentioned in Clarke
County, Al and De Soto Parish, La records.
James m. 2nd Elizabeth Daniel, a niece of his

---

        85. Alabama, Clarke County, Marriage Book
B, page 12, Only the date license was issued is
given.
        86. Texas, Jefferson County, Clerk's File
726, Deed Book 48, pp. 212-213.
        87. Alabama, Clarke County, Marriage Book
A, page 261.

first wife, in De Soto Parish. James and Narcissa had:

196. Easter Howell b. 1836 d. aft 1850
197. Henry Howell b. 1837 d. aft 1850
198. Daniel Howell b. 1841 d. aft 1850
199. Sarah G. Howell b. 1844 d. aft 1850

40. Estridge Daniel b. 1816 in Clarke County, Al d. 1 Oct 1866 in Harris County, Texas. He married[88] Minerva Ann Porter 15 Nov 1835 in Clarke County, Alabama. She b. 1819 in Alabama d. aft 1880. He probably cared for his parents in their old age. He moved to De Soto Parish, La by 1850 and later Hardin County, Texas by 1860. He died in Harris County, Texas where his wife, Minerva Ann, was appointed administratrix[89] of his estate. His date of death may actually be 1 Aug 1866 since the appointment of his wife as administratrix is dated Sep 1866. At the time of his death he owned several hundred acres of land in Hardin County and land in Harris County. I have found no other records pertaining to his estate. Minerva was living in Harris County in 1870 and Hays County in 1880 with her children. Estridge and Minerva had:

200. Martha Jane Daniel* b. 8 Oct 1837 d. 23 Nov 1906
201. Pickens Daniel b. 1842 d. bef 1866
202. Jonah Daniel b. 1845 d. aft 1866
203. Walter Daniel b. 1848 d. bef 1860
204. Aaron Kinsey Daniel* b. July 1850 d. aft 1910
205. James Hampton Daniel b. 1854 d. aft 1866
206. John Daniel* b. 1857 d. aft 1880
207. William Daniel* b. 1861 d. aft 1880

---

88. Alabama, Clarke County, Marriage Book B, page 15.
89. Texas, Harris County, Probate Book R, page 485.

41. Francis Marion Daniel b. 1821 in Clarke County, Al d. aft 1870. He moved to De Soto Parish, La with his family and owned land there. He was in Jefferson County, Texas with his brothers Aaron Kinsey and James in 1850. He is difficult to research because he went by his initials, F., F.M., Francis and Marion.

I believe he is the F. M. Daniel who married[90] Margaret Williams 6 Jan 1852 in Jefferson County. This may be supported by the fact that he was granted 476 acres land[91] by A. and M. Williams, et al, in 1854 in Jefferson County, Tx. The Daniels were listed next to a Williams family in the 1850 Jefferson County census and Margaret Ann, a daughter aged 17, was with this family. He is also probably the Marion living in Hardin County in 1870 with several children but no wife but this is not certain. The Matilda Daniel who married Henry Cravy 26 Mar 1877 as recorded in Hardin County records[92] may be their daughter. There were also a Francis and Margaret Daniel living[93] in Live Oak County, Tx in 1860 that closely fit the information I have about this man and his wife. His wife was not with the family in 1870 and may have died before then. They may have had:

    208. Mahalie Daniel b. 1855 d. aft 1870
    209. Matilda Daniel b. 1858 d. aft 1870
    210. Lewis Daniel b. 1863 d. aft 1870
    211. Victoria Daniel b. 1867 d. aft 1870

42. Mahala Daniel b. 29 Sep 1822 in Clarke County, Alabama d. 2 Mar 1897. She married[94]

---

90. Texas, Jefferson County, Marriage Book B, page 50, #196.
91. Texas, Jefferson County, Deed Book K, page 65.
92. Texas, Hardin County, Marriage Book 1, page 49.
93. Texas, Live Oak County, 1860 Census, page 370, Family #496.
94. Louisiana, De Soto Parish, Marriage Book A, page 9.

Willis Paschal Allan 4 July 1844 in De Soto
Parish, La. He b. 10 Mar 1819 in Alabama and d.
12 Feb 1856 in De Soto Parish. He was the
brother of Nancy Davenport Allan who married
Mahala's brother James. They were the children
of Willis and Elizabeth Allan. Mahala next m. a
man named Monk who apparently died before 1860.
She was living with her son in Hardin County,
Texas in 1860 and 1870. Mahala is buried in the
Daniel Cemetery at Kountze, Texas. Mahala and
Willis had:

> 212. Willis Paschal Allan b. 1845 d. aft
> 1870

43. James Daniel b. 24 May 1826 in Clarke
County, Al d. 8 Nov 1862. He married[95] Nancy
Davenport Allan 13 Dec 1847 in De Soto Parish,
Louisiana. She b. 24 Nov 1829 in Alabama d. 24
May 1899 in Hardin County. They are both buried
in the Daniel Cemetery near Kountze, Texas. He
owned land in De Soto Parish, La. He was a
Confederate soldier and was killed in action.
After his death his wife m. Richard D. Evans.
James and Nancy have several descendents in the
vicinity of Hardin County . They had:

> 213. Sarah Adelaide Daniel* b. 27 Nov 1848
> d. 9 May 1921
> 214. James Willis Daniel* b. 18 Sep 1851
> d. 7 Aug 1913
> 215. Narcissa Davenport Daniel* b. 10 Dec
> 1853 d. aft 1870
> 216. Mary Elizabeth Daniel* b. 1 Apr 1862
> d. 7 Aug 1897
> 217. William Aaron Daniel* b. 1 Apr 1862
> d. 10 Oct 1920

---

95. Louisiana, De Soto Parish, Marriage
Book A, page 48.

55

55. John Daniel b. 26 Sep 1832 in Champaign
County, Oh d. 14 Nov 1930 in Ansley, Custer
County, Nebraska. He married[96] Elizabeth
Adelphia Loso 22 May 1882 in Champaign County,
Il. Their marriage record says this was her
second marriage. She was the daughter of Peter
and Ann Metsker Loso. John was listed as a
merchant and resident of Paxton, Il in their
marriage record. Elizabeth was b. Mar 1853 in
Ohio or Illinois and d. 8 Apr 1920 in Ansley,
Custer County, Nebraska. John came to Illinois
with his family about 1844. He was in every
census until 1880. In 1870 he was living with
his brother Colwell and his family in Kerr Twp,
Champaign County. He was listed as an invalid.
In the 1870s he became a partner with his
brother, Hiram, in the Daniel Brother's Well
Boring Company. This company was dissolved upon
his brother's death. I have a copy of John's
signature from his brother's estate records[97]
in Ford County. He and his wife were in the
1920 Custer County, Nebraska census. According
to his wife's will they had one adopted son.
John's death was mentioned on two separate days
in Ansley newspapers:

14 Nov: JOHN DANIELS, who celebrated his
birthday of 98 years on Sept. 26, passed away
Friday morning at Ansley, after being in poor
health for the past ten years. Mr. Daniels has
been a resident of Ansley and Custer County,
for a large number of years. He was the oldest
man in Ansley, if not in Custer County. His
health has been so poorly the past year, he has
not been downtown Ansley since he came down at
the Presidential Election to vote for Mr.
Herbert Hoover.

---

96. Illinois, Champaign County, Marriage
Book 4, page 143, License #1522.
97. Illinois, Ford County, Administrator
File #98, Daniel, Hiram.

John Daniel

16 Nov: John Daniels was born near Urbana in Champaign County, Ohio on Sept. 26, 1832 and died in Ansley on 14 Nov, 1930, aged 98 years, 1 month and 18 days. On May 22, 1882 he was married to Elizabeth Loso and in 1885, they came to Nebraska, living first at Keanney and later coming to Mason City and Ansley, where he has since resided. His wife died April 8, 1920. He was converted 37 years ago and with his companion and a brother and sister McGregor formed the first Free Methodist Church in this vicinity at Algernon. Aside from his nephew, E. J. Daniels of Ansley, he leaves several other nephews and nieces and relatives. The funeral was held at the Free Methodist Church in Ansley Sunday at 2 p.m. by Rev. Alfred Randall, pastor, assisted by Rev. W. H. Lee and Rev. A. Hodson and burial was made in Ansley Cemetery. Relatives attending were another nephew, Edward T. Groom of Hunter, Okla., a niece Mrs. Lon Miller of Cabool, Mo. and a great granddaughter, Mrs. Reginold Bauer of Hastings, Nebraska.

John and Elizabeth adopted:

218. Wayne Goddard Daniel b. Dec 1899 d. aft 1920

Colwell T. Daniel

56. Colwell Travis Daniel b. 1 Apr 1836 in Logan County, Ohio d. 12 Dec 1897 at Ansley, Custer County, Ne. He is buried next to his wife in Lot 15 in the Janesville Cemetery in Custer County. His name is sometimes spelled Caldwell, but he signed it Colwell T. He

married[98] Minewell Arvilla Francis 7 Dec 1864
in Ford County, Il. She b. 30 Nov 1846 in
Illinois d. 7 Oct 1916 at Lincoln, Ne.
Colwell was a Union soldier, serving as a
corporal in Co. D, 3rd Mo. Cav. He participated
in several battles and the pursuit of the
Confederate, Price. He served in Missouri very
near where my great grandfather, James Quincy
Daniel, had settled. My great grandfather and
his close relations sympathized with the
Confederate cause. Colwell received bounty
money in Champaign County, Il and was
discharged on 25 Jan 1863 by reason of
disability. The cause of this disability was
cited as a hereditary predisposition to a form
of tuberculosis which Colwell testified had
caused the deaths of his father and sister. He
was granted an invalid pension[99] of six
dollars a month for disease of the lungs
starting in July 1881. His widow received a
widow's pension[100] after his death. Colwell's
pension file gives his description as; five
feet nine inches high, dark complexion, grey
eyes and dark hair.
Colwell was farming in Kerr Township,
Champaign County, Il in 1870. He was a grocer
and confectioner in Pellsville, Vermilion
County, Il in the 1870s and 1880s. He was also
postmaster there after his brother Marion. This
town no longer exists. He has a biography[101]
in the History of Vermilion County, Il and is
mentioned in the History of Rankin, Il. The
Rankin history relates that he sold the best
candy in town and an old woman wove rugs in his
store. I believe that at some point he was in

---

98. Illinois, Ford County, Marriage Book
A, #146.
99. Washington, D.C., National Archives,
Union Pension File, Certificate #192,728,
Colwell Daniels.
100. Washington, D.C., National Archives,
Union Pension File, WC460.624, Daniel, Colwell
(Minewell Daniel, widow).
101. The History of Vermilion County, Il
by Hiram W. Beckwith, Chicago, 1879, page 1014.

59

partnership with his brother Marion in the
grocery business. I have copies of his
signature from the estate records of his father
and brother Hiram and his pension file. His
widow and sons were living in Custer County, Ne
in 1900. He had an obituary[102] in a Custer
County newspaper. His biography and obituary
follow:

C.T. Daniel, Pellsville, grocer and
confectioner, was born in Logan County, Ohio,
on the 1st of April, 1836, and spent his early
days on a farm. He moved with his father from
Ohio to this state in 1844, and settled in
Champaign County. He came to this county in
1874, settling in Pellsville, where he still
resides. Mr. Daniel enlisted in the late war,
in 1861, in Co. D, 3d Mo. Cav., and was in the
pursuit of Price and in the battles of
Hartswell (Missouri), Springfield and Pilot
Knob. He married on the 7th of December, 1864.
His wife was born in Vermilion county,
Illinois, on the 30th of November, 1845. They
are the parents of three children: Thomas W.,
Priscilla W., and Mary. Mr. Daniel has held the
office of school director for five years. He is
a republican and a Methodist.

C. T. Daniel

Last Sunday afternoon about 1 o'clock, the
sad intelligence flashed over the town that our
fellow-townsman, Mr. C. T. Daniels, had passed
beyond this vail of tears, away from this world
with its pain and sorrow, its troublesome
strife and duties tiring, to that land that is
fairer than day, where he shall bask in the
light of the great white throne and remember
its troubles no more.
Death is a monster we cannot overcome. In
journeying the weary path of life, we find
rocks and thorns here, - sometimes a rose. But
roses are so few and far apart that we seldom

---

102. Nebraska, Custer County, Mason City,
The People's Advocate, 17 Dec 1897.

inhale their sweet perfume. And so we travel on and on, knowing not whither we go, ever and anon quenching our thirst at the fountain of ambition. All at once and without a note of warning, the monster punches upon us and we are slain.

The Deceased was 61 years of age and he leaves a wife, and two sons who have grown to manhood. Paralysis was the cause of death.

The funeral services were held at the Methodist Church by Rev. W. H. Forsyth, and Rev. Alfred Gilson preached the funeral sermon. The GAR laid the remains at rest in the Janesville Cemetery on Tuesday.

CARD OF THANKS

We wish to extend our heart-felt thanks to those who so kindly assisted us during the sickness and after the death of our beloved husband and father. - Mrs. C. T. Daniels & Children.

School was dismissed in the high school room last Tuesday morning for a short time, so as to be able to let the pupils attend the funeral services for our beloved friend, Mr. Daniels.

Colwell and Minewell had:

219. Thomas Wilbur Daniel* b. 4 Oct 1865 d. 20 Sep 1935
220. Ira A. Daniel b. 15 Feb 1868 d. 19 Sep 1869
221. Priscilla A. Daniel b. 11 Aug 1872 d. 1 Jan 1885
222. Helen May Daniel* b. 4 Feb 1875 d. 19 May 1894
223. Oscar A. Daniel b. 4 Jan 1880 d. 15 Jul 1880
224. Austin G. Daniel* b. 4 Jan 1880 d. 15 Mar 1918

Thomas T. Daniels

57. Thomas Tipton "Tip" Daniel b. 2 Feb 1839 in
Logan County, Ohio d. 4 Jul 1916 at Ansley,
Custer County, Ne. He is buried in the

THOMAS TIPTON AND EMILY JANE HANKINS DANIELS

Ansley Cemetery. He married[103] Elizabeth J.
Lucas 23 Feb 1871 in Ford County, Il. She b. 24
May 1845 d. 1 Dec 1873 at Pellsville, Il. They

---

103. Illinois, Ford County, Marriage Book
A, #556.

had one daughter that died as an infant. Elizabeth and her daughter are buried in the Pellsville Cemetery in Vermilion County, Il. Thomas next married[104] Emily Jane Hankins Daniel, widow of his brother Hiram, on 2 Feb 1876 in Vermilion County. She b. 14 Sep 1847 in Williamsport, Indiana d. 30 Jun 1926 at Ansley, Ne. They raised her two children by her marriage to his brother.

Thomas was a Union soldier, serving as a private in Co. I, 2nd Il. Cavalry Volunteers and was in several battles and skirmishes. He received bounty money in Champaign County, Il and a pension[105] for his service. His pension file gives the following description of him: 5 foot 11 1/2 inches high, light complexion, brown hair, and blue eyes.

Thomas was a hardware merchant in Pellsville, Il in the 1870s and 1880s. He has a biography[106] in the History of Vermilion County, Il. Thomas moved to Custer County, Ne with his brothers and their families. He was active in GAR Post 180 in Ansley, Ne. I have copies of Thomas and Emily's signatures from the estate records of Hiram Daniel and Thomas' pension file. His biography and obituary[107] from an Ansley newspaper follow:

T.T. Daniels, Pellsville, hardware and agricultural implements, was born in Logan County, Ohio, on the 2nd of February, 1839. He remained on the farm until nineteen years of age, at which time his father died. He came to this state in 1844, and settled in Champaign County, where he remained until 1858. On the

---

104. Illinois, Vermilion County, Marriage Book D, page 15, #623.
105. Washington, D.C., National Archives, Union Pension File WC813.535, Daniels, Thomas T.(Emma Daniels, widow).
106. The History of Vermilion County, Il, by Hiram W. Beckwith, page 1017.
107. Nebraska, Custer County, Ansley, The Ansley Herald, Friday, 7 Jul 1917, Volume 25, Number 28.

29th of July, 1861, he enlisted in Co. I, 2d
Ill. Cal. Vol., and was in the battles of Holly
Springs, Franklin, Clinton (Louisiana),
Greenville (Alabama), and at the sieges of
Vicksburg and Ft. Blakely, also in several
skirmishes. He has been twice married: first to
Elisabeth J. Lucas in 1870. She was born in
Indiana in 1845, and died in 1873. They had one
infant, now deceased. He was then married to
Emma Jane Hankins, on the 2d of February, 1876.
She was born in Indiana in 1849. They have by
this marriage one child, Marse, born on the 4th
of March, 1878. Mr. D. is a good business man
and well respected in this community.

T. T. DANIELS

An Old Citizen, Civil War Veteran Passes On

T. T. Daniels passed on and died at his
home in Ansley, Nebraska on Monday evening,
July 3, 1916, aged 77 years, eight months and 2
days.
It was Mr. Daniels request that his
obituary in the newspaper be brief, in keeping
with his simple manner of life, but in justice
to a good man that is gone, it is difficult to
convey in brief words the death of so long and
useful a life.
He was born in Logan County, Ohio in 1839.
When a young man, he answered the call to serve
in the Civil War. He moved to Custer County,
Nebraska in the early days here, being a
pioneer of Nebraska.
But he is gone! Another name is stricken
from the ever-lessening roll of our old
soldiers and settlers, and a solitary woman in
the sunset of life and a lonely home are left
to attest how sadly they will miss him. It must
be so; these tender human ties cannot be
severed with a pang. Yet, is such a death there
is no cause for grief. His life work was done
and well done. He had met old age cheerfully
but wearied with life's duties and cares, he
laid down to rest.

64

It was our good fortune to have known him long and well, and we only knew him to esteem him more highly as the years passed by. Today, we miss him, his kindly smile and friendly greeting.

The funeral services were held at the home Wednesday at 3:30 p.m., with Rev. E. Johnson, officiating and paying a beautiful tribute to the memory of the deceased. The interment was made in the Ansley cemetery.

I also include Emily's obituary[108] as she was married to two Daniel boys and the obituary is very informative about both families:

Mrs. T. T. Daniels

Emma Hankins was born in Williamsport, Indiana, Sept. 14, 1847. She married Hiram Daniels Oct. 26, 1867. To This union two children were born, Charles of Spanaway, Washington and a daughter, Clara, who died May 10, 1903. This home was broken by the death of the father, Hiram, who died Nov. 30, 1874.

February 2, 1876, Mrs. Daniels was born two children, Mose of York and Ernest of Ansley, Nebr. (**The Custer County Historical Society sent this obit to me and noted that although it appeared in the paper this way, a couple of lines relating to her second marriage were probably omitted.)

Through the death of her daughter in 1903, Mrs. Daniels inherited a 3rd family of children, 3 grandchildren being taken into her home and cared for. Hazel Insko and Maude Olsen of Broken Bow and Jim Sims of Washington.

Mrs. Daniels was blind the last year of her life and in great suffering. June 29, 1925 Mrs. Daniels died, preceded by her husband, the late Thomas T. Daniels who died July 4, 1916.

Thomas and Emily had:

---

108. Nebraska, Custer County, Ansley, The Ansley Herald, 2 July 1925.

225. Edmond Mose Daniel* b. 4 May 1878 d.
11 Jan 1947
226. Earnest Jesse Daniel* b. 6 Jul 1880
d. 11 May 1962

58. Rachel Ann Daniel b. 1841 in Logan County,
Ohio d. 1861 in Champaign County, Il. She was
mentioned in the estate records of father and
appeared in census records. She married[109]
Elijah Galloway 11 Sep 1858 in Champaign
County, Il. He b. 1834 in Pa. d. aft 1860. She
died while her father's estate was being
administered. Her mother and stepfather were
raising her son in 1870. I did not find a stone
for her in the cemeteries where the other
Daniels are buried but think she is probably
buried near her father. They had:

227. John Charles Galloway b. 1861 d. aft
1870

59. Hiram Daniel b. 3 Aug 1844 in Logan County,
Ohio d. 30 Nov 1874 in Ford County, Il. and is
buried in the Pleasant Grove Cemetery, Button
Township, near his first wife and several
relatives. Hiram married[110] Sarah Emeline
Jones in Vermilion County, Il 25 Apr 1865. She
b. 27 Mar 1843 d. 24 May 1868 and is buried in
the Pleasant Grove Cemetery in Ford Co. Hiram
and Sarah had three children that died as
infants and are buried near their mother. Hiram
next married[111] Emily Jane Hankins 26 Oct
1869 in Ford County. She b. 14 Sep 1847 in
Williamsport, Warren County, Indiana and d. 30

109. Illinois, Champaign County, Urbana
Free Library, Box A, File G.
110. Illinois, Vermilion County, Marriage
Book B, page 15.
111. Illinois, Ford County, Marriage Book
A, #424.

Jun 1925 in Custer Co., Ne. She later married his Hiram's brother, Thomas.
Hiram was a Union soldier[112] in Co. K, 76th Il. Inf., serving two and one half years and being discharged by reason of disability. He and his brother John were partners in the Daniel Brother's Well Boring Company as shown in his estate[113] records. I have copies of his signature from his and his father's estate records. His estate records also give his children's birth dates and full names. Hiram's obituary[114]:

Died - Hiram Daniels an estimable man and prominent farmer, personally known to many of our citizens, died at his residence in Button, of typhoid fever last Monday evening.

Hiram and Emily had:

228. Charles Henry Daniel* b. 14 Jul 1870 d. aft 1925
229. Clara Emma Daniel* b. 14 May 1872 d. 10 May 1904

60. Miriam Daniel b. 1845 in Champaign County, Il d. aft 1870. She married[115] Alexander G. Mattox 28 Nov 1864 in Ford County, Il. He b. 1843 in Indiana d. aft 1870. They were in the 1870 Ford County, Il census in Button Twp where the Daniel family was most active. I have not located them after 1870. Alexander was a farmer. They had:

230. Margaret Mattox b. 1865 d. aft 1870

---

112. Illinois, Ford County, County Courthouse, GAR Record Book.
113. Illinois, Ford County, Administrator File #98, Daniel, Hiram.
114. Illinois, Ford County, Paxton Record, 3 Dec 1874, page 1.
115. Illinois, Ford County, Marriage Book A, #143.

Marion Daniel

62. Marion Francis Daniel born[116] 5 Feb 1847
in Champaign County, Il d. of angina pectoris
23 Jan 1921 in Cabool, Texas County, Mo. He was
married[117] 17 Sep 1868 to Miss Ellen J.

FRONT ROW LEFT TO RIGHT: MARION, GUSSIE, EDITH
PEARL AND ELNORA GROOM DANIELS. BACK ROW:
LILLIE, EVA AND MAUD DANIELS.

Wilson in Ford County, Il. She b. 1851 in New
York d. aft 1875. After Ellen died Marion next
m. Elnora Lucretia Groom 10 Apr 1879 at
Winfield, Ks. Elnora's brother, James, was the
husband of Marion's sister, Sarah. Elnora was
b. 20 Nov 1859 in Rome, Peoria County, Il and

---

116. Illinois, Champaign County, Urbana,
Urbana Free Library, Guardianship File #162, 17
Apr 1863.
117. Illinois, Ford County, Marriage Book
A, #343.

68

d. 25 Mar 1940 at Cabool, Texas County, Mo.
From the estate records of his brother, Hiram,
I have a copy of his signature and a store
letterhead from the M. Daniel & Bro. Grocery
and Confectionery in Pellsville, Il dated 1875.
I suspect the brother in this letterhead was
Colwell Daniel. I found more documents
containing his signature in his guardianship
file. Marion Daniel was postmaster[118] of
Pellsville, Il in 1870 and was succeeded by
Colwell T. Daniel. Marion and Ellen were living
in Ford County in 1870.

Marion moved to Cowley County, Ks about
1877 and then to Texas County, Missouri in
1902. He and his wife were members of the
Methodist Church. Marion pursued the career of
farmer. A cousin sent me a copy of his obituary
and noted it probably came from a Cabool, Mo
newspaper:

Marion Daniels was born in Champaign
county, Illinois, February 5th 1847, died
January 23rd 1921, being at the time of his
death 73 years 11 months and 18 days old. He
went from Illinois to Kansas in 1877 and in
1879 was married to Ella Le Grom to which was
born two girls, Mrs. Gussie Moldenhauer of
Mound Valley, Kansas and Mrs. Pearl Miller of
Cabool and three daughters by a former
marriage, Mrs. Harcourt of Springfield, Mo.,
Mrs. Maud Smith of Greenwich, Kans. and Mrs.
Eva Allman of Mound Valley, Kansas. Five girls
all living with 20 grand children and 9 great
grand children.

Mr. Daniels was a great home lover,
devoted to wife and children, always looking on
the bright side of life. He had been a member
of the Methodist Church for forty-five years
and was a class leader for several years, he
always loved singing and working in the church
in his younger days.

Mr. Daniels was only sick in bed one week
but had not been well for several years. There

---

118. The History of Vermilion County, Il,
by Hiram W. Beckwith, page 1013.

is left to mourn his loss a wife, five
children, one brother of Ashley, Nebraska, one
sister, Mrs. James Groom and a host of friends.
There was a song and prayer at the country
home at 2 p.m. Wednesday the funeral proper was
conducted at the home of Mr. Daniel's daughter,
Mrs. Pearl Miller in Cabool.

Marion and Ellen had:

231. Lillie Daniels* b. aft 1868 d. aft
     1921
232. Maud Daniels* b. aft 1868 d. aft 1921
233. Eva Daniels* b. aft 1868 d. aft 1921

Marion and Elnora had:

234. Gussie Daniels* b. 11 Nov 1880 d. 21
     Apr 1966
235. Edith Pearl Daniels* b. 14 Apr 1885
     d. 26 Feb 1958

63. Sarah Ann "Sade" Daniel b. 12 Aug 1850 in
Champaign County, Il d. 5 Aug 1929 at Wilmot,
Cowley County, Ks. She married[119] James
Pierson "Jim" Groom 7 Nov 1869 in Ford County,
Il. James was b. 27 Mar 1848 in Cole County,
Mo, the son of Samuel Dabney and Lucinda
Thompson Groom, and d. 9 or 10 Jan 1923 in
Cowley County, Ks. James Groom sold land to
John Daniel in Champaign Co., Il in 1870. This
was land that Sarah had received as her share
in her father's estate. They moved to Wilmot,
Cowley County, Ks before 1872.
     According to family tradition some of
James' family moved to Cowely County, Ks in
1869 and about a year later James and Sarah
followed. They got as far as Olathe, Ks when it
became necessary for Sarah to stop to give
birth to their first child. She reportedly
remained in Olathe while James went on to ready
the farm for her arrival. He brought her there

---

119. Illinois, Ford County, Marriage Book
A, #431.

70

JAMES PIERSON AND SARAH ANN DANIEL GROOM

in the spring. Her obituary[120] appeared in a
Winfield, Kansas newspaper:

Sarah A. Groom

Short Funeral Services at the Winfield
home followed by a church service at the Wilmot
Christian church were held Wednesday for Mrs.
Sarah A. Groom who died Monday.
    The Rev. E. T. Franks of Rock conducted
the services, assisted by the Rev. T. Earl Mead

---

120. Kansas, Cowley County, Winfield,
Daily Courier, Thursday, 8 August 1929.

of Dallas, a son-in-law of Mrs. Groom. At the
church, the Floral male quartet composed of
Jake Fife, John Dicken, W. O. Bender and Leroy
Sturm sang "In the Garden" and Mr. Dicken sang
as a solo "That Wonderful Mother of Mine."

Pallbearers were six grandsons and were
Glenn Groom, Lynn Groom, Gelston Groom, Gilmer
Groom, Wilbur Groom and Frank Harp.

Surviving Mrs. Groom are seven children,
Mrs. Minnie Harp, of Fairview, Okla.; Mrs.
Alice Mead, of Dallas, Texas; Edward Groom, and
Ray Groom, of Hunter, Oklahoma; Frank Groom and
Arthur Groom of Wilmot; and the Rev. J. Paul
Groom of Cunningham all of whom were present
for the funeral services.

Other out of town relatives who attended
the services Wednesday were Mrs. Eva Allman and
son of Mound Valley; Perry Harp of Wakita,
Okla.; Mrs. Marion Kelly of Cunningham; Mr. and
Mrs. George Wall and family of Wichita; Frank
Harp, and family of Wellington; H. S. Groom and
family of Atlanta, and the Rev. Ray Harp, of
Duncan, Okla.

Mrs. Groom was born in Champaign county,
Ill., Aug. 12, 1850 and married there to J. P.
Groom on Nov. 7, 1864. Starting soon after they
were married Mr. and Mrs. Groom came to Kansas,
locating first at Olathe, and after one year
taking a claim in Richmond township. The old
homestead is still in possession of the Groom
family and the government patent for the claim
is hanging on the wall of the Winfield home.
Mr. Groom died in 1923. Mrs. Groom moved to
Winfield in 1910 and made her home at 1416 East
Sixth avenue.

Sade and Jim had:

236. Minnie Myrtle Groom b. 1 Jan 1871 d.
     29 Jan 1950
237. Edward Tipton Groom b. 3 Dec 1872 d.
     bef 1940
238. Samuel Bennet Groom b. 3 Dec 1874 d.
     21 Nov 1879
239. Lela Maud Groom b. 3 Nov 1876 d. 30
     Dec 1878

240. Ellahu Francis Groom b. 11 Dec 1878
     d. 5 Aug 1971
241. Arthur Lee Groom b. 16 Jun 1881 d. 6
     May 1969
242. Perry Elmer Groom b. 22 Aug 1883 d. 1
     Mar 1972
243. James Paul Groom b. 26 Jul 1887 d. 14
     Mar 1977
244. Alice Lenora Groom b. 21 Jul 1891
245. Ray Allen Groom b. 5 Apr 1895 d. Oct
     1967

67. Martha Jane Daniels b. 12 Apr 1842 in
Champaign County, Ohio died[121] 5 May 1893 in
Barkley Township, Jasper County, In. She is
buried in the Smith Cemetery in that township.
She m. John L. Nichols 25 Oct 1859. I think
they were probably married in Jasper County,
Indiana but I did not find a record of their
marriage there. John L. Nichols was b. 16 Dec
1838 in Champaign County, Ohio, a son of George
and Rebecca Lewis Nichols, and died 31 Dec 1931
in Rensselaer, In and is buried in the Weston
Cemetery there. They were mentioned in the
estate records of her father and were
enumerated in several censuses in Barkley
Township, Jasper County, Indiana. John was a
farmer. He married twice after his first wife's
death but all of his children were by Martha
Jane. He has a lengthy biography[122] in a
Jasper County, In history. She had an
obituary[123] in a Rensselaer, In newspaper:

Mrs. Martha Nichols, wife of John L.
Nichols, one of our best known citizens, died
last Friday, at her home in the north part of
Rensselaer, of consumption, after a long

---

121. Indiana, Jasper County, Barkley
Township, Smith Cemetery, Tombstone.
122. A Standard History of Jasper and
Newton Counties, Indiana, Lewis Publishing Co.,
Chicago, 1916 Volume 2, pp. 434-435.
123. Indiana, Jasper County, Rensselaer
Republican, Vol XXV, Thursday, May 11, 1893,
No. 37, page 1, col 4.

illness. Her age was 55 years and 20 days. The
funeral was held at Trinity M.E. Church, Sunday
forenoon, and the remains were then taken to
Smith cemetery, Barkley tp., for interment. She
leaves a husband, three sons and two daughters
to mourn her loss. She was raised in Barkley
township and was a sister of William, George
and Horace Daniels of the township.

Martha and John had:

246. Angeline Nichols b. 1862 d. bef 1931
247. Wallace Nichols b. 26 Mar 1865 d. 22
     Jul 1897
248. Mary Ellen Nichols b. 3 Aug 1867 d. 1
     Dec 1867
249. Cynthia Nichols b. 2 Apr 1869 d. 15
     Aug 1872
250. Jesse E. Nichols b. 21 Aug 1871 d. 21
     Nov 1924
251. Dallas Nichols b. 23 Sep 1875 d. 29
     May 1908
252. Hattie Nichols b. 1878 d. aft 1931
253. Chattie Nichols b. 1 Jan 1883 d. 18
     Jan 1883

William Daniels

68. William H. Daniels b. 18 Dec 1843 in
Champaign County, Ohio died[124] 22 Dec 1911 in
Rensselaer, Jasper County, Indiana. His middle
name is not known and there is some confusion
as to his middle initial, which has also been
reported as F. He married[125] Sarah Elenor Ott
7 Jun 1866. She was b. 11 Apr 1849 in
Pennsylvania the daughter of Michael and Eliza
Ann Burns Ott and died[126] 27 Mar 1923 in

---

124. Indiana, Jasper County, Death Book
CH-15, page 34.
125. Indiana, Jasper County, Marriage Book
1, page 48.
126. Indiana, Jasper County, Death Book
CD-3, page 54.

Rensselaer, Indiana. William and Sarah are buried in the Weston Cemetery in Rensselaer.

SONS OF SHELBY AND MARY ENGLISH DANIELS AND THEIR SPOUSES. BACK ROW: THOMAS T. AND ADA JONES DANIELS, JOHN CHARLES AND ALICE DUNBAR DANIELS AND HORACE G. AND CERILDA GINN DANIELS. FRONT ROW: WILLIAM AND SARAH E. OTT DANIELS, GEORGE AND AMANDA J. OTT DANIELS.

William served as a Union soldier during the Civil War and both he and his widow received a pension[127] for his service. He was a member of Co. E 135th and Co. H 154th Indiana Infantry Regts, which are inscribed on his tombstone, and also the 9th Regt. of Militia. I have copies of his signature from his pension file and the estate records of his father. He was discharged with the rank of Corporal from the 154th at Stevenson, Virginia on 4 Aug 1865. His discharge certificate is included in his pension file and gives his description: five

---

127. Washington, D.C., National Archives, Union Pension File WC737.303, Daniels, William.

feet nine 1/2 inches high, dark complexion, blue eyes, auburn hair.

I have two pictures of him and several of his wife. According to family members Sarah was a stern, but kindly woman, of Pennsylvania Dutch ancestry. She was very religious and during her lifetime none of her family were allowed to perform any work on Sunday that was not absolutely necessary. She has a lengthy obituary in the Rensselaer Evening Republican on the day of her death. William's illness was mentioned in the newspaper on the day before his death and his obituary appeared in the Rensselaer paper[128] on the day of his death:

William Daniels Now in a Very Critical Condition

William Daniels is now in a very critical condition and apparently the end is near at hand. His son Guy, came again from Rock Island, Ill., arriving on an early morning train. Mr. Daniels is today suffering much agony and hypodermic means of quieting him have been necessary.

DEATH CAME TO WILLIAM DANIELS FRIDAY MORNING

Excellent Citizen Passed Away After Long Sickness - Barkley Resident For Many Years.

William Daniels, for several years a resident of Rensselaer and prior to removing here a farmer for many years in Barkley township, died this Friday morning at about 5 o'clock, having passed from sleep to death. He has been a sufferer for a long time and for several months the family had realized that he could not last long. Dropsy and Bright's disease were the causes of death. Prior to two years ago he had been strong and in excellent

---

128. Indiana, Jasper County, Rensselaer, The Evening Republican, No. 301, 21 Dec 1911, Vol XV, page 4 col 2. No. 301, 22 Dec 1911, Vol XV, page 1 col 3.

health. He was 68 years of age and served during the civil war in the 9th, 135th and 134th Indiana regiment. He was one of the kindliest and most universally liked citizens of Rensselaer. He leaves a widow and six children, viz; Mrs. J.F. Payne, Korah Daniels, Mrs. James Price, Guy, Pearl and Elmer Daniels. The latter two are at home; Guy lives at Rock Island, Ill., and the others reside in Jasper County. He also leaves four brothers, viz: George, of Barkley township, Charles of Craig, Colo., who arrived here Thursday; Tom, of Hammond and Horace, of Marion township.

The funeral will be held Sunday afternoon at 2:30 O'clock at the Christian church, being conducted by Rev. C.L. Harper. Burial will be made in Weston cemetery.

William and Sarah had:

254. Flora Jane Daniels* b. 2 Aug 1867 d. 30 Nov 1952
255. Korah Daniels* b. 4 Feb 1870 d. 3 Jul 1949
256. Mary Ann Daniels* b. 16 Feb 1872 d. 1949
257. Harvey Daniels b. 7 Aug 1874 d. 18 Feb 1876
258. Grace Daniels b. 12 Aug 1876 d. 16 Mar 1878
259. Roy Daniels b. 24 Dec 1881 d. 23 Dec 1882
260. Melvin Guy Daniels* b. 8 Nov 1884 d. 17 Jun 1939
261. Alice Pearl Daniels* b. 25 Jan 1887 d. 23 Feb 1972
262. William Elmer Daniels* b. 23 Feb 1892 d. 14 Sep 1966

70. Mary Ellen Daniels b. 15 Jun 1847 in Champaign County, Ohio died[129] 2 Jun 1874 in Jasper County, Indiana. She is buried in the

---

129. Indiana, Jasper County, Barkley Township, Smith Cemetery, Tombstone.

Smith Cemetery, Barkley Twp. She married[130] Stephen T. Comer 9 Nov 1871 in Jasper County. He b. 14 Feb 1848 in Jasper County and d. there 20 Sep 1917. He was the son of William C. and Phoebe DeWitt Comer. He has a biography[131] in a Jasper County history. Mary and Stephen had:

    263. William Shelby Comer b. 15 Jan 1873
        d. 18 Oct 1959

George Daniels

71. George Daniels b. 16 Feb 1850 in Jasper County, Indiana died[132] 16 Jan 1917 in Rensselaer, Indiana. He married[133] Amanda Jane Ott in Jasper County 13 Mar 1879. She b. 13 Dec 1857 in Pennsylvania, daughter of Michael Ott and Eliza Ann Burns, and d. 14 Dec 1920 in Jasper County. They are buried in the Smith Cemetery in Jasper County as are some of their children. He was a well known farmer in Jasper County but retired to Rensselaer. His biography[134] is in "A Standard History of Jasper and Newton Counties, Indiana". I have two pictures of him and his wife and a copy of his signature from his brother, William's, pension file. His biography follows:

George Daniels. The well kept and productive farm of George Daniels lies in a fertile tract of Barkley Township, with the village of Parr

    130. Indiana, Jasper County, Marriage Book 1, page 211.
    131. A Standard History of Jasper and Newton Counties, Indiana, Lewis Publishing Co., Chicago, 1916, Volume 2, pp. 520-522.
    132. Indiana, Jasper County, Death Book H-10, page 98.
    133. Indiana, Jasper County, Marriage Book 1, page 496.
    134. A Standard History of Jasper and Newton Counties, Indiana, Lewis Publishing Co., Chicago, 1916, Volume 2, page 632.

as his postoffice. Mr. Daniels has lived in Jasper County all his life, and by industry and close attention to business affairs has reached a position of substantial independence and has provided well for the family which has grown up around him and the members of which are now established in homes of their own with one exception.

It was on the old Daniels homestead in Jasper County that George Daniels was born February 16, 1850, a son of Shelby and Mary (English) Daniels, who in the very early days came to Western Indiana from Champaign County, Ohio, and secured a quarter section, 160 acres, direct from the Government, paying $1.25 per acre. That land is now highly improved and it is worth many times its original cost. On the old homestead they reared a family of eight children named Martha, William, Ellen, Rody, George, Charles, Thomas and Harris. Of these sons the oldest, William, saw active service in the Civil War as a member of an Indiana regiment, and after the war came back to the old home farm, where subsequently, he bought the interests of the other heirs. The father died in 1877, and the mother in 1876.

Reared in Jasper County during the decades of the '50s and '60s, and attending such schools as then offered their facilities to the growing children, George Daniels had made farming his regular vocation, and after leaving the home of his parents began by hard work to improve a place of his own. On March 13, 1879, he married Miss Mandy Ott. To their marriage have been born six children: Voida, deceased; Alonzo; Roy; Walter; John and Ira. Among the possessions which Mr. George Daniels prizes because of family associations is an old flintlock musket which originally belonged to his grandfather, and which is now nearly 200 hundred years old. Mr. Daniels' father had occasion to use this same gun about 1861 or 1862 when there was reported to be a conspiracy among the sympathizers in this section of Indiana to capture Rensselaer.

79

His obituary[135] appeared in a Rensselaer, Indiana newspaper:

BARKLEY PIONEER DIES SUDDENLY

George Daniels Passed Away At His Home Suddenly This Wednesday Morning In Barkley Tp.

Uncle George Daniels, 66 years of age, a pioneer of Barkley township, passed away at his home this Wednesday morning after an illness that lasted only a few hours. Death was thought to be due to heart failure. Mr. Daniels had worked all day Tuesday hauling hay and was apparently in as good health as usual when stricken.

Mr. Daniels was born on the old Daniels homestead in Jasper county, Feb. 16, 1850. His entire life was spent in Jasper County, making farming his regular vocation during that time, and by close attention to business affairs reached a position of substantial independence. Mr. Daniels came of a family who were among the early settlers of this country and the name has been connected throughout Jasper county's history. On March 13, 1879, he was married to Miss Mandy Ott.

Deceased leaves to mourn their loss, his wife, four sons, namely, Alonzo and John, of this county; Roy Daniels of North Dakota; Walter, of Royal Center, Ind., and Ira, also of this county; three brothers survive, Charles of Colorado; Thomas of Hammond, Ind., and Horace G., of this county.

The funeral arrangements had not been made at this time, but will be published in a later issue.

George and Mandy had:

264. Voida Daniels b. 31 Jan 1880 d. 15 Dec 1880

---

135. Indiana, Jasper County, Rensselaer, The Evening Republican, Vol XXI, No. 13, Wednesday, 17 Jan 1917, page 1, col 4.

265. Roy Daniels* b. 15 Jul 1881 d. 23 Mar
1959
266. Motty Alonzo Daniels* b. 2 Nov 1882
d. 29 Mar 1952
267. Walter E. Daniels* b. 27 Mar 1884 d.
abt 1960
268. John Lawson Daniels* b. 7 Jul 1889 d.
11 Feb 1925
269. Ira Melvin Daniels* b. 18 Jan 1898 d.
17 May 1943

73. Rhoda Jane Daniels born[136] 23 Jun 1856 in
Jasper County, Indiana d. 11 Dec 1889 in Jasper
County. She m. James Campbell 1 Apr 1885. Her
birth, death and marriage dates and the name of
her spouse all come from her tombstone. She is
buried in the Smith Cemetery, Barkley Township,
Jasper County. I have not found any record of
children for her.

74. John Charles Daniels b. 26 Jul 1858 in
Jasper County, Indiana[137] d. 4 Apr 1933,
probably in Craig, Colorado. There were a John
C. and Alice Daniels in the 1920 Santa Monica,
Ca census that match what I know of this
couple, so they may have retired to that place.
I have two pictures of him. His approximate
date of death was remembered by his great
nephew, William Louis "Bill" Daniels (#533).
Bill remembers him from a visit to Rensselaer
about 1925. He was alone on this visit. He
married[138] Alice Dunbar but I have not found

---

136. Indiana, Jasper County, Rensselaer,
Daniel Family Bible in possession of Margaret
Shroyer Ellis in 1994. Also Jasper County,
Indiana Family Bible Records compiled by
Margaret B. Paulus, General Van Rensselaer
D.A.R., 1944, page 18. Genealogy #G9772977.
137. Indiana, Jasper County, Rensselaer,
Daniel Family Bible in possession of Margaret
Shroyer Ellis in 1994.
138. History of Jasper County, Indiana,
Jasper-Newton Counties Genealogical Society,
Taylor Pub. Co., 1985, page 52. Jasper County
Public Library.

a record of this marriage. He was a rancher near Craig, Co and purchased 700 acres of land from the government for one dollar per acre. Charles and Alice had:

    270. U. M. Daniels
    271. Pearl Daniels

75. Thomas Tipton Daniels b. 1 Nov 1861 in Jasper County, Indiana[139] d. Aug 1929 probably in Hammond, Indiana. He married[140] Ada Jones 23 Apr 1891 in Hammond, Indiana. Ada was born in Jan 1871 in Indiana and d. aft 1920 when she was in the census. Thomas and Ada were living in Lowell, Lake County, In in 1900. They were living with his mother-in-law, Alice Jones, in Hammond, in 1920. There was only one child in their home then but there may have been others besides the two daughters I have identified. There is no record of his burial in Jasper County funeral home or cemetery records or reports of his death in newspapers there so he may be buried at Hammond. When I visited the City Record Center in Hammond in 1994 the book that should contain his death record was out being rebound. Thomas and Ada had:

    272. Rubie Daniels b. Jan 1895
    273. Edna Daniels b. 1902 d. aft 1920

76. Horace Greely Daniels b. 28 Aug 1865 in Jasper County, Indiana and died[141] there 23 Sep 1943. Horace was raised by Job and Roda English of Brook, In after the death of his

---

139. Indiana, Jasper County, Rensselaer, Daniel Family Bible in possession of Margaret Schroyer Ellis of Rensselaer, In, 1994.
140. Indiana, Lake County, Marriage Book E, page 458. Also History of Jasper County, Indiana, Jasper-Newton Counties Genealogical Society, Taylor Pub. Co., 1985, page 52.
141. Indiana, Jasper County, Death Records, Book D-11, page 271.

parents. He married[142] Malinda Ellen Pullins 28 Jul 1888. She b. 14 may 1866 in Indiana and d. 8 Apr 1891 in Jasper County, a daughter of John J. Pullins. She is buried near Horace in the Smith Cemetery, Jasper County. Horace next married[143] Cerilda Ginn 11 Oct 1894. She b. Oct 1868 in Jasper County died 9 Oct 1950 in Rensselaer[144]. Horace was a well known farmer in Barkley Township. His biography[145] appears in "A Standard History of Jasper and Newton Counties, Indiana". He was a member of the Independent Order of Odd Fellows. Horace and Cerilda are buried next to each other in the Smith Cemetery in Barkley Township, Jasper County. I have a photocopy of the original of his will. His biography:

Horace G. Daniels. It is one of the oldest and best known families of Barkley Township that Horace Daniels is a representative, and his own active career has been pursued with substantial benefit to himself and the community for more than thirty years.

Born August 28, 1865, on the old Daniels homestead in Jasper County, he is a son of Shelby and Mary (English) Daniels, who were early settlers of Jasper County, having come to this section from Ohio, and secured a quarter section of land direct from the Government. Horace was the youngest of eight children, the others being Martha, William, Ellen, Rhoda, George, Charles and Thomas.

When Horace Daniels was still an infant his mother died, and his father died when Horace was about twelve years of age. Both he and his brother, George, attended the old Burns school

---

142. Indiana, Jasper County, Marriage Book 2, page 340.
143. Indiana, Jasper County, Marriage Book 3, page 175.
144. Indiana, Jasper County, Death Records, Book D-11, page 367.
145. A Standard History of Jasper and Newton Counties, Indiana, Lewis Publishing Co., Chicago, 1916, Volume 2, pp. 379-380.

in Barkley Township and his early education was
limited in time of attendance and in quality of
instruction. After growing up to manhood Horace
Daniels married, in 1888, Malinda Pullins,
daughter of John and Mary Pullins. Mrs. Daniels
died April 8, 1892, having been the mother of
two children; Chattie, now deceased; and Mary,
who is married and lives in a home of her own.
Mr. Daniels was married October 11, 1894, to
Cerilda Ginn. They also have two children,
named Dora and Omar. Mr. Daniels is a member of
the Independent Order of Odd Fellows, No. 143,
at Rensselaer, Indiana.

Horace G. Daniels

His obituary appeared in a Jasper County
newspaper[146]:

HEART ATTACK TAKES LIFE OF H.G. DANIELS.

Pioneer Jasper County Farmer Dies Last Night
of Stroke; Services to Be Held Monday

Horace G. Daniels, who shared prominently
in the country's agricultural life over a long
span, died suddenly at his home at the north
edge of Rensselaer about eleven o'clock last
night.
Death was almost instantaneous and was
ascribed by Coroner M.D. Gwin as the result of
a heart block. Although Mr. Daniels had not
been in good health for several months he was
as well as usual yesterday when he engaged in
minor work about his farm. Mrs. Daniels said
that the stroke was almost immediately fatal.
Mr. Daniels had not complained of feeling ill
when he retired. He suddenly experienced pain,
she said, and died almost instantly.

---

146. Indiana, Jasper County, Rensselaer
Republican, Vol 46, No. 225, Friday, 24 Sep
1943, page 1 col 2.

Mr. Daniels was born in Jasper county on
August 28, 1865, the son of Shelby and Mary Ann
(English) Daniels. He was born and reared on a
farm and it was natural he should follow
farming pursuits, which he did so well through
a long period of years. During the latter
period of his lifetime he alternated residence
between his Barkley township farm and
Rensselaer. He moved to the farm where his
death occurred about five years ago.

On October 11, 1894 Mr. Daniels was united
in marriage with Cerilda Ginn, the ceremony
being performed in Rensselaer.

Mr. Daniels was of a large family, only
one of whom, his sister, Mrs. Rilla Gray, of
Hobart now survives.

Other survivors are the widow, a son,
Omar, of near here, a daughter, Mrs. Elmer
Schroyer of Union township and six
grandchildren.

Mr. Daniels was member of the Odd Fellows
lodge for a period of forty-eight years. He
also held membership in the Rebekah lodge.

The death of this estimable man coming so
unexpectedly came as a severe shock to his many
friends throughout the county who admired him
so much. He was a quiet, hard working man who
contributed greatly to the constructive
enterprises of community life.

The funeral services will not be held
until Monday afternoon at 2 o'clock at the W.J.
Wright Chapel. Three of the six grandchildren
are in military service and the delay in the
funeral services is to permit their arrival
here in time for the services. Burial will be
at Smith cemetery. The remains will be taken to
the late residence this evening.

Horace and Malinda had:

274. Chattie Daniels b. 4 May 1889 d. 11
     Jul 1890
275. Mary Daniels* b. 29 Apr 1890 d. 1916

Horace and Cerillda had:

276. Dora Fern Daniels* b. 8 Apr 1896 d. 4
Apr 1989
277. Omar Horace Daniels* b. 1 Mar 1897 d.
1 Mar 1955

77. Aurilla "Rilla" Daniels b. 1869 in Jasper
County, Indiana she d. aft 1943. She
married[147] John A. Gray 19 Feb 1888. I know
she had children because I met a descendent of
hers in Rensselaer in 1993. They had:

278. RESERVED

78. Alice Daniel b. 1857 in Illinois d. bef
1900. She may have been born in one of the
counties where her Daniel uncles settled. The
biography of her mother in an 1883 Piatt
County, Il history gives her husband's name as
Richard Cresse and their residence as Iowa. An
R. L. Cressa and an Alice Daniels were
married[148] 22 Mar 1877 in Mason County, Il
and this may be them. They were living at
Gravity, Taylor County, Ia in 1881 where I
found a record for one child for them, though
there may have been others. Alice and Richard
had:

279. Arthur E. Cresse b. 18 Jun 1881

79. Emo May Daniel born[149] Aug 1859, Van Wert
County, Oh, and d. 13 Oct 1902 in Bement, Piatt
County, Il of uremic poisoning which was
contributed to by diabetes mellitus. She is
buried in the Bement Cemetery in the same plot
as her mother and two of her children. Her name
is unusual but is written this way on her
tombstone and in Piatt County records. I have
not found a record of her marriage but an 1883
Piatt County history names her spouse, year of

---

147. Indiana, Jasper County, Marriage Book
2, page 328.
148. IGI, Illinois, Mason County, Marriage
Records.
149. Illinois, Piatt County, Death
Certificate, #1409.

marriage and children. She m. Simon Reinhart in
1877. He was b. 1842 in Wurtemburg, Germany and
d. 23 Aug 1903 at Cardington, Oh. He was living
with his father, first wife and children in Van
Wert County, Ohio in 1870. Emo and Simon were
in the 1880 Piatt County census. Simon was
working as a tailor in Van Wert, Oh and Bement,
Il. He may have suffered a debilitating injury
or illness as several Piatt County deeds are
indexed as "Emo Reinhart & husband." They had
three children who died as infants; Emo Alice,
Sidney and Daniel. May and Simon had:

> 280. Roxie Pauline Reinhart b. 1877 d.
> 1923
> 281. Leo S. Reinhart b. Jul 1879 d. aft
> 1900
> 282. Lloyd Cresse Reinhart b. Nov 1880 d.
> 7 Jul 1953

80. Frances Gertrude Daniel b. Jun 1861,
probably in Van Wert County, Oh, d. aft 1925.
She married[150] Sidney Grant 24 Aug 1882 in
Piatt County, Il. He b. Jul 1852 in England and
d. 1915. She attended school and worked as a
seamstress during the 1880 census. Frances and
Sidney lived in Bement and Decatur, Il. The
1900 Piatt County census shows that they had
two children, one deceased before then. She
probably moved to Rockford to live with her son
after leaving Decatur. Gertrude and Sidney had:

> 283. Roscoe Sidney Grant b. Jun 1888 d.
> aft 1922

81. Dell Libbie Daniel born[151] 6 Aug 1863 in
Van Wert County, Oh d. of diabetes mellitis 12
Mar 1922 at Bement, Piatt County, Il. Her death
certificate names her parents as Thomas and

---

150. Illinois, Piatt County, Marriage Book
B, page 53.
    151. Illinois, Piatt County, Bement
Cemetery, SW section, Plot #214, tombstone.

Elizabeth Yost Daniels. She married[152] Grow L. Burgess 30 Oct 1887 in Piatt County. He b. 31 Oct 1864 in Illinois, the son of Henry B. and Mary Miller Burgess, and d. 17 Sep 1939. They are buried in the Bement Cemetery. Her obituary[153] appeared in a Bement newspaper:

Funeral services for Mrs. G. L. Burgess, who died Sunday morning, Mar. 12 were conducted at the home Tuesday afternoon at 2:00 by Rev. Wilbert Dawson of Springfield, assisted by Rev. R. S. Fairchild of the Bement Methodist Church of which Mrs. Burgess had long been a member.
Mrs. J. R. Bower, Mrs. W. R. Camp, Mrs. Earl Folk, Roy Jones, and Rev. Fairchild sang. At the cemetery, a quartet sang "Abide With Me" in compliance with a request made by Mrs. Burgess.
Dell L. Daniel was born in Van Wert, Ohio Aug. 6, 1863. In 1879, she came after her father's death, with her mother and two sisters to Bement.
She was united in marriage to Grow L. Burgess Oct 18, 1887. To this union, four children were born, Leila, Elizabeth, Kenneth, and Marjorie, all of whom are living. Besides her husband and children, Mrs. Burgess leaves one sister, Mrs. Sidney Grant of Decatur.
Mrs. G. H. Burgess, L. C. Burgess, and James Webster of Monticello; Mrs. Sidney Grant of Decatur; Mrs. Wilbert Dawson of Springfield and Mr. and Mrs. Roscoe Grant of Rockford were among those from out of town who attended the funeral.

Grow and Dell had:

284. Helen Leila Burgess b. Sep 1892 d.
     aft 1922
285. Mary Elizabeth Burgess b. Mar 1894 d.
     aft 1922

---

152. Illinois, Piatt County, Marriage Book B, page 86.
153. Illinois, Piatt County, The Bement Register, 16 March 1922.

286. Kenneth Bennett Burgess b. Mar 1898
     d. 17 Jan 1966
287. Marjorie Burgess b. Mar 1900 d. aft
     1922

MIRIAM "MARM" DANIELS

90. Miriam "Marm" Daniel b. 21 Dec 1850 in
Champaign County, Ohio d. 17 Aug 1929 in
Vermilion County, Il. She is buried in the
Fairchild Cemetery in Vermilion County. She
married[154] John Edmund Elkins 1 Jan 1870. He
b. 1851 in Ohio d. bef 1875. She next

---

154. Illinois, Vermilion County, Marriage
Book B, page 59.

married[155] Joseph M. Cox 2 Jul 1875. He b. 1
Nov 1843 in Indiana d. 11 Feb 1902 in Vermilion
County. He was a disabled Union veteran and
received a pension for a wound in his left
shoulder. She next m. Charles Hoth. I have
several pictures of her and one of Charles Hoth
and two stepsons. I have copies of her
signature from the estate records of her sister
Harriet. Marm and John Elkins had:

288. Sylvester Elkins b. 1872 d. aft 1946

Miriam and Joseph Cox had:

289. Benona Cox b. 30 Aug 1876 d. 25 Nov
     1955
290. Evan O. Cox b. 1878 d. aft 1880
291. Noah Cox b. Feb 1880 d. 22 Dec 1934
292. David Cox b. 2 Feb 1884 d. 23 Jan
     1957

91. Mary Jane Daniel b. 11 Dec 1852 in
Champaign County, Ohio d. 9 Dec 1885 in
Vermilion County Illinois. She married[156]
Henry Atwood 25 Feb 1872. He b. 14 Mar 1850 in
Illinois d. 23 Apr 1928. They are both buried
in the Pentecost Cemetery in Vermilion County.
This cemetery is abandoned and very overgrown
but was accessible in 1993. After her death he
married her sister Louisa. They had:

293. Ina Belle Atwood b. 5 Dec 1872 d. 25
     Dec 1906
294. William Atwood b. 23 Dec 1873 d. 4
     Jun 1890
295. Clara Atwood b. 18 Feb 1879 d. 25 May
     1929
296. Ira Atwood b. 13 May 1881 d. 25 Apr
     1917
297. Infant b. 12 Oct 1885 d. 12 Oct 1885

---

    155. Illinois, Vermilion County, Marriage
Books.
    156. Illinois, Vermilion County, Marriage
Book B, page 78.

93. Harriet Rebecca Daniel b. 18 May 1856 in Champaign County, Il d. 9 May 1895 in Vermilion County, Il. She is buried in the Fairchild Cemetery in Vermilion County. A short obituary[157] for her appeared two days after her death in the Danville, Il "Evening Commercial News". Even though she did not marry I am devoting this space to her in order to mention that the records of her estate provided several signatures and some interesting information about this family. Her obituary:

Miss Harriet R. Daniels, aged 39 years, died of consumption at 3 o'clock Thursday evening at her home 5 miles northwest of the city. The funeral services were conducted at 2 o'clock yesterday afternoon at Union Chapel by Rev. Gravett. Burial in Fairchild graveyard.

I have visited her grave at that cemetery. An Illinois State government project is allowing many old cemeteries in that state to return to natural prairie grasses to preserve them and this cemetery is one of those.

94. Napoleon Daniel b. 10 May 1858 in Vermilion County, Il d. 24 Nov 1939 in Danville, Il. He married[158] Laura Gritton 24 Aug 1879. She b. Sep 1858 d. 6 Aug 1941. They are buried in the Johnson Cemetery in Vermilion County. They separated in later years. She was reportedly a disagreeable woman. I have pictures of them both. Napoleon was a farmer a few miles north of Danville but retired to that city. Family members report that he was a large man. His obituary[159] appeared in the Danville Commercial News:

157. Illinois, Danville, The Evening Commercial News, Volume 49, page 8, col 4, 11 May 1895.
158. Illinois, Vermilion County, Marriage Book 1, page 52, License #2010.
159. Illinois, Vermilion County, Danville Commercial News, 24 Nov 1939, page 4, col. 8.

NAPOLEON DANIELS (CENTER)

Aged Retired Farmer Dead - Napoleon Daniel
- Death came early Friday, Nov. 24, 1939, to
Napoleon Daniel, 81, retired farmer and life
resident of Vermilion County.

Mr. Daniel died at 3:30 a.m. at his home,
7 Pine St. He had been under a doctor's care
but was up and around the house Thanksgiving
Day.

He was born in Blount Township, northwest
of the city, son of Eastridge and Caroline
Kiser, moving to Danville upon retirement from
the farm. He married Miss Laura Gritton, who
survives.

Also surviving are the following sons and
daughters: Mrs. Jennie Henry and Mrs. Cora Van
Vickle, Danville; Roy, Everett and William
Daniel, Gary, Ind., and Mrs. Wilbur Phillips,
Plymouth, Ind. Two sisters, Mrs. Louise Atwood,
Danville rural route, and Mrs. Nan Holtz,
Muscatine, Iowa, survive also.

He was a member of the Nazarene Church.

LAURA GRITTON DANIELS (WIFE OF NAPOLEON)

The body was removed to Edmund & Dickson Funeral Home to remain until funeral arrangements are completed.

Napoleon and Laura had:

298. Stella Ann Daniels* b. 1 Nov 1880 d. 18 Nov 1972
299. Jennie May Daniels* b. 28 Jan 1882 d. 3 Jan 1974
300. William Marion Daniels* b. 14 Oct 1884 d. 1972
301. Everett Edward Daniels* b. 30 Aug 1891 d. 1973

302. Nellie Daniels* b. Sep 1894 d. aft
     1939
303. Roy E. Daniels* b. 18 Dec 1900 d. aft
     1939

LEFT TO RIGHT: LOUISA M. ATWOOD, NAN HOLTZ AND
MIRIAM HOTH. (DANIELS SISTERS)

95. Etna Daniel b. 24 Sep 1860 in Vermilion
County, Il d. 9 Sep 1882. She married[160]
Homer Allen 20 Oct 1879. He was a farmer in
Vermilion County. They had three children that
died mysteriously as infants. After she died
her family found finger marks on her throat
suggesting she had been strangled. Her husband
had insisted on burying their children in the
garden of their farm. He apparently repeated
this pattern in a later marriage. The family
there tells the story that later occupants of
the house said that the ghosts of these infants
could be heard crying in the night. The family,
being unable to rent the house because of its

---

        160. Illinois, Vermilion County, Marriage
Book 1, page 58.

94

reputation for being haunted, had it torn down. I have one picture of Homer and Etna.

97. Nancy Ann "Nan" Daniel b. 4 Oct 1864 in Vermilion County, Il d. 7 Nov 1958 Muscatine, Muscatine County, Ia. She was married[161] to Henry Holtz 22 Oct 1885 in Muscatine. I have several pictures of them. Henry was a farmer. They had:

    304. Ray Holtz b. aft 1885 d. aft 1920
    305. Roy Holtz b. aft 1885 d. aft 1920
    306. Bessie Holtz b. aft 1885 d. aft 1920

ATWOOD FAMILY, LEFT TO RIGHT: JOHN HENRY, HENRY, WILMA, LOUISA M. DANIELS, NOAH, CELESTA, ARTHUR, CAROLINE KISER (WIFE OF EASTRIDGE DANIEL).

98. Louisa Matilda Daniel b. 25 Nov 1866 in Vermilion County, Il and d. there 29 Jan 1949. Her name was pronounced Loo-eye-za. She

Louisa M. Atwood

---

    161. Notes of my cousin, Viola Cundiff, Danville, Il.

married[162] Robert Thornton Caster 25 Sep 1884 in Urbana, Il. He b. 20 Jan 1864 in Illinois d. 5 Oct 1886. Next, she m. Henry Atwood husband of her late sister, Mary Jane. Henry and Louisa operated the Henrietta Hotel in Blount Township, Vermilion County in the late 1890s. I have several pictures of Louisa and Henry and a copy of her signature from the estate records of her sister Harriet. Louisa is buried in the Fairchild Cemetery and Henry in the Pentecost Cemetery in Vermilion County. Louisa and Robert had:

307. Elmer Evert Caster b. 15 Jun 1885
308. Luvena May Caster b. 24 Dec 1886

Louisa and Henry had:

309. Arthur Green Atwood b. 2 Apr 1889 d. 22 Dec 1960
310. Noah Franklin Atwood b. 22 Jan 1891
311. Daisy Caroline Atwood b. 7 Oct 1892
312. Ethel Elsie Atwood b. 7 Oct 1894 d. 22 Aug 1910
313. Celesta Laverne Atwood b. 30 Sep 1896
314. Emma Edith Atwood b. 5 Jan 1898
315. John Henry Atwood b. 26 May 1905 d. aft 1994
316. Wilma Clarice Atwood b. 12 Oct 1907

Frank Daniel

99. Frank Daniel b. 27 Aug 1869 in Vermilion County, Il d. 22 Aug 1898. Against the wishes of his family he went to work in a coal mine in Vermilion County. He was crushed to death in a mining accident. His accident was reported in the Danville "Evening Commercial News" on the next two days after his death. One of these

---

162. Illinois, Champaign County, Urbana, Urbana Free Library, Marriage Book for Sep 1884.

articles says that he was buried in the
Fairchild Cemetery, but an elderly family

FRANK DANIEL

member told me that he was buried in the
Pentecost Cemetery about eight feet from his
sister Mary Jane. His sister, Louisa, took his
death very hard and always cried in later years
when she talked about it or saw his picture. I
have a photo of a very fine charcoal drawing of
him and a copy of his signature from the estate
records of his sister Harriet. From the
Danville Commercial News:

23 Aug 1898 - KILLED IN THE MINE - Frank
Daniels Crushed By Two Tons Of Slate - Frank

97

Daniels, aged about 25 years, was instantly killed at A.H. Bonnet's coal mine, in Pilot Township, by falling slate yesterday at 10:30. He was engaged in removing a prop when a section of roof gave down and a mass of slate weighing two tons fell upon him killing him instantly. It is said that it was his own fault, for if he had taken the precaution to put in another prop before he removed the one which he desired out of the way, the roof would have remained intact.

Owing to Coroner Stansbury being at Rankin holding an inquest over a railroader who was killed in the I.E. & W. yards Sunday night, no inquest over the miner's body could be held.

24 Aug 1898 - Funeral of Frank Daniels - The funeral of Frank Daniels, the man who was killed in Bonnett's mine last Monday morning, was held yesterday afternoon at 4 o'clock at the family residence, eight miles northwest of the city. There was a very large attendance at the services. Rev. Snyder officiated. Interment occurred in the Fairchild Cemetery. The floral offerings were many and beautiful, mutely attesting the esteem in which the deceased was held by his friends.

103. Allen G. Daniel b. 9 Aug 1850 in Champaign County, Ohio d. 30 Mar 1893 in Ojai, Ventura County, Ca. He and several family members are buried[163] in the Nordhoff Cemetery in Ojai. His name and dates also appear on his parent's tombstone. He was a Presbyterian minister. From the estate records of his mother it is apparent that he had at least three children and Nordhoff Cemetery records indicate one more. The estate records of his mother in 1903, Nordhoff Cemetery records and the 1900 Ventura County, Ca census indicate his spouse's name was Margaret S. Parsons. She was b. Jul 1849 in New York and d. Sep 1932 probably in Ojai. She

---

163. California, Ventura County, Ventura, Genealogical Society Quarterly, Jun 1992, pp. 43-44.

was living with her children and mother, Sophia
Parsons, in Ojai, Ventura County, Ca during the
1900 census. Her mother was born Jan 1822 in
Canada or England. Allen's widow, daughter Mary
and son Harold were living in Ventura, Ca in
1903 and son Raymond was living in Oakland.
They may have had a son named Clarence who died
before 1903. They had:

> 317. Raymond Safford Daniels* b. Dec 1879
> d. aft 1903
> 318. Mary Playter Daniels b. 18 Aug 1884
> d. 3 Jan 1972
> 319. William DeForest Daniel b. 2 Jun 1888
> d. Aug 1888
> 320. Harold Daniels* b. Apr 1889 d. aft
> 1903

Sarah Daniels

104. Sarah Alice Daniels b. 1852 in Champaign
County, Ohio d. aft 1904 in Champaign County.
She apparently never married and lived with her
family until after 1903 when her mother died. I
have a copy of her signature from the estate
records of her mother.

Margery Baker

105. Margery Daniel b. Dec 1853 and d. aft 1904
in Champaign County, Ohio. She married[164]
Levi Johnson Baker 4 May 1881. He b. Dec 1850
in Champaign County, Ohio d. aft 1904. He was a
merchant in Urbana, Ohio where they were
enumerated in the 1900 census. He was appointed
guardian to the children of his wife's brother,
William Thomas Daniel, when their grandfather
Wilson died. This guardianship bond gave the
birth dates of all of these children who were

---

164. Ohio, Champaign County, Marriage Book
I, page 118.

living. I have a copy of her signature from the
estate records of her mother. Levi and Margery
had:

321. Mabel M. Baker b. Jan 1882 d. aft
     1900
322. Harry D. Baker b. Jul 1885 d. aft
     1900
323. Herbert T. Baker b. Aug 1887 d. aft
     1900
324. Robert J. Baker b. Jul 1889 d. aft
     1900
325. Louis A. Baker b. Jul 1894 d. aft
     1900
326. Ruth Baker b. Jul 1897 d. aft 1900

MARY ADELIA DANIEL WILSON

106. Mary Adelia Daniel b. 1855 in Champaign
County, Oh d. aft 1904 when she was residing in
Corning, Ca. She m. James H. Wilson b. 1854 d.
aft 1902 in California. I have pictures of her
and a copy of her signature from the estate
records of her mother. Her husband was a
businessman in California. They did not have
children.

W. T. Daniel

107. William Thomas Daniel b. 15 Jul 1858 in Champaign County, Oh d. 23 Mar 1944 at Ardmore, Carter County, Ok after being hit by a car. He was a resident of Durant, Bryan County, Ok at the time of his death.

He married[165] Emma Catherine Wilson 23 Sep 1880 in Champaign County. She was b. 26 Oct 1857 in Champaign County and d. there 1 May 1895 of typhoid. She is buried in the Springhills Cemetery with her son William Allen Daniel who died of the same illness two weeks earlier. She was a cousin of the Wilson boys who married her husband's sisters. William was the family black sheep because he deserted his family sometime after the death of his wife. His brother-in-law Levi J. Baker was appointed guardian to their children but they were living with various relatives in 1900. I have a copy of William's signature from the estate records of his mother. He was living in Dayton, Oh when his mother died.

William m. second Georgeanna Van Kirk before 1898. Georgeanna was b. 15 Dec 1872 at DeGraff, Logan County, Oh and d. 4 May 1961 at Wichita, Sedgwick County, Ks and is buried at the Wichita Park Cemetery there. She was the daughter of Samuel F. and Catherine Kelly Van Kirk. She was a member of the Trinity Methodist Church. William moved with his second wife and their family to Comanche County, Kansas. He later left his second family. Family members told me that he would arrive unexpectedly at their home for visits and then leave the same way. The family never knew where he was between these visits. He was apparently a wanderer. I have a photocopy of his death certificate courtesy of one of his grandchildren. His burial was handled by the Bettes Funeral Home

---

165. Ohio, Champaign County, Marriage Book I, page 56.

101

in Ardmore, Ok. No pictures of him have been
found. A news article concerning his death
appeared in an Ardmore newspaper on the day of
his death:

Durant Man Is Killed by Car

**William T. Daniels Meets Death on 77 in
Arbuckle Mountains**

A man about 80 years old, identified as
William T. Daniels, who formerly lived at 308
East Third, Durant, was fatally injured at 9 p.
m. Wednesday as he walked along the highway 14
miles north of Ardmore in the Arbuckle
mountains.
Driver of the car has not been located.
According to Bert Powers, highway
patrolman, who with Theo Cobb, another highway
patrolman, investigated the case, the man
suffered a fractured skull, broken legs and
other injuries. He was brought to the Hardy
sanitarium at Ardmore and died at 7 a. m.
Friday.
He was apparently traveling toward Ardmore
and several witnesses were found who had seen
him walking along the highway prior to the
accident.
A passerby found the injured man beside
the road and notified officers.
The battered sidelight off an old model
car was found near the scene of the accident.
Patrolmen are in search of the car involved.
Powers said that Durant reported the man
to be an old age pensioner who had lived with a
family named Morrison at Durant. The body was
being held pending investigation.

Next day:

Body Held for Burial

Body of W. T. Daniels, Durant, who was
killed in a highway accident Wednesday night,
is being held at Bettes funeral home pending
burial arrangements. Daniels died Thursday

102

morning. He is survived by two nephews in
California.

William and Emma had:

327. Rollo Wilson Daniel* b. 4 Nov 1881 d.
     1946
328. John M. Daniel b. 22 May 1883 d. 1913
329. William Allen Daniel b. 6 Nov 1884 d.
     18 Apr 1895
330. Harry Ernest Daniel* b. 14 Jan 1888
     d. 15 Dec 1951
331. Perry Louis Daniel* b. 12 Mar 1890 d.
     Oct 1953
332. Fred Elden Daniel* b. 14 Oct 1893 d.
     2 Oct 1983

William and Georgiana had:

333. Myrtle Daniel* b. 1898/9 d. abt 1930
334. Walter Thurman Daniel* b. 12 Jan 1904
     d. 11 Jan 1948
335. Harold Robert Daniel b. 25 Sep 1906
     d. 20 May 1964
336. Opal A. Daniel b. 22 Apr 1908 d. 7
     Jul 1978

Margaret R. Daniels,

108. Margaret R. "Maggie" Daniels b. Jun 1860
in Champaign County, Oh d. aft 1904 when she
was residing in West Liberty, Ohio. She did not
marry. I have a copy of her signature from the
estate records of her mother. She was a boarder
in the home of Elizabeth Clarke in 1900 in Los
Angeles.

109. Minnie E. Daniel b. 23 Jan 1863 in
Champaign County, Oh d. 30 Oct 1938 in Long
Beach, Ca. She married[166] Solomon Donley
Wilson 18 Mar 1885 in Champaign County, Ohio.

---

166. Ohio, Champaign County, Marriage Book
J, page 27.

SOLOMON DONLEY AND MINNIE E. WILSON

He b. 21 Feb 1856 in Champaign County d. 14 Dec
1939 in Long Beach, Ca. They are buried in the
Sunnyside Memorial Cemetery in Los Angeles, Ca.
I have pictures of them and a copy of her
signature from the estate records of her
mother. They had:

337. Clarence Elba Wilson b. 2 Dec 1886 d.
     1 Nov 1985
338. Margaret Miriam Wilson b. Dec 1888
339. Perry Donley Wilson b. 15 Jan 1903 d.
     18 Oct 1989

Anna. M. Daniels.

110. Anna May Daniel b. Aug 1865 in Champaign
County, Oh d. between 1943 and 1945 Los
Angeles, Ca. She never married. She was deaf
which was a family trait. I have pictures of
her and a copy of her signature from the estate
records of her mother. She was a favorite aunt

of the families who lived in California and
apparently got along very well despite her
handicap and the era of time in which she
lived. She was a roomer in the house of Charles
Moore in Los Angeles in 1900.

ANNA MAY DANIELS

111. Miriam Daniel b. 1844 in Logan County,
Ohio d. aft 1884 when she was living in Putnam
County, Indiana. She married[167] Jacob M.
Couchman 7 Oct 1863 in Champaign County, Ohio.
I was not able to find them in the 1880 Putnam
County, Indiana census. He ran a tile and saw

---

167. Ohio, Champaign County, Marriage Book
F, page 336.

mill in Fincastle, In and was a prominent man in that area and has a biography[168] in a history of that county. He was listed in the 1900 census of Putnam County, In but I do not know if Miriam was still living then or not. I have not been able to determine dates or places of death for them as yet. They had:

340. Infant b. aft 1863
341. infant b. aft 1863
342. Amos A. Couchman b. aft 1863
343. John Taylor Couchman b. 20 Jan 1866
     d. 2 Apr 1944
344. George William Couchman b. aft 1866
345. Sarah E. Couchman b. aft 1866
346. Arthur Leon Couchman b. aft 1866
347. Ida M. Couchman b. aft 1866
348. Margaret Bertha Couchman b. aft 1866
349. Harriet E. Couchman b. aft 1866
350. Emma L. Couchman b. aft 1866
351. Henry Couchman b. aft 1866

112. Almira Daniel b. 9 Aug 1845 in Logan County, Ohio she d. 11 Apr 1898 at Russellville, Ind and is buried in the Russellville Cemetery. She was living with her mother in Russellville, Putnam County, Indiana in 1880. She probably lived with her mother until she died. She outlived her mother by about five years. I do not know how she made a living but may have depended on her sister, Miriam's, family.

113. Robert Francis Daniel b. 1849 in Logan County, Ohio d. aft 1880 when he was still living there. He married[169] Clara B. Runyon 2 Sep 1871 in Logan County. She b. 1850 in Ohio d. aft 1880. They may have been the couple

---

168. Biographical and Historical Record of Putnam County, Indiana, Lewis Publishing Co., Chicago, 1887, pp. 491-492.
169. Ohio, Logan County, Marriage Book D, page 199.

living in Allen County, Ohio[170] in 1900 with children born after 1880. I include these children here, even though there is no proof of their relationship, to aid future researchers; Pearl b. May 1882, Alma b. Dec 1886 and Roza b. Apr 1889. Robert Francis was living in Quincy Township, Logan County in 1870 occupied as a wagonmaker and was with his family there in 1880 working as a painter. Robert Francis and Clara had:

> 352. Edward Daniel b. 1872 d. aft 1880
> 353. Margira Daniel b. 1874 d. aft 1880
> 354. Ira Z. Daniel b. 1876 d. aft 1880
> 355. Charles Daniel b. 1879 d. aft 1880

114. Nancy Jane Daniel b. 19 Sep 1855 in Ohio d. 1 Dec 1906 and is buried at Ransom Cemetery, Ness Co., Ks. She married[171] Andrew Jackson Gullett 27 Mar 1875 in Champaign Co., Oh. They moved to Ness County about 1886. Nancy was with her Uncle John and Aunt Miriam Daniel Taylor in 1860 in Champaign Co., Oh and in 1870 was listed as their domestic servant. Andrew and Nancy had seven children. I was contacted by a descendent after this book had gone to the publisher so was not able to list all of these children but list the ancestor of the family member who contacted me.

> 356. Ethel Gullet b. 17 Oct 1888 d. 1973

115. Dora E. Daniel b. 1857 Logan County, Ohio d. aft 1879 when she was living in Putnam County, Indiana. She pressed a suit[172] for division of her father's estate in 1879 in Logan County, Ohio. She was not with her mother and sister in the 1880 Putnam County, Indiana census. She may have married.

---

170. Ohio, Allen County, 1900 Census, ED. 4, Sheet 20, Line 48.
171. Ohio, Champaign County, Marriage Book G, page 520.
172. Ohio, Logan County, Deed Book 58, page 407. Deed Book 59, page 17.

357. RESERVED

129. William Estridge Daniel b. 18 Apr 1834 in
Montgomery County, Ky d. 11 Jun 1928 Platte
County, Mo. He is buried in the Riverview
Cemetery there. He married six times but all of
his children were by his first wife. He m.
first Allie Jane Wright 23 Jul 1853 in
Montgomery County, Ky. She b. 22 Jun 1837 in
Montgomery County d. 22 Apr 1888 in Platte Co.,
Mo. She is buried in the Brown Cemetery there.
She was the sister of Mariam Boone Wright who
married William's uncle James Quincy Daniel and
were my great grandparents. Allie and Mariam
were daughters of Meredith and Sarah Calbraith
Wright of Montgomery County, Ky. William and
Allie's dates come from a cousin in Kansas
City, Mo. All are probably verifiable in
records there except, perhaps, for their date
of marriage. I have the names and marriage
dates of all of William's wives but list only
his second wife also. She was Senna Fox[173],
daughter of Harrison Fox who was a son of John
and Elizabeth Hoffmman Fox. John Fox was
probably a brother of Mary Samantha Fox who
married Estridge Daniel (#6). William's picture
and a short biography[174] appeared in a Platte
City newspaper and later William had an
obituary in the same newspaper[175]:

PLATTE COUNTY OLD TIMERS

    William E. Daniel, 93 years old, is a
member of an old Kentucky family that located
in Platte County in 1854. He is now living in
Camden Point. His children are Mrs. Hiram
McComas of Fairfax; Mrs. Fannie Moore, Wheeler;
Mrs. Armilda Cox and William Daniel, all living
in Platte county.

------

    173. Kentucky, Montgomery County, Marriage
Book 1864-1900, page 318.
    174. Missouri, Platte County, The Platte
City Landmark, 5 Sep 1927, page 2.
    175. Missouri, Platte County, The Platte
City Landmark, 15 Jun 1928, page 4.

WILLIAM ESTRIDGE DANIEL

W. E. DANIEL DEAD

William E. Daniel died at his home in
Camden Point June 11, 1928, at the age of 94
years. He was the son of Shelby and Cynthia Ann
Daniel and was born in Montgomery county,
Kentucky, April 18, 1834. He married in 1853 to
Ollie J. Wright and to this union were born
nine children, four dying in infancy, and one
married daughter, Mrs. Cynthia Marshall also
preceding him in death. The surviving children
are Mrs. Mamie B. McComas, Mrs. Armilda
Rinehart, Mrs. Fannie Moore and William Daniel.

He also leaves a sister, Mrs. Mary Hanks of
Smithville. If the writer mistakes not, Mr.
Daniel was married six times, all his wives
preceding him in death. When a young man he
united with the Christian church. He was a man
of most pleasing personality and highly
respected.
Funeral services were conducted at the
Platte City Christian church Tuesday by Rev. W.
M. Mundell and burial was in the cemetery here
under McComas of Smithville.

William and Allie had:

358. Cynthia Ann Daniel* b. 14 Mar 1857 d.
     12 Feb 1901
359. Mariam Boone Daniel* b. 27 Feb 1859
     d. 4 Jul 1929
360. Armilda J. Daniel* b. 7 Sep 1862 d.
     1960
361. Mary Frances Daniel* b. 8 Oct 1864 d.
     aft 1920
362. William Meredith Daniel* b. 22 Feb
     1874 d. 1959

130. James Harvey Daniel b. 7 Dec 1835 in
Montgomery County, Ky d. 24 Jan 1920 in Platte
County, Mo. He married[176] Missouri Ann
Flannery 10 May 1866 in Platte County. She was
born 14 Dec 1846 in Platte County and died
there in 1904. They are both buried[177] in the
Riverview Cemetery in Platte City, Platte
County. Missouri Ann was the daughter of Thomas
and Fannie Brunts Flannery. Both the Daniel and
Flannery families are mentioned in the "Annals
of Platte County" by Paxton, the Flannery's in
great detail. James was a farmer and owned the
farm next to his father's. He was a Confederate
soldier and may be the James Daniel who
served[178] in Company R, 8th Missouri

    176. IGI, Missouri.
    177. Platte County, Missouri Cemeteries,
Seattle, Wa Public Library.
    178. National Archives, Confederate
Military Service Records, Daniel, James H.

Cavalry until the end of the war. He had a lengthy obituary in a Platte City newspaper[179]:

James H. Daniel Passes

Another Landmark has gone to his reward. James H. Daniel was born December 7, 1835 in the state of Kentucky, and with his father came to Missouri at an early age and grew to manhood a few miles west of Platte City. When the Civil War broke out, he shouldered his gun and went forth to do service for the Confederate cause. After the conflict was over he returned to his home and on the 10th day of May 1866, was married to Missouri A. Flannery, a sister of our fellow townsman, Judge T. B. Flannery. To this union was born two children, B. F. Daniel of Kansas City and Miss Issie Daniel, who is in the service of the government at Pittsburg, Pa., and was not able to be present at the funeral of her father. Besides these two children he leaves one brother, William E. Daniel of Ferrelview and one sister, Mrs. Mary Hanks of Smithville, two grandchildren and a host of other relatives and friends that mourn his departure.

For some time "Uncle Jimmie" as he was familiarly known, had made his home with his niece, Mrs. Ruth Zeigler, whom upon the death of her mother, when James H. Daniel had a home of his own, he had taken as a little child and reared. Mrs. Zeigler, showing her appreciation and her gratitude for the kindly ministrations of her uncle, gave to Uncle Jimmie the tenderest care, and no trouble or pains were spared to make his old age pleasant and happy. Here in this home on the morning of January 24, 1920, he wrapped the drapery of his couch about him and lay down to peaceful slumber. Some weeks ago Mr. Daniel's suffered an attack of smallpox, but had recovered from this and had returned home from the hospital. His death was

---

179. Missouri, Platte County, The Platte City Landmark, 30 Jan 1920, page 2.

111

the result of blood poisoning, caused probably from the scratching of the smallpox scares. He was 84 years, one month and 17 days of age.

In early life he united with the Christian Church, and lived a consistent Christian life to his death. The remains were brought to Platte City Sunday, where services were conducted at the grave by Rev. W. H. Adams of the Methodist church, and the remains laid to rest.

Uncle Jimmie Daniel was a familiar character here for many years, a retiring, modest gentleman, whom all loved and admired. He passed thru many hardships and endured them all with a patience that was Christian and heroic. We who admired him much are happy in this thought that a niece, who did not forget, made his last days pleasant ones. We lived by Uncle Jimmie for a short time, and he won our esteem by his gentle, ever pleasant manner. He loved to tell of the war days and live again in reminiscence the old days of long ago. He appreciated the smallest favor shown, and to serve him was a pleasure always. We shall not soon forget him.

James and Missouri had:

363. Benjamin Franklin Daniel* b. 19 Sep 1869 d. 9 Dec 1963
364. Issie F. Daniel b. 15 Nov 1879 d. 1920

131. Armilda Jane Daniel b. 10 Oct 1837 in Montgomery County, Ky d. 24 Feb 1900 in Platte County, Mo. She married[180] Almanza Hon (#120), her first cousin, 23 Sep 1855 in Powell County, Ky. He was the son of Moses and Malinda Daniel Hon. Almanza Hon b. 1 Sep 1830 in Montgomery Co., Ky d. 2 Dec 1913 in Platte Co., Mo. Both are buried in the Platte City Cemetery. It is through their daughter Mary that sketchy descriptions of Estridge (#6) and

---

180. IGI, Kentucky, Powell County, Marriage Records.

Mary Fox Daniel have been handed down to us.
Her obituary appeared in a Platte City
newspaper[181]:

Mrs. Almanza Hon.

Died, at her residence, four miles east of
Platte City, Saturday, Feb. 24, 1900, Mrs.
Almanza Hon.
Mrs. Hon, whose maiden name was Armilda J.
Daniel, was a daughter of Shelby Daniel of
Kentucky. She came with her parents to
Missouri, where she married Almanza Hon, and
they have lived on their farm east of Platte
City for many years. Mrs. Hon was a quiet,
unassuming christian woman, and possessed a
host of friends who will miss her cheerful face
and kindly deeds of charity. She attended to
her household duties as a faithful and loving
wife, and raised her children in the fear and
love of the blessed master. Her home was ever a
pleasant place made so to a great degree by her
ever cheerful and lovable disposition. She, in
early life, united with the Christian church
and was a faithful member of that denomination.
She leaves behind her heartbroken husband,
three sons, Shelby, Quincy and Lee, and Miss
Minta. Mrs. Hon was a sister of W. E. Daniels
who lives east of Platte City, and our fellow
townsman James H. Daniels. Her remains were
brought Sunday to the Christian church in
Platte City, where, after religious services
conducted by Rev. Lockhart of St. Joseph, they
were interred at the city cemetery.

Almanza and Armilda had:

365. Isaac Shelby Hon b. 4 Sep 1856 d.
     1928
366. James Quincy Hon b. 11 Nov 1858 d.
     1936
367. Mary Elizabeth Hon b. 6 Feb 1864 d.
     22 Oct 1950

---

181. Missouri, Platte County, The Platte
City Landmark, 2 March 1900, page 4.

368. Enos Hon b. 3 Oct 1868 d. 23 Jan 1924
369. Arminta Hon b. 26 Jun 1871 d. 28 Apr
1947
370. Nora Hon b. 11 Sep 1874 d. 9 Aug 1875
371. Lee Cortis Hon b. 30 Sep 1876 d. 25
Oct 1950

LEFT TO RIGHT: RANDALL RICHARDSON DANIEL,
DONNIE A. DANIEL, HOUSAN HUNN.

132. Randall Richardson Daniel b. 23 Mar 1839
in Montgomery County, Ky d. 6 Dec 1917 in
Kansas City, Mo. He married[182] Susan Edwin
Coons 22 Mar 1869 in Platte County, Mo. She b.
14 Sep 1849 in Missouri d. 24 Oct 1938 in
Kansas City, Mo. She was the daughter of Joseph
Frederick and Katherine H. Gaines Coons.
Randall and Susan are buried in the Elmwood
Cemetery in Kansas City. His nickname was given
as "Boss" in the "Annals of Platte County, Mo"
by Paxton. I have one picture of him. Susan was
living with her daughter Katherine and her
husband, Charles H. Doane, in the 1920 census

---

182. IGI, Missouri, Platte County,
Marriage Records.

of Kansas City, Mo. There is a very brief mention of his death in a Kansas City newspaper:

The funeral of Randal R. Daniels, who died yesterday morning, will be held at 3626 Brooklyn Friday afternoon at 2:30. Burial will be in Elmwood cemetery.

Randall and Susan had:

372. Joseph Shelby Daniel* b. 29 Dec 1866 d. 23 Sep 1938
373. Ermina Katherine Daniel* b. 3 Apr 1869 d. 1965
374. Mary Ellen Daniel* b. 27 Jun 1873 d. aft 1938
375. Almanza B. Daniel* b. 18 Sep 1878 d. 18 Oct 1960

133. Mary Lucretia Daniel b. 20 Feb 1847 in Montgomery County, Ky d. 9 July 1933 in Platte County, Mo. She is buried in the Riverview Cemetery there. She m. Edwin Otis Wren 24 Sep 1867. He d. Sep 1873 and she m. second Gallatin Searcy Hanks 21 Mar 1876. Her obituary appeared in a Platte City newspaper[183]:

MRS. HANKS DEAD

Mrs. Gallatin Hanks died at the home of her son, Clint Hanks, near Linkville, Sunday, July 9, 1933. Mrs. Hanks was advanced in years. On account of the rainstorm last Friday night Mrs. Hanks arose to see about the windows, becoming confused in her direction, and fell down a flight of steps. She sustained injuries bad enough to result in her death Sunday.
Mary L. Daniel was the daughter of Shelby and Cynthia Daniel who came to Platte County from Kentucky in the early fifties. She first married Edwin O. Wren, who preceded her in death. Two children were born to them. Mrs.

---

183. Missouri, Platte County, The Platte City Landmark, 14 July 1933, page 1.

Richard Oldham of Kansas City, who survives, and Mrs. Davis Ramey, deceased. She was a sister of Mrs. Armilda Hon. Her second marriage was to Gallatin Hanks, who also preceded her in death. She has since made her home with her children. There were several children by the second marriage.

She was a member of the Christian Church, and funeral services were held at the Second Creek church Monday afternoon. Burial was in the Platte City cemetery.

Mary and Edwin had:

376. Lillie Wren b. 18 Feb 1869 d. 10 Oct 1894
377. Mary Eddie Wren b. 1872 d. 1946

Mary and Gallatin had:

378. Thomas Clifton Hanks b. 28 May 1877 d. 1968
379. Charles Hanks b. 19 Aug 1881

134. William Jameson Daniel b. 20 Mar 1841 in Montgomery County, Ky d. 14 Oct 1907. This man apparently lived his whole life in Montgomery County, Ky. He reportedly did not marry. I am sure more information is available concerning this man in the records of his county. He was at his mother's home in 1900.

135. James Estridge Jameson Daniel b. 11 Mar 1843 d. 29 Jul 1858 in Montgomery County. He is probably buried in the Daniel family cemetery there but may have no stone. He died during a brief period[184] when death records were kept in that county. His cause of death was given as scrofula which is tuberculosis of the lymph glands of the neck.

136. Pleasant Jameson Daniel b. 19 Aug 1845 in Montgomery County, Ky and died there 15 Aug

---

184. Kentucky, Montgomery County, Vital Statistics, 1852-1862.

LEFT TO RIGHT: PLEASANT J. DANIEL, ARMINA J. DANIEL COX AND HARVEY J. DANIEL.

1929. I have two pictures of him and one of his wife. He was a farmer and a life long resident of Montgomery County and his family is shown in censuses there. He married[185] Mary Ellen Cockerham 19 Aug 1891 in Montgomery County. Mary was born Apr 1875 in Kentucky and died aft 1906. The birth dates of their children show that he did not marry until fairly late in

---

185. Kentucky, Montgomery County, Marriage Book 1864-1900, page 358.

life. He had a brief obituary[186] in a Kentucky newspaper:

DEATH OF P. J. DANIEL

P. J. Daniel, aged 84, died Thursday afternoon at his home at Camargo. Funeral services were held at his late residence Saturday morning by Elder B. W. Trimble. Burial took place in the family graveyard. He is survived by his wife and several children.

Pleasant and Mary had:

380. Arthur Franklin Daniel* b. 4 Aug 1892 d. 30 Jun 1958
381. William Leonard Daniel* b. 16 Feb 1895 d. 13 Mar 1985
382. Alger Wheeler Daniel* b. 5 Mar 1897 d. 4 Apr 1979
383. James Daniel b. 7 Sep 1900 d. 7 Sep 1900
384. Gillian Frances Daniel* b. 20 Oct 1903 d. aft 1994
385. Bradley Lee Daniel* b. 23 Oct 1906 d. 11 Mar 1993

137. Armina Jameson Daniel b. 4 Apr 1848 Montgomery County, Ky d. 17 Jun 1921 at Crawfordsville, In. She married[187] Winfield Scott Cox 1 Dec 1870 in Montgomery County. He probably died in Crawfordsville as well since his name and dates are also inscribed on her tombstone. He was b. 1849 in Montgomery County, a son of David and Margaret M. Cox, and d. 1889. I found no obituary for Armina but her death was recorded in the death records of Montgomery County, In. She was occupied as a dressmaker in 1900. She and her daughter, Bettie, were living at 610 Binford St, Crawfordsville then. Bettie was living at this

---

186. Kentucky, Montgomery County, Mt. Sterling Advocate, 20 Aug 1929.
187. Kentucky, Montgomery County, Marriage Book 1864-1900, page 76.

address in 1947 when she died and her
obituary[188] appears in the newspaper there.
Bettie had been working as a sales lady at a
local store for many years. Bettie and her
parents are buried in the Oak Hill Cemetery,
Union Township, Montgomery County, In.
According to the 1900 census Armina had three
children but one was deceased by then. I have
one picture of her with brothers, Harvey and
Pleasant. Winfield and Armina had:

386. Bettie Bland Cox b. 15 Sep 1871 d. 14
Mar 1947
387. Margaret Lon Cox b. 6 Aug 1873 d. aft
Mar 1947

139. Columbus Quincy Daniel b. 14 Jul 1852 in
Montgomery County, Ky and d. 11 May 1910 in
Bourbon County, Ky. His middle initial was
given as "Q" in the record[189] of his birth
but is sometimes listed as "J". I am guessing
that his middle name was Quincy after his uncle
James Quincy but may later have been changed to
Jameson, the same as his siblings. He was known
as the "Bluegrass King" but I don't know
exactly why. He owned land in the rich
Bluegrass region of Kentucky between Mt.
Sterling and Paris on the Paris Road. He
married[190] Eliza Prather 31 Mar 1874 in
Montgomery County, Ky. She b. Aug 1853 d. aft
1910. His date of death comes from the Daniel
family bible in possession of descendents in
Montgomery County. He had an obituary[191] in a
Kentucky newspaper:

---

188. Indiana, Montgomery County,
Crawfordsville Journal and Review, Vol.
XVIII, No. 129, Saturday, 15 Mar 1947, Page 1
Col 6.
189. Kentucky, Montgomery County, Vital
Records, 1852.
190. Kentucky, Montgomery County, Marriage
Book 1864-1900, page 116.
191. Kentucky, Bourbon County, The
Kentuckian-Citizen, 14 May 1910.

DANIEL

Mr. C. J. Daniel, aged 58 years, residing at New Forest, near Paris, died Wednesday morning, of stomach trouble, after a protracted illness.

The deceased was a native of Montgomery county, was the son of the late Harvey Daniel, and was an honorable and highly esteemed citizen.

He married Miss Eliza Prather, also of Montgomery, who survives, with three children, Mr. Woodford Daniel, Mr. Holt Daniel and Miss Sarah Daniel.

The funeral services were held at the residence Thursday afternoon at 3 o'clock, and were conducted by Elder R. H. Crossfield, of Lexington. The interment was in the Paris cemetery.

The pall-bearers were: Sidney G. Clay, E. M. Dickson, V. K. Shipp, John H. Roseberry, James McClure and U. S. G. Pepper.

Columbus and Eliza had:

388. Sarah "Sallie" Daniel* b. May 1884
     d. aft 1910
389. Woodford C. Daniel* b. Oct 1889 d.
     aft 1912
390. Holt Daniel* b. Oct 1891 d. aft 1910

140. Harvey Jameson Daniel b. 18 Aug 1854 in Montgomery County, Ky d. 12 Jan 1930 in South Boston, Virginia. He married[192] Leora Jeffries Gilkey 21 Oct 1880. She b. 19 Dec 1860 in Montgomery County d. 9 Nov 1908 in Richmond, Va and is buried in the Oakridge Cemetery, South Boston, Va with her husband. Harvey m. second Marian Seaman. She was b. 28 Mar 1893 and d. 12 Jan 1943 and is buried in the Oak Ridge Cemetery. Harvey and Leora were in the 1900 census of Montgomery County. I have one picture of him. He was a dairy farmer near Mt.

---

192. Kentucky, Montgomery County, Marriage Book 1864-1900, page 184.

Sterling, Ky. Some time after 1900 they decided to move to another state. Since many of his cousins had moved west he probably considered doing so as well and made an unknown number of visits to cousins in Kansas and Missouri. His wife's cousin had located in Kansas and many Daniels and others settled in Missouri. His wife was against moving west so Harvey went to Virginia and using the services of a real estate agent located and purchased a property called "Maplewood" in Halifax County. Information on the descendents of Harvey and Leora come from the notes of Mary and Caroline Walker[193] of Richmond, Va. Harvey and Leora had:

391. Mary Florine Daniel* b. 19 Aug 1881 d. 6 Nov 1970
392. Georgia Clay Daniel* b. 14 Aug 1883 d. 21 Dec 1982
393. Marguerite May Daniel* b. 23 Jul 1886 d. 10 Jan 1979
394. Charles Gilkey Daniel* b. 7 Aug 1888 d. 15 Feb 1938
395. Anna Lee Daniel b. 28 May 1893 d. 9 Dec 1905
396. Elizabeth Harvey Daniel* b. 24 Jul 1898 d. 19 Jan 1981
397. Arthur Daniel b. Jan 1890 d. Jan 1890
398. Gifford Daniel b. Feb 1891 d. May 1891

141. Mary Jameson Daniel 21 Jan 1857 d. 28 Oct 1921 in Montgomery County, Ky. She m. Nelson Wills abt. 1901 in Menifee County, Ky. Nelson b. 9 May 1842 in Morgan County, Ky the son of Shelton and Cordelia Wills. She had one child before marrying Wills. Mary had:

399. Richie Daniel* b. 29 Jan 1890 d. 21 Dec 1955

Mary and Nelson had:

---

193. Mary and Caroline Walker, 4624 Hanover Ave., Richmond, Va 23226.

121

400. Harrison Wills b. aft 1901

145. Narcissa Daniel b. 1841 in Montgomery
County d. aft 1870. She married[194] William A.
McKnab 25 Jan 1860 in Bath County, Ky. He b.
1840 in Kentucky d. aft 1870. Her mother was
living with them in Bath County in 1870. They
may have moved to Missouri as many of her
cousins did. I believe Narcissa's sister
married William's brother. They had:

    401. James McKnab b. 1862 d. aft 1870
    402. William McKnab b. 1865 d. aft 1870
    403. Ida McKnab b. 1868 d. aft 1870
    404. Leonard McKnab b. Apr 1870 d. aft
    1870

148. Joseph Daniel b. 1845 in Kentucky may have
been the man who was living in Bath County, Ky
in 1880 with his five children, brother, mother
and nieces whose last names were Daniel and
Crouch. His mother was named Mary and was the
right age to be the widow of Isom Daniel.

The only problem with this is that his
brother in this census was named Shelton Daniel
and aged the same as his brother John C.
Daniel, who was in the 1850 census, would have
been. This Joseph and Shelton Daniel were in
the 1860 census of Clark County, Ky, probably
as laborers, living with a man named Daniel
Wade. Shelton was in the 1870 Bourbon County,
Ky census with a wife named Lizzie and an Emily
Daniel who was probably his sister. A John S.
Daniel married[195] Elizabeth F. Anderson 29
Jan 1868 in Bourbon County, Ky. An Emily Daniel
was married in Bath County after 1870. Arminta
Jane Daniel, the sister of Joseph's father,
Isom Daniel, had a son named William Shelton
Alexander.

---

194. Kentucky, Bath County, Marriage
Returns, 1811-1866, Part 3, page 93.
195. Kentucky, Bourbon County, Marriage
Book 1852-1900, page #165.

My instinct tells me that this Joseph is
the son of Isom and Mary Daniel so I will
include these children with a caution that I
have no proof. I have found no record of a
marriage for Joseph or Shelton Daniel. I have
not found any record of Joseph or Shelton in
censuses after 1880. Joseph and his wife had:

405. Lizzie L. Daniel b. 1864 d. aft 1880
406. John C. Daniel b. 1868 d. aft 1880
407. Emma S. Daniel b. 1870 d. aft 1880
408. James Daniel b. 1874 d. aft 1880
409. Joseph Daniel b. 1877 d. aft 1880

149. Leroy Daniel b. 1847 in Montgomery County,
Ky d. aft 1884 when he was living in Audrain
County, Mo. He married[196] Martha Lucinda
Byrnes 21 Dec 1876. She was b. in Audrain
County in 1852 and d. there 21 Jul 1884 of
somatitis matima after an illness of six
months. She was the daughter of William Byrnes
who deeded land to her in 1878. According to
death records in Audrain County she is buried
in Rum's Cemetery. He may have been the Leroy
Daniel in the 1860 Morgan County, Ky census
living with individuals named Dennis and
Nester. His mother's sister was married to man
named Dennis in Bath County, Ky and that family
was from Morgan County. The birth record[197]
of Leroy's son, Charles, noted that he was the
third child born to this family. There was one
child in their home in the 1880 Audrain County
census. His wife went by her middle name,
Lucinda. Leroy's uncle, James Quincy Daniel,
lived in this county from 1857 to 1878. This is
more guesswork. Lucinda and Leroy had:

410. Naomi Daniel b. 1879
411. Charles Andrew Daniel b. 6 Feb 1884

---

196. IGI, Missouri, Audrain County,
Marriage Records.
197. Missouri, Audrain County, Birth
Records, Book 1, #311, pp. 23-23a.

150. Mary L. Daniel b. 1849 in Montgomery County, Ky d. aft 1850. She may be the M. L. Daniel that married[198] Wm T. Crouch in Bath County, Ky 13 Jan 1870. They were married at the home of John Moore in Menifee County. The Nagie Crouch in the home of Joseph Daniel in the 1880 Bath County census and listed as his niece could be her child. A guess.

412. RESERVED

151. Emily A. Daniel b. 1851 in Montgomery County, Ky d. aft 1870. Emily A. Daniel married[199] A. W. McNab in Bath County, Ky 3 Dec 1873 at the home of Jack Crouch. Her sister, Narcissa, married a William A. McKnab in Bath County in 1860. Another guess.

413. RESERVED

152. Luther C. Daniel b. 11 Mar 1853 in Montgomery County, Ky d. aft 1910 possibly at Columbus, Ohio. He was born during a brief period when birth records were kept in Montgomery County. I found no record of him again until the late 1880s when he started appearing in Bath County, Ky records when he witnessed several marriages and was mentioned in deed records. A cousin, Herbert Pergram, b. in 1899, knew of this family and knew, Luther's, son Tinsley and confirmed Luther was a son of Isom and Mary Pergram Daniel. Herbert or Herbie, as he is known, said that this family moved to Ohio. Luther m. a woman named Lucinda before 1892 and they were in the 1900 and 1910 censuses of Bath County. She was b. Oct 1873 in Kentucky. She may be the Lucinda Daniel with daughter Lavinia and son Wilson Y.

---

198. Kentucky, Bath County, Marriage Returns, 1867-1917, page 64.
199. Kentucky, Bath County, Marriage Returns, 1867-1917, page 141.

Daniel, aged 8, in the 1920 Columbus, Ohio
census[200]. They had:

414. Lillie L. Daniel b. May 1892 d. aft
1910
415. Tinsley Daniel* b. Sep 1895 d. aft
1910
416. Emilu C. Daniel b. 1901 d. aft 1910
417. Lavinia M. Daniel b. 1901 d. aft 1910
418. RESERVED

162. John Meredith Daniel b. 22 Feb 1850 in
Montgomery County, Ky d. 26 Dec 1891 in
Moberly, Mo. He married[201] Anna Belle Goodwin
8 Aug 1877 near Monroe City, Mo and their
marriage is recorded at Paris, Mo. She was the
daughter of James M. and Virginia A. Martin
Goodwin of Virginia. Virginia A. Martin was the
sister of James Martin who married John
Meredith Daniel's sister, Sarah. Anna was b. in
1854 in Missouri and d. 7 Feb 1887 in Clay
County, Mo. John later remarried but the name
of his second wife is unknown. There is a
marriage[202] recorded at Paris, Mo for John
Daniel and Cladee Lambirth 14 Aug 1890 that may
be for this man.
    He went to work in the mines near
Keytsville, Mo where he became ill. He moved
his family to Moberly, Mo. where he died of "a
complication of diseases". A sister, probably
Sarah, traveled there by train to claim his
body and move his family to Clay County where
he was buried. His death is mentioned in
newspapers in Moberly[203] and Liberty,

---

200. Ohio, Franklin County, Columbus, #47
E. Rick St., 1920 Census, ED 148, Vol 77, Sht
2, Ln 77.
    201. Missouri, Monroe County, Marriage
Book 3, page 271.
    202. Missouri, Monroe County, Marriage
Book 6, page 311.
    203. Missouri, Randolph County, Moberly
Daily Monitor, Volume XIX, No 296, Dec 26,
1891, Saturday Evening, page 2. Volume XIX, No
297, Dec 28, 1891, Monday Evening, page 3.

Mo[204]. Family tradition says that his condition was contributed to by injuries sustained in a train accident sometime earlier. John may have had a child by his second wife. He is buried in the Barry Cemetery, Barry, Mo in a plot with his first wife and brothers George and Albert. This is a six grave plot but these cousins, my great uncles and aunt, share the same stone, which is a pillar type stone, about four feet tall and inscribed on three sides. I mention this because on my visit there I had some trouble locating the stone as I was expecting several stones or something more imposing. The stone is in very good condition. The notices from the Moberly paper and John's obituary from Liberty, Mo follow:

An Object of Sweet Charity.

A Monitor reporter while on his rounds this morning learned of a case of extreme destitution, and one which appeals to the christian people of our city. Some two weeks ago a man named Daniels, with his family consisting of a young wife and three boys, children of a former wife, the oldest being 12 and the youngest about 1 year old, arrived here in a destitute condition from one of the mines near Keytsville where he had been working, and moved into a house at 510 Roberts street, East Moberly. About a week after the man was taken ill, and he died last night. Since their arrival here the city has given them fuel, etc., while generous neighbors have supplied them with food. But we are informed that the children have hardly enough clothing to cover them, and that there is no stove in either of the two rooms of the house, and they are huddled together to keep from freezing. A sister of the man has been telegraphed for, but it is believed she has no means to assist them and the man will, in all probability, be buried as a pauper.

---

204. Missouri, Clay County, Liberty Tribune, 8 Jan 1892.

The Daniels Family

The case of the Daniels family, living at 510 Roberts street, East Side, to which reference was made in our issue of Saturday, is indeed a pitiable one. The family was in deepest destitution - having lived on nothing but "ship stuff" for more than a week, with no fire at all to warm their almost clotheless bodies. An appeal in their behalf was made to our people from the various pulpits of our city on last evening, when the following collections were received: M.E. Church...$5.60, M.E. South Church...3.80, Salvation Army...5.30, C.P. Church...16.00, Christian Church...17.00.

We failed to get the reports from the other churches.

The committee having this case in hand will use what money is needed to meet their immediate wants and secure the family passage back to their home and friends in Kansas City and the remainder will be placed in the city poor fund. This prompt and liberal response is but another evidence of our people, who are ever ready and willing to answer the calls of those in distress and contribute to the wants of the needy.

Later

The sister of the man Daniels above referred to, came, and by the assistance of the committee was enabled to take the remains of her brother to Harlem this p.m. for interment.

Obituary

John M. Daniels died at Moberly on Dec. 26th, of a complication of diseases. His remains were brought to Barry and buried in our cemetery on Dec. 29. Funeral services by Elder Dan Carpenter. He was 42 years old and 24 years a member of the Christian church. He left a widow and three children.

John and Anna had:

419. Beulah Mae Daniel* b. 4 Sep 1878 d.
     16 Dec 1957
420. Myrtle Meredith Daniel* b. 6 Apr 1881
     d. 13 Apr 1951
421. Onie St. Elmo Daniel* b. 5 Jul 1883
     d. aft 1905
422. Alicia Pearl Daniel* b. 10 Sep 1885
     d. 16 Mar 1978

SARAH ELEANOR ISABEL DANIEL MARTIN

163. Sarah Eleanor Isabel "Sally" Daniel b. 15
Apr 1852 in Montgomery County, Ky d. 5 May 1916

in Ralls County, Mo. She married[205] James A.
Martin 5 Oct 1873 in Audrain County, Mo. James'
sister, Virginia Martin Goodwin, was the
mother of the wife of Sarah's brother, John
Meredith Daniel. James was b. Jun 1844 in
Virginia d. before 1910, in 1906 according to
family tradition, in Ralls County, Mo.
According to the notes of Alicia Pearl Daniel
(#422) he was buried at Ariel Chapel Cemetery,
Ralls County but I could find no stone for him
there. Aunt Sally was buried somewhere around
Lakenan, Mo. where she had been living with one
of her sons. James and Sarah lived mostly in
western Ralls County, Mo where James was a
farmer. I have one picture of Sarah and one of
each of her sons as young men. Their son,
Frank, administered his Aunt Allie Martin's
estate in Ralls County, Mo. Aunt Sally seems to
have been well thought of by the family from
what I have gathered in conversations with
various relatives. James and Sally had:

> 423. Albert Quincy Martin b. Jan 1876 d.
> 1951
> 424. Frank C. Martin b. 3 Sep 1878 d. aft
> 1919

164. Estridge Shelby Daniel b. 7 Nov 1854 in
Montgomery County, Ky d. 16 Apr 1857 in Audrain
County, Mo. I mention him because he was buried
near his grandmother, Mary Fox Daniel on the
farm of James Quincy Daniel. Her tombstone had
disappeared by 1936 but a tree planted where
Estridge Shelby was buried was still there then
and the graves were cared for. This information
comes from the notes of Alicia Pearl Daniel
(#422) as told to her by Estridge Shelby's
brother, James Edwin Daniel (#165). Although no
one living at this time knows the location of
these graves the tree may be a clue. It is
possible that Mary's stone is still there but
is buried under the surface now. Estridge
Shelby's mother had a liking for cedar trees

---

205. IGI, Missouri, Audrain County,
Marriage Records.

and planted a row of them along the side of
their farm house, the stumps of which are still
visible in 1994. I have briefly visited this
farm a couple of times and questioned the
present occupants and a neighbor but could find
nothing.

JAMES EDWIN AND WILLIE HUNN DANIEL

165. James Edwin "Ed" Daniel b. 10 Jan 1858 in
Montgomery County, Ky d. 10 Mar 1952 at Osborn,
DeKalb County, Mo. He married[206] Willie
Hausen Hunn 22 Sep 1880 in Clay County, Mo. She
was the daughter of Hausen W. and Nancy E.

---

206. IGI, Missouri, Clay County, Marriage
Records.

Davis Hunn who are buried in the Barry Cemetery near where three of James Edwin Daniel's brothers are buried. Willie Hausen Hunn b. 15 Feb 1861 Harrison County, Mo d. 16 Nov 1931 at Fairport, Mo. James and Willie are buried at the Fairport Cemetery in Fairport, Mo. Both have substantial obituaries in the DeKalb County Herald. Copies[207] of these notices may be obtained from the DeKalb County Historical Society in Maysville, Mo. I have many pictures of the Hunns and James and Willie Daniel from about 1885 until they were elderly. Willie Hunn's sister married Joseph Shelby Daniel (#372), a cousin of James Edwin. James Edwin was an enterprising man. He farmed, ran a hotel, a restaurant and a general store at various times. Uncle Ed and Aunt Willie raised two of his nephews and two of their grandchildren as their own children. They all called him Papa Ed. Through my dad I know him as Uncle Ed. Several cousins have told me that Ed and Willie were talented and avid dancers and were well known for performing a dance called the "Shondee". These same cousins told me that all of the Daniels of this generation danced. His obituary[208]:

James Edwin Daniel Rites Held Friday - Services For Osborn Man Who Died March 10 Held At Fairport Methodist Church Friday - James Edwin Daniel, son of James Quincy and Mariam Boone Wright Daniel, was born near Mexico, January 10, 1858, and died March 10, 1952 at Osburn, at the age of 94 years and two months.
He was united in marriage to Willie H. Hunn, September 22, 1880. She preceded him in death, Nov 16, 1931.
He leaves to mourn his passing two daughters, Mrs. A.L. Perry of Osburn, and Mrs. C.F. Moss of Maysville, and one son George E.

---

207. Missouri, DeKalb County, Weatherby, DeKalb County Historical Society, Family Folders, Daniel Surname.
208. Missouri, DeKalb County Herald, 20 March 1952, page 10, col 1.

Daniel of Glendale, California; ten grandchildren, Gladys E. Tate, St. Joseph, Chas. W. Perry, Fairport, Arthur E. Perry, Osborn, Covell Daniel, Downey, California, Homer and John E. Moss and Mrs. Bonnie Moulton, Pontiac, Michigan, George G. Moss of South Bend, Indiana, Mrs. Norma Johnson, Salina, Kansas, and Mrs. Willie Thompson of Fairport, who was reared in his home as one of his children; twenty-four great-grandchildren; eleven great-great grandchildren.

One grandson, Earl Moss, and one granddaughter, Carol Daniel, preceded their grandfather in death.

He was the last of a family of nine children, two sisters and six brothers having preceded him in death.

In his youth he united with the Christian Church at Barry, Missouri, and later transferred his membership to the Fairport Methodist Church. He had made his home with his son-in-law and daughter, Mr. and Mrs. A.L. Perry of Osborn, since the death of his wife. The following poem was read at the service, entitled "Jesus Is Always There."

Sometimes our skies are cloudy and dreary,
Sometimes our hearts are burdened with care,
But we may know, whate'er may befall us,
Jesus is always there.
When in the midst of life with its problems,
Bent with our toil and burdens we bear;
Wonderful thought and deep consolation,
Jesus is always there.
When we are walking through the green pastures,
Or over mountains rugged and bare;
Precious the thought and sweet the assurance,
Jesus is always there.

"Lo I am with you always" is written God
will not fail to answer our prayer

132

Trusting his word, we rest in His promise
- Jesus is always there.

Never a burden that he doth not carry,
Never a sorrow that he doth not share;
Whether the day be sunny or dreary,
Jesus is always there.

Funeral services were held at the Fairport
Methodist Church Friday, March 14th at 2 p.m.,
conducted by Rev. Fred Nold, assisted by Rev.
S.O. Borland of Osborn. Soloist was Emory
Sweiger, who sang "Without a Cloud" and "Good
Night and Good Morning" and was accompanied by
Mrs. Vest Hewitt.
Pallbearers were great-grandsons, J.B.
Tate, A.J. Perry, Jack Brice, R.B. Sandgren,
L.L. Boyer, A.T. Estes.
Burial was in the Fairport Cemetery under
the direction of the Bram Funeral Service.

Ed and Willie had:

425. Linnie Maude Daniel* b. 6 Jul 1881 d.
     15 Feb 1976
426. Lora Lee Daniel* b. Nov 1883 d. 1975
427. George Edwin Daniel* b. 27 May 1897
     d. 22 July 1967

166. Charles Daniel b. 7 May 1861 in Mexico,
Audrain County, Mo d. 19 Dec 1936 in Oakwood,
Mo. He married[209] Frieda Anna Margaret
Bastian, daughter of Friedrich Wilhelm August
Bastian and Sophia Christina Stengel. Charles
and Frieda, or Charlie and Freedy, m. 16 Sep
1900 in Ralls County, Mo. She b. 5 Mar 1882 at
Hannibal, Marion County, Mo, where her father
operated a furniture store, and died there 14

---

209. Missouri, Ralls County, Marriage Book
F, page 94.

133

July 1975. She was a midwife and delivered many
babies.

When he first saw his future wife, Charles
was working as a stock broker and traveled
extensively. Her father's farm was in western

CHARLES AND FRIEDA ANNA MARGARET BASTIAN DANIEL

Ralls County, Mo and Charles was there buying
stock. He was about 5 foot 6 inches tall and
had black hair and "steely blue" eyes which he
inherited from his father. He was later a
farmer but moved to town in 1929 due to ill
health. My father remembered this move very
well and also recalled taking a large box of
the Daniel family pictures to his mother and
her direction to take them down and throw them

in the creek as she "didn't want to haul them around". This probably explains the scarcity of pictures of the family of James Quincy Daniel and his descendents. The few that I have I found in the hands of the descendents of Charles' siblings.

Charles smoked cigars and grew his own tobacco which was called "Green Mule". He had been working as a night watchman and laborer in a large plant nursery in the months before he died of edema. He died on a very stormy night, sitting upright in a chair. He was a strong man and his heart beat for several minutes after he stopped breathing. His brothers, Bob and Ed, and other family members were present. His wife died of the diseases of old age at 93 years. Both have obituaries in The Hannibal Courier Post shortly after their deaths. These newspapers are on microfilm, copies of which are held by the Hannibal, Mo Public Library. Charlie and Frieda are buried in the Grandview Cemetery near Hannibal, Mo.

Charles and his first cousin, Harvey Jameson Daniel, bore a striking resemblance to one another. Charles and Frieda were my grandparents and I have many mementos and documents concerning them and copies of their signatures. His obituary[210]:

AGED OAKWOOD RESIDENT DIES - CHARLES DANIEL HAD BEEN ILL YEAR - FUNERAL TO BE SUNDAY - Following a year's illness, Charles Daniel died in his home, 1507 Viley Avenue, Oakwood, at 1:45 o'clock this morning at the age of 75 years.

Mr. Daniel had lived in Ralls County for many years, coming to Oakwood seven years ago.

The remains were removed to Schwartz's funeral home and prepared for burial. Services will be held Sunday afternoon at 1:30 o'clock at the Oakwood Christian church with the Rev. John W. Golden in charge. Interment will be in Grand View burial park. The remains were taken

---

210. Missouri, Marion County, Hannibal Courier Post, 19 Dec 1936, page 1.

to the family home this afternoon and will be removed to the church at 11 o'clock Sunday morning to lie in state until the time of the service.

Mr. Daniel was born March 7, 1861, in Mexico, Mo., the son of James Quincy and Mariam Wright Daniel. He was a member of the Spalding Christian Church.

Surviving are his wife, Mrs. Freda Daniel; seven children, Fred C., of Columbus, Ohio; Cecil of Hannibal, John and George of Oakwood; Mrs. Eldred Reed of Hannibal; Mrs. Vincent Lappin of Oakwood and Theda Ruth Daniel at home; two brothers, James Edward of Denver, Mo., and Robert of Fort Collins, Colo.; a sister, Mrs. Elmyra Taylor of Beardstown, Ill.; six grandchildren.

Charlie and Freedy had:

428. Frederick Charles Daniel* b. 21 Sep 1901 d. 20 Dec 1968
429. Cecil Earl Daniel* b. 15 Apr 1905 d. 3 Jan 1968
430. George Albert Daniel* b. 21 Dec 1907 d. 9 Dec 1986
431. Thelma Rita Daniel* b. 23 Nov 1909 d. aft 1994
432. Elva Mariam Sophia Daniel* b. 24 Jun 1912 d. 3 Jul 1993
433. John Quincy Daniel* b. 24 Dec 1915 d. aft 1994
434. Theda Ruth Daniel* b. 6 Nov 1923 d. aft 1994.

167. Elmyra Webster "Myra" Daniel b. 22 Feb 1864 in Audrain County, Mo d. 5 Dec 1949 in Denver, Co. She married[211] Jefferson Davis Taylor in Clay County, Mo 30 Jan 1884. There was a notice of their marriage in the Clay County Liberty Tribune. He was b. 13 Apr 1861 d. 26 Apr 1936 in Ft. Collins, Co. They lived in Missouri until at least 1910. Jefferson was

---

211. IGI, Missouri, Clay County, Marriage Records.

known as Uncle Buck or Jeff and Elmyra as Myra or Aunt Myra. I have a note written by her and several pictures of them both. This note mentions William Meredith Daniel (#362) and shows that, though divided by distance and

LEFT TO RIGHT: MYRA DANIEL TAYLOR, DAUGHTER MAYME LOUISE TAYLOR CALDER AND JEFF TAYLOR

widening familial ties, there was still a sense of family among these people nearly one hundred years after migrating from Kentucky. My father mentioned to me that his father had contact with cousins in Kentucky but Dad did not know the particulars of this.

Aunt Myra was a tiny woman, like her mother. She was very well liked by those who knew her. Her daughter married and was

stepmother to her new husband's three sons.
Mrs. Irene Calder of Beardstown, Il, the widow
of one of these stepsons, told me in a
conversation in 1993 that Myra was grandmother
to her children and so spoiled them with
attention that she could not compete. She was
not complaining and said this with a laugh only
to illustrate what a good woman she thought
Myra was. After Jeff died Myra lived with her
brother, Bob, in Ft. Collins, Co until he died.
Myra and Jeff had:

> 435. Mayme Louise Taylor b. 20 Mar 1890 d.
> Aug 1964

ALBERT RINGO DANIEL

168. Albert Ringo Daniel b. 31 Mar 1867 in Audrain County, Mo d. 16 Jun 1896 in Clay County, Mo. He is buried in the Barry Cemetery near Liberty, Mo. in the same plot as brothers John and George. He was known as Bert Daniel. I have one picture of him as a teenager from the pictures of his first cousins, Lora Lee and Linnie Maude Daniel. The note written on the back says "Uncle Bert Daniel son of Quincy and Mariam Daniel". He has a brief obituary[212] in the Liberty Tribune but it does not give a cause of death. He did not marry. His death is something of a mystery to me and I hope to discover more about him from area newspapers. His middle name probably came from Webster Ringo who was supposedly a partner with his father in the stock business. Bert's obituary:

Barry - The remains of Bert. Daniel of Linden were buried in Barry Cemetery last Wednesday, June 17. Funeral services were held at the Methodist chapel at Linden by Rev. Walters, after which the remains were brought here for internment.

169. George Martin Daniel b. 18 Jul 1870 in Audrain County, Mo d. 7 Apr 1897 at Linden, Clay County, Mo. He married[213] Minnie Denny in DeKalb County, Mo 21 Oct 1896. She b. 27 Mar 1879 in Grant Township, DeKalb County, Mo d. 21 Nov 1949 and is buried at Oak Grove Cemetery there. Her family was well known in the area for having large dances and being very musical. They may have met at one of these dances. George and Minnie had been married only six months when he died of consumption. He has a brief obituary[214] in the Liberty Tribune of Clay County, Mo. He was buried in the Barry Cemetery, Barry, Mo in a plot with his brothers

---

212. Missouri, Clay County, Liberty Tribune, 26 Jun 1896.
213. Missouri, DeKalb County, Marriage Book G, page 81.
214. Missouri, Clay County, Liberty Tribune, 16 Apr 1897.

John and Albert. I have one picture of Minnie
copied from a DeKalb County, Mo History. She
next married[215] Charles W. Flanders. George's
obituary:

Died near Linden, the 7th of April, 1897,
Mr. George Daniels, aged 26, of that dread
disease consumption. His death in the bloom of
early manhood and with many bright prospects in
life opening before him, brought grief to his
young wife, only 18, and they had only been
married six months.
Truly it was a sad scene, at the church at
Linden, as the solemn rites were performed by
Bro. Waters of Liberty.

FIRST ON LEFT: CHARLES DANIEL. SECOND FROM
LEFT: ROBERT Q. DANIEL. FAR RIGHT: ANNA
BASTIAN.

170. Robert Quincy "Bob" Daniel b. 7 Sep 1874
in Audrain County, Mo d. 15 Apr 1943 in Ft.
Collins, Co. He farmed in Missouri and lived in

---

215. Missouri, DeKalb County, Marriage
Book H, page 100.

Ralls County near his siblings, Charlie, Myra
and Sallie. He was in love with Anna Bastian,
whose sister was the wife of his brother
Charles. Her father did not approve of the
match and ordered her to break off their
courtship, which she did. Bob never married. My
father remembered him from visits to Hannibal,
particularly on the occasion of his brother
Charles' death, as a short man whose hair stood
straight up on the top of his head. Bob Daniel
and his sister Myra lived together after her
husband died. There is a brief mention[216] of
his death in the DeKalb County, Mo. Herald on
the 22nd of April 1943. My father remembers
that he and his brothers and sisters each
received forty-four dollars from their Uncle
Bob's estate. I have several pictures of him
from about the age of thirty-five on. He
greatly resembled his father. From a DeKalb
County, Mo newspaper:

Attended Funeral

J.E. Daniel received word Friday of the
death of his brother, Bob Daniel, of Fort
Collins, Colorado. He left Friday night for
Fort Collins to attend the funeral services. He
is survived by one sister, Mrs. Myra Taylor,
who made her home with him, one brother, J.E.
Daniel, and several nieces and nephews.

His obituary[217] from a Ft. Collins
newspaper:

Robert Q. Daniel Is Taken by Death

Robert Q. Daniel of 810 West Mountain
avenue died at his home last night having been

---

216. Missouri, DeKalb County, Maysville,
DeKalb County Historical Society, Family
Folders, Daniel Surname.
217. Colorado, Larimer County, Ft. Collins
Express Courier, Friday, 16 Apr 1943, page 2,
col. 2.

confined to his bed for 10 days. His health had
been poor for almost two years.
Mr. Daniel was born Sept. 7, 1874, in
Mexico, Mo., and was of a family of nine
children. In 1920 he came to Ft. Collins and
for 13 years was employed by the Espelin Floral
company. He is survived by a sister, Mrs.
Elmire Taylor of Fort Collins, a brother, Ed
Daniel of Maysville, Mo., and several nieces
and nephews. One niece, Mrs. C. F. Calder of
Dixon, Ill., is expected to come for the
funeral.
The service will be conducted Monday at 2
p. m. at the Day-Rice funeral home by the Rev.
R. L. Decker. Burial will be in Grandview
cemetery.

171. Amos R. Daniel b. 1825 in Clarke County,
Alabama d. aft 1851. He is probably the man who
married[218] Christina Skinner 10 Aug 1851 in
De Soto Parish, La. I have not located them
after this time. He was in the 1850 De Soto
Parish census living with his mother and
siblings. I reserve this number for their
children:

    436. RESERVED

172. Elizabeth Daniel b. 1828 Clarke County, Al
d. abt 1866 De Soto Parish, La. She
married[219] James Howell 20 May 1847 In De
Soto Parish. He was the husband of her late
aunt, Narcissa Daniel. They were in the 1850 De
Soto Parish census. Elizabeth and James had:

    437. Celia R.A. Howell b. 1858 d. aft 1860
    438. John E. Howell b. 1859 d. aft 1860

173. Sarah Daniel b. 12 Feb 1830 in Clarke
County, Al d. 1 Mar 1901 in De Soto Parish, La.

------

    218. Louisiana, De Soto Parish, Marriage
Book A, page 104.
    219. Louisiana, De Soto Parish, Marriage
Book A, page 34.

She married[220] James Jones 28 Oct 1851 in De Soto Parish. He b. 30 Oct 1830 in Mississippi d. 4 Sep 1906. They were in the 1880 census of De Soto Parish, La with three of the children of her brother Giles. Sarah gave her father's birthplace as Virginia. Sarah and James had:

439. Leodossia Jones b. 1852 d. aft 1870
440. Martha Jones b. 1853 d. aft 1870
441. Amanda Jones b. 1856 d. aft 1870
442. Rufus Jones b. 1858 d. aft 1870
443. Katy Jones b. 1860 d. aft 1870
444. James Jones b. 1862 d. aft 1870
445. Wilburn Jones b. 1869 d. aft 1870

175. Thersa Daniel b. 1836 Clarke County, Al d. aft 1857. She married[221] William W. Tatum in De Soto Parish, La 28 Mar 1857. I have not traced them after their marriage. I have also seen her name spelled Thirza. I reserve:

446. RESERVED

176. Giles Daniel b. 1838 Clarke County, Al d. abt 1875. He m. Nancy Jane Oates abt 1860 possibly in Shelby County, Tx. He is reportedly buried at Cold Springs, San Jacinto Co., Tx. She was b. 1841 in North Carolina d. abt 1870, a daughter of James and Mary A. Oates, and is reported to be buried in the Oates Cemetery in Polk County, Texas. The notes of a cousin indicate a Giles Daniel enlisted in the Confederate infantry and may have been this man. Giles and Nancy were in the 1870 Polk Co., Tx census. Giles married[222] second Catherine Bennett 11 Aug 1871 in San Jacinto County, Tx. She may be the Catherine Daniel in De Soto Parish, La deed records around 1900. A correspondent sent me copies of the records of

---

220. Louisiana, De Soto Parish, Marriage Book A, page 110.
221. Louisiana, De Soto Parish, Marriage Book A, page 93.
222. Texas, San Jacinto County, Marriage Records.

both of these marriages. Much of the information for Giles Daniel, his siblings and descendents comes from the notes of Mrs. Juanita Christian Parker, whose husband was a descendent of Giles and Nancy Daniel. Giles and Nancy had:

447. Giles David Daniel* b. May 1862 d. 1912
448. Amos James Daniel* 31 Dec 1863 d. 7 Apr 1941
449. Robert Monroe Daniel* b. 19 Sep 1870 d. 7 Jul 1946
450. Mary Jane Daniel* b. 1866 d. aft 1895

Giles and Catherine had:

451. Alfred Daniel b. abt 1875

178. Mary Daniel b. 1842 in Caddo Parish, Louisiana d. aft 1866. She married[223] J. C. Taylor 16 Nov 1867 in De Soto Parish, La. I have not tried to locate them in records yet. I do not know if they had children.

452. RESERVED

179. Emily Daniels b. 1845 De Soto Parish, Louisiana d. aft 1871. She may be the Emma C. Daniels who married[224] Joseph Taylor 9 Oct 1871 in De Soto Parish, La. She was probably the Emma Daniel in the home of Sally (Celia) Daniel in the 1870 De Soto Parish census.

453. RESERVED

187. James Willis Daniel b. 1838 in Clarke County, Alabama d. 1863. He may have been a Confederate soldier. A suit against his parent's estate in Jefferson County, Tx gave his date of death and name of his child but not

---

223. Louisiana, De Soto Parish, Marriage Book 1, page 157.
224. Louisiana, De Soto Parish, Marriage Book 2, page 194.

his spouse's name. A J.W. Daniel married[225] M.C. Dicken 24 Oct 1860 in Hardin County, Tx where many of the Daniels settled. This may be a record of his marriage. He was with his family in Jefferson County, Tx in 1850. He had:

454. Henry Daniel b. bef 1863

189. John C. Daniel b. 1843 in Louisiana d. abt 1894. His date of death is given in a suit against his parent's estate in 1901. This suit does not say if he had children, perhaps because they died before 1901. He may have been the J.C. Daniel who married[226] Missouri Jordan 25 Nov 1874 in Hardin County, Tx. There are several members of the Jordan family buried in the Daniel Cemetery in Hardin County, Tx and also records of several Daniel/Jordan marriages in records of that county.

190. Aaron Kinsey Daniel b. 1844 in De Soto Parish, La. d. 1875. He may be the A. K. Daniel who married[227] Susan Drake 10 Jan 1870 in Hardin County, Tx. He may be the A. K. Daniels in the 1870 Hardin County, Tx census with wife Susan. He was aged 25, she 28 and there were a Henry aged 12 and Tally, male, aged 9 in their home. These may have been children of his brother, James Willis Daniel. The same suit mentioned in the records of his brothers names his child. He had:

455. Elizana Daniel b. bef 1875

191. Eastridge M. Daniel b. 1846 in De Soto Parish, La d. aft 1912. He was living with his wife who was named Annie in Harris County, Tx in 1870. She was b. 1836 in Mississippi. The family of his uncle, Estridge Daniel, was

---

225. Texas, Hardin County, Marriage Book 1, page 28.
226. Texas, Hardin County, Marriage Book 1, page 23.
227. Texas, Hardin County, Marriage Book 1, page 28.

living nearby. He initiated a suit[228] in 1901 in Jefferson County, Tx to divide his parent's estate. He was living with his sister, M.E. Kirby, in Jefferson County during the 1910 Texas census. He was listed as married but his wife was not present. He was employed as a truck farmer.

456. RESERVED

193. Mary E. Daniel b. 1852 in Jefferson County, Tx and d. aft 1910, probably in Beaumont, Tx where she was in the 1910 census. She m. J. W. Kirby, probably in Jefferson County. They are mentioned in the suit settling her parent's estate in 1901 in that county. In this suit Kirby attested that he had married Mary Daniel. The 1910 census shows that she was widowed and had four children, two of whom were deceased. Mary and J.W. had:

457. Ruby Kirby b. 1891
458. Ratston Kirby b. 1895

194. Benjamin Franklin Daniel b. 1853 in Jefferson County, Tx d. abt 1878. The suit mentioned among the records of his siblings also names his child but does not name his spouse. He may have been married in Jefferson County, Tx. He had:

459. Benjamin Daniel b. bef 1878

195. Sarah C. Daniel b. 1856 in Jefferson County, Tx married[229] William D. Laird 29 Jun 1877 in Hardin County, TX. They are mentioned in the suit involving her siblings. I don't know if they had children. They d. after 1901.

460. RESERVED

---

228. Texas, Jefferson County, Clerk's File 726, Deed Book 48, pp. 212-213.
229. Texas, Hardin County, Marriage Book 1, page 50.

200. Martha Jane Daniel b. 28 Oct 1837 in Clarke County, Alabama d. 23 Nov 1906, probably in Hays County, Texas. She married[230] Edward John Riley 1 Dec 1853 in Jefferson County, Texas. He b. 21 Feb 1834 in Covington, Mississippi the son of William John and Nancy Collins Riley and d. 4 Dec 1876 at Barton Creek, Hays County, Tx. He was a farmer. She next m. Warren J. Collins in 1880. He b. 1854 in Mississippi. Martha and Edward had:

461. Tillamon E. Riley b. 10 Nov 1855 d. 1861
462. Amanda E. Riley b. 11 Dec 1857 d. aft 1870
463. Willis Paschal Riley b. 10 Jul 1860 d. 28 Mar 1933
464. William E. Riley b. 20 Jul 1864 d. Aug 1906
465. Seleta J. Riley b. 18 Feb 1867 d. Jun 1930
466. John M. Riley b. 6 Sep 1869 d. aft 1916
467. Nellie C. Riley b. 20 Apr 1872 d. 1911
468. Nora Victoria Riley b. 1 Mar 1875 d. 10 Jun 1940

204. Aaron Kinsey Daniel b. Jul 1850 in De Soto Parish, Louisiana d. aft 1910, possibly in Travis County, Tx. He married[231] Missouri Jula Runnels, abt 1878 in Hays County. She b. 1853 d. aft 1910. The 1880 Hays County, Tx census noted that she had rheumatism. Aaron was in Harris County, Tx with his mother and siblings in 1870, Hays County in 1880 and 1900 and Travis County in 1910. In 1910 he and his wife were living with their son-in-law and daughter. Aaron was a farmer. There is the record of a birth of a Benjamin Franklin Daniel 2 Oct 1875 in Hays County, Tx, the son of A. R.

230. Texas, Jefferson County, Marriage Records.
231. Texas, Hays County, Marriage Book C, page 235.

and M. J. Daniel. It is possible that this was their child but according to the 1910 census they were not married then. He may also be the Aaron K. Danill who applied for a pension[232] in 1910 for service in Capt. Caulfield's Company of Texas Minute men, 1870-72. Aaron and Missouri had:

469. Alva J. Daniel b. Oct 1879 d. aft 1900
470. Eva D. Daniel* b. Jul 1881 d. aft 1910
471. Willie L. Daniel b. Sep 1886 d. aft 1900
472. Ira E. Daniel b. Mar 1888 d. aft 1900
473. Frank Daniel b. Jun 1890 d. aft 1900

205. James Hampton Daniel b. 1854 Hardin County, Tx d. aft 1870. He was with his mother and siblings in 1870 Harris County, Tx and he is mentioned in the estate records of his father in 1866. The only clue I have to his life after 1870 is the record of a marriage[233] for a Hampton Daniel in Monroe County, Mississippi in 1881. The IGI shows many Daniels in this county during that time period so this record is probably for a man in that family but may it be worth checking.

474. RESERVED

206. John Daniel b. 1857 in Hardin County, Tx and d. aft 1880. He was in the 1860 through 1880 censuses with his family. He was occupied during the 1880 Hays County census as a school teacher. I have no other data on this man but since he was a school teacher he may be mentioned in county records.

232. Daniel Discoverer and Documenter, Jan 1988, Issue 49, page 4, Union Pensioners copied from GS Film #0540866, Danill, Aaron K., Capt Caulfield's Co. Tex Min Men 1870-72; filed 1910, Dec 18, Indian Ser. #18914, filed in Tx.
233. IGI, Mississippi, Marriage Records.

475. RESERVED

207. William Daniel b. 1861 in Hardin County, Tx d. aft 1880. He was working as a cowboy in 1880 and living with his mother and siblings, including sister Martha Jane, her children and new husband, in Hays County, Tx. I have no information pertaining to him after this time.

476. RESERVED

213. Sarah Adaline Daniel b. 27 Nov 1848 in De Soto Parish, La and d. 9 May 1921 in Hardin County, Tx. She married[234] George W. Williford 24 Oct 1867 in Hardin County. He. b. 25 Feb 1846 in Mississippi and d. 9 Oct 1921. They are buried in the Daniel Cemetery near Kountze, Tx. They were in the 1880 Hardin County, Tx census with some of their children. There may have been more children later. Sarah and George had:

> 477. Litha D. Williford b. 1870
> 478. Willis H. Williford b. 15 Dec 1873 d. 1 Jun 1896
> 479. Rosha A. Williford b. 1877

214. James Willis Daniel b. 18 Sep 1851 in Jefferson County, Tx d. 7 Aug 1913 in Hardin County, Tx. He married[235] Louisa O. Patterson 13 Jun 1875 in Hardin County. She b. 27 Mar 1858 in Florida d. 22 Apr 1940 in Hardin County. They are both buried in the Daniel Cemetery near Kountze, Tx. He was a farmer. His obituary[236] appeared in a Beaumont, Tx newspaper:

---

234. Texas, Hardin County, Marriage Book 1, page 31.
235. Texas, Hardin County, Marriage Book 1, page 20.
236. Texas, Jefferson County, Beaumont Daily Journal, Vol XVII, No. 38, Friday, 8 Aug 1913, page 10, cols. 5-7.

Funeral of James Willis Daniels.

Out in the old family cemetery in Hardin county, upon his own tract of land, there was laid to rest yesterday afternoon all that was mortal of James Willis Daniels, who died on Wednesday afternoon upon the same land and practically the same place where he had been born nearly 63 years ago.

He had spent all of his life on this farm, had a raised a family of seven children; all of them living and respected by all who knew them, and leaves behind him that which is the only thing the best and greatest can leave and many do not, a good unspotted name.

James Willis Daniels is also survived by his wife, whom he married in early youth and who was Lou Patterson of the well known Patterson family of the state of Florida, as well as a brother, Wm. A. Daniels of Burke, Angelina County, and two sisters, Mrs. George Williford of near Kountze and Mrs. Burle Eason, who also resides near Kountze.

The children of the deceased are well known in Beaumont and community. Two sons, W. P. Daniels and George Daniels, are residents of this city, while James D. Daniels and Carl Daniels still reside near Kountze, as well as three daughters, Mrs. Henry Shepard and the Misses Clara and Josie Daniels.

James and Nancy had:

480. Nancy Mahala Daniel* b. 19 Dec 1876 d aft 1910
481. William Paschal Daniel* b. 25 Feb 1878 d. aft 1910
482. George Oscar Daniel* b. 29 Nov 1879 d. 1958
483. James Littleton Daniel* b. 15 May 1882 d. 1955
484. Sarah Elizabeth Daniel b. 23 Nov 1884 d. 11 Oct 1885
485. Clara Emily Daniel b. 20 Jan 1888 d. aft 1910

        486. Carl Wilburn Daniel* b. 24 Nov 1890
        d. 24 Dec 1972
        487. Josie Vernice Daniel* b. 19 Dec 1892
        d. aft 1910

215. Nancy Davenport Daniel b. 10 Dec 1853 in
Jefferson County, Tx. I believe she is the N.
D. Daniel who married[237] Joseph M. Rountree
12 Jan 1870 in Hardin County, Tx. He and a
child may be buried in the Daniel Cemetery near
Kountze, Tx. She was not with her siblings in
the 1870 Hardin County census. The obituary of
her brother James Willis Daniels indicates that
she married Burl Eason bef 1913. This was
probably a second marriage.

        488. RESERVED

216. Mary E. Daniel b. 1 Apr 1862 in Hardin
County, Tx d. 7 Aug 1897. She married[238] R.
W. Williford 30 May 1880 in Hardin County. She
is buried in the Daniel cemetery near Kountze,
Tx. They were not in the 1880 Hardin County
census. I am guessing that the child I am
listing was theirs because his grave is next to
theirs. They may have had other children. They
had:

        489. William Doucla Williford b. 28 May
        1886 d. 13 Jan 1911

217. William Aaron Daniel b. 1 Apr 1862 in
Hardin County, Tx d. 10 Oct 1920. He is buried
in the Daniel Cemetery near Kountze, Tx. He was
with his sister Sarah's family in 1880. I do
not know if he married. His brother James'
obituary reports that he was living at Burke,
Angelina County, Tx in 1913.

---

        237. Texas, Hardin County, Marriage Book
1, page 39.
        238. Texas, Hardin County, Marriage Book
1, page 71.

        151

FIFTH GENERATION

219. Thomas Wilbur Daniel b. 4 Oct 1865, probably in Champaign County, Il d. 20 Sep 1935 at Gordon, Sheridan County, Ne. He is listed in the 1900 Merna, Kilfail Township, Custer County, Ne census with his wife, Daisy Pearl Lowe. She was b. 4 Mar 1875 in Hampton, Iowa, the daughter of John and Marcilla Davis Lowe, and d. 13 Dec 1960 at Los Angeles, Ca. They were married[239] 4 Oct 1891 at Berwyn, Custer County, Ne. Her brother, Will Lowe, aged 58, was in their home in 1920 when they were listed in the census at Gordon, Sheridan County, Ne. Wilbur and Daisy had:

   490. George Colwell Daniel* b. 22 Jul 1893
        d. 1965

222. Helen May Daniel b. 4 Feb 1875 at Pellsville, Vermilion County, Il and d. 19 May 1894 Custer County, Ne. She married[240] Oliver Cross 19 Mar 1893 at Broken Bow, Ne. He was b. 1872 in Iowa, the son of John H. and Melissa Bullock Cross. May died in childbirth and is buried in the Janesville Cemetery, Custer County, next to her father. May and Oliver had:

   491. Florence Helen Cross b. 19 May 1894

224. Austin G. Daniel born[241] 4 Jan 1880 at Pellsville, Vermilion County, Il d. 15 Mar 1918 and is buried in the Ansley Cemetery, Custer County, Ne. His twin brother Oscar A. Daniel died[242] 15 Jul 1880 and is buried in the Pellsville Cemetery near Rankin, Il. Austin was

-----

239. Nebraska, Custer County, Marriage Book 3, page 46.
240. Nebraska, Custer County, Marriage Book 3, page 295.
241. Illinois, Vermilion County, Birth Book 1, page 127.
242. Illinois, Vermilion County, Death Book 1, page 60, #707.

153

living in Ansley, Ne in 1900 with his mother. They had taken in boarders so may have been running a boarding house or trying to make ends meet after the death of Colwell Daniel. Austin married[243] Katherine V. Baker 28 Aug 1902 in Custer County. She was b. in 1882 in Westerville, Ne the daughter of Thompson and Sarah Huffman Baker and d. aft 1920. Katherine and their two children were living in Custer County in 1920. Austin and Katherine had:

    492. Velda E. Daniels* b. 11 Jul 1903 d.
        22 Sep 1971
    493. Edsel E. Daniels b. 1918 d. 1945

225. Edmond Mose Daniels born[244] 4 May 1878 at Pellsville, Vermilion County, Il d. 11 Jan 1947 at Tacoma, Wa. His father gave his name as both Mose E. and Moses E. in his Union pension file. Edmond married three times. He first married[245] Nita O. Miller 25 Apr 1890 at Broken Bow, Ne. She was b. Aug 1878 in Nebraska the daughter of Cyrus H. and Elizabeth Hendricks Miller. I have found no record of children for them. Edmond next married Nancy Estella Barto who was b. 1886 and d. 23 Mar 1919 in Great Falls, Mt. She was the daughter of Charles Truman Barto and Estella Beckwith Cooley. Edmond next married Mahalia Olmstead. She was b. 1878 in Illinois. Edmond was living in Custer County, Ne in 1900 and in Thomas County, Ne in 1920. He and his family lived in South Dakota between 1918 and 1920. Edmond and Nancy had:

    494. Clifford Edmond Daniels* b. 21 Oct
        1912 d. 11 Nov 1981
    495. Thomas Jackson Daniels* b. 23 Jul
        1914 d. aft 1994

243. Nebraska, Custer County, Marriage Book 5, page 609.
244. Illinois, Vermilion County, Birth Book 1, page 25.
245. Nebraska, Custer County, Marriage Book 5, page 286.

EDMOND MOSE DANIELS

496. Ethel Anna Daniels b. 1916 d. aft
     1994
497. Doris Irene Daniels* b. 10 Apr 1918
     d. aft 1994

Edmond and Mahalia had:

498. Betty Daniels b. 10 Nov 1922 d. aft
     1994

226. Earnest Jesse Daniel born[246] 6 July 1880 at Pellsville, Vermilion County, Il d. 11 May 1962 at Broken Bow, Ne. He married[247] Libbie Scott 24 Oct 1906 in Custer County, Ne.

EARNEST JESSE AND LIBBIE SCOTT DANIELS

She was born 1883 in Iowa, the daughter of John W. and Emma Bardick Scott. She died 15 Nov 1956, aged 74, and is buried in the Ansley Cemetery next to her husband. Earnest was living in Thomas County, Ne in 1920 during the

---

246. Illinois, Vermilion County, Birth Book 1, page 154.
247. Nebraska, Custer County, Marriage Book 7, page 145.

156

census and his wife's name was given as Martha
E. and she was born in Iowa in 1883 so it
appears that Libbie was her nickname. Earnest's
niece, Betty, told me that Earnest and Libbie
owned and operated a cafe in Ansley, Ne.
Libbie's hobby was painting china. Earnest
apparently had no obituary but one was written
for his wife in an Ansley newspaper. Earnest
and Libbie had:

> 499. Kenneth William Daniels* b. 2 Sep
> 1911 d. 6 Jan 1976

228. Charles Henry Daniel b. 14 July 1870 in
Button Township, Ford County, Il d. aft 1925.
He moved to Custer County, Ne with his family.
He m. a woman named Bertha in Nebraska bef
1900. She was b. in Aug 1875 in Nebraska. When
his mother died in 1925 her obituary reported
him to be living in Spanaway, Wa. Using this
information I believe I located his family in
the 1920 Pierce County, Washington census. They
moved to Washington state between 1903 and
1907. Charles and Bertie had:

> 500. Tulsa I. Daniels b. Nov 1897 d. aft
> 1900
> 501. Eugene Daniels b. 1903 d. aft 1920
> 502. Harold Daniels b. 1907 d. aft 1920
> 503. Helen Daniels b. 1910 d. aft 1920
> 504. Thomas T. Daniels b. 1914 d. aft 1920
> 505. Robert L. Daniels b. 1918 d. aft 1920

229. Clara Emma Daniels b. 14 May 1872 in
Button Township, Ford County, Il and d. 10 May
1903 or 1904 at Tulsa, Ok. She married[248]
Edmond W. Sims 13 Nov 1889 at Ansley, Custer
County, Ne in the Methodist Episcopal Church
there. Edmond was b. 1866 in Iowa the son of
Albert and H. Stalkop Sims. He witnessed his
father-in-law's Union pension application.
Clara and Edmond moved to Tulsa, Ok about 1894.

---

248. Nebraska, Custer County, Marriage
Book 2, page 221.

After Clara's death her mother raised her children. Clara and Edmond had:

506. Hazel Sims b. 1890 d. aft 1975
507. Maude Ida Sims b. 10 Oct 1893 d. 6 May 1975
508. Jim Sims b. aft 1889 d. bef 1975

231. Lillie Daniels b. aft 1868 d. aft 1921. She m. a man named Harcourt and they were living in Springfield, Mo in 1921. I do not know if they had children.

509. RESERVED

232. Maud Daniels b. aft 1868 d. aft 1921. She m. a man named Smith and they were living in Greenwich, Ks in 1921. I do not know if they had children.

510. RESERVED

233. Eva Daniels b. aft 1868 d. aft 1921. She m. a man named Allman and they were living in Mound Valley, Ks in 1921. Her mother's obituary indicates that she had at least one son.

511. RESERVED

234. Gussie Daniels b. 11 Nov 1880 in Cowley County, Ks and d. 21 Apr 1966 at Parsons, Labette County, Ks. She m. Frank Ludwig Moldenhauer 12 Apr 1900 in Cowley, Ks. He b. 8 Aug 1874 in Sun Prairie, Wi and d. 18 Mar 1933 in Parsons, Ks. I am using the birth dates for her children which were sent to me by a cousin but the dates for the first two children seem confused. Gussie and Frank had:

512. Gladys Elnora Moldenhauer b. 11 Dec 1906 d. 24 Dec 1977
513. Dorothy Louise Moldenhauer b. 29 May 1906 d. 16 Oct 1989
514. Frank L. Moldenhauer b. 8 Jan 1919

235. Edith Pearl Daniels b. 14 Apr 1885 in Cowley County, Ks and d. 26 Feb 1958 in Cabool, Mo. She m. William Lonzo Miller 2 Mar 1904 in Cabool, Mo. He b. 24 Aug 1869 in Douglas County, Il and d. 5 May 1947 in Springfield, Mo. They are buried in the Cabool Cemetery. Edith and William had:

    515. Marion Elbert Miller b. 24 Dec 1904
         d. 8 Jul 1979
    516. James Lee Miller b. 5 Apr 1906 d. 3
         May 1978
    517. William Arthur Miller b. 27 Jul 1908
    518. Fay Elnora Miller b. 24 Nov 1909

254. Flora Jane Daniels b. 2 Aug 1867 in Jasper County, Indiana died[249] in Marion, In 30 Nov 1952. She married[250] John E. Forguson "Forg" Payne 9 Sep 1886 in Jasper County. He b. 1 Mar 1862 in Jasper County and d. there 8 Nov 1928, the son of George W. and Nancy Combess Payne. He was a farmer in Barkley Township. They are buried in the Weston Cemetery, Rensselaer, Indiana. I have pictures of both. She had an obituary[251] in a Rensselaer newspaper:

Former Resident Of City Dies At Marion Sunday

Mrs. Flora J. Payne Succumbs after 4-Year decline; Services Here Tuesday

    Mrs. Flora Jane Payne, until 14 years ago a continuous resident of the Rensselaer area where she was born in 1867, died at her home in Marion at 11:30 O'clock Sunday morning. The widow of John F. Payne, she had been in slow decline for four years.

---

    249. Funeral Home Records of Rensselaer, In and surrounding areas, November 1917 - May 15, 1990, Joyce I. Lane, 1990, Rensselaer, In Public Library.
    250. Indiana, Jasper County, Marriage Book 2, page 249.
    251. Indiana, Rensselaer Republican, Vol 55, No. 282, Monday, 1 Dec 1952, page 1, col 4.

Born in Barkley township August 2, 1867, she lived there continuously until going to Marion; home of her son Clifford Payne, fourteen years ago. She was a daughter of William Daniels and Sarah (Ott) Daniels. She was educated in the Barkley schools and on September 9, 1886, she was united in marriage to John F. Payne on September 9, 1886, a farmer of this community. He died November 8, 1928.

Mrs. Payne was a member of Barkley Methodist church, the Pythian Sisters of Marion and Eastern Star chapter of Upland.

Surviving besides the son are two grandchildren, a brother, Elmer Daniels of Rensselaer, and a sister, Mrs. Bart Grant, also of Rensselaer. She was preceded in death by a daughter, Mrs. Arthur Waymire, four brothers and two sisters.

Funeral services will be held from Jackson Funeral Chapel here at one o'clock Tuesday with the Rev. Dale Hamilton of Barkley Methodist church officiating. Interment will be at Weston cemetery. Friends may call at the Chapel after 11 a. m., Tuesday.

Flora and Forg had:

519. Clifford Payne b. aft 1886 d. aft 1952

255. Korah "Korrie" Daniels b. 4 Feb 1870 Jasper County, In d. 3 Jul 1949 in Chicago, Il. He married[252] Margaret Ellen Abbott 9 Sep 1890 in Jasper County. She was b. May 1867 and d. 15 Nov 1927 in Berrian County, Mi. They are buried in the Weston Cemetery, Rensselaer. He was a farmer and carpenter in Jasper County, In. He and his son Fred often sat together on a bench under a large tree on the courthouse lawn when they were in Rensselaer. They later moved to Chicago. Korrie and his son Fred died the same year. I have a couple of pictures of

---

252. Indiana, Jasper County, Marriage Book 2, page 451.

Korah. Korah's obituary[253] appeared in a Rensselaer newspaper:

Korah Daniels Dies In Chicago At Age Of 79

Former Rensselaer Resident Succumbs Sunday afternoon; Rites Here Tomorrow.

Korah Daniels, son of a pioneer Jasper county couple who made his home in Rensselaer until going to Chicago 22 years ago to reside, died at Franklin Boulevard hospital in Chicago Sunday afternoon. The death of Mr. Daniels followed a prolonged decline and came about two months after the death of his son, Fred, who died suddenly of a heart attack at his East Chicago home.

Mr. Daniels was born in Jasper county February 2, 1870, a son of William Daniels and Sarah (Ott) Daniels. His boyhood and early adult life was spent on the farm, after which he came to Rensselaer and engaged in the carpenter trade for many years. He was married to Miss Margaret Ellen Abbott of this community and this city was their place of resident throughout their married life. Soon after the death of his wife, Mr. Daniels went to Chicago to make his home. Until a few years ago when he retired from active life, Mr. Daniels, was employed as a nightwatchman in the Marshall Field store in that city.

The immediate survivors include two daughters, Mrs. George F. Brown of Oak Park, Ill., and Mrs. E.S. Engberg of Chicago, one brother, Elmer Daniels of Rensselaer, and three sisters, Mrs. Bart Grant of Rensselaer, Mrs. James Price of LaPorte and Mrs. Flora Payne of Marion.

Mr. Daniels was a man of quiet mannerisms whose industrious ways, public spiritedness and progressiveness, combined with his high character and loyalty and friendliness earned

_____

253. Indiana, Rensselaer Republican, Vol 52, No. 156, Tuesday, 5 Jul 1949, page 1, col 4.

him the respect and friendship of everyone. He was a citizen who gained a community's admiration.

The funeral services will be held from the W.J. Wright Chapel in Rensselaer at 4 o'clock, DST, Wednesday afternoon, with the Rev. Earl Moore in charge. Interment will be at Weston cemetery.

Korah and Margaret had:

520. Bertha Alice Daniels* b. 19 Jul 1891
     d. 8 Jul 1951
521. Fred Douglas Daniels* b. 31 May 1893
     d. 6 May 1949
522. Alice Pearl Daniels* b. 28 Sep 1895
     d. Apr 1979

256. Mary Ann "Mellie" or "Mel" Daniels b. 16 Feb 1872 Jasper Co., In d. 1949. She married[254] James W. Price 14 July 1888. He b. 1867 d. 1938. He was a farmer. They and several children are buried in the Prater Cemetery, Jasper County. The record of some of these children comes from the personal knowledge of William Louis Daniels, her nephew, of Rensselaer. A search of birth records in Jasper County will probably disclose more information about this family. Mel and James appear in a Daniel family reunion photo in my possession. Mel and James had:

523. Guy E. Price b. 12 Jan 1889 d. 16 May
     1908
524. Alma M. Price b. 23 May 1892 d. 14
     Jun 1892
525. Infant b. 11 Dec 1893 d. 11 Dec 1893
526. Effie Price b. aft 1889 d. aft 1920
527. Maude Price b. aft 1889 d. aft 1920
528. Earl Price b. aft 1889 d. aft 1920
529. Infant b. 30 Jul 1905 d. 7 Aug 1905

---

254. Indiana, Jasper County, Marriage Book 2, page 342.

Guy M Daniels (signature)

260. Melvin Guy Daniels b. 8 Nov 1884 in Jasper
Co., In d. 17 Jun 1939 in Rensselaer, In. He is
buried in the Weston Cemetery, Rensselaer, In.
He m. Ella C. Denman, of Toledo, Oh, 11 Oct
1922. They adopted two children. He was a WWI
veteran and served in France. I have several
pictures of him, one in uniform, and some of
his wife, as well. He strongly resembled his
grandfather, Shelby Daniel. Records of the
probate of his estate are in Jasper County
records. Their adopted children did not
maintain their relationship with the family. He
met his prospective spouse in Washington, D.C.
where they both worked in the government
offices that were later part of the Pentagon.
He received a lengthy obituary[255] with a
front page headline in a Rensselaer newspaper.
This obituary fails to mention that one of
those he was conversing with when he died was
his brother, Elmer Daniels, according to
Elmer's son, Bill. Guy's obituary:

Guy Daniels, World War Officer, Dies

END COMES AS HE VISITS ON CITY STREETS

Barkley Farmer Falls Lifeless While
Conversing With His Friends Here Saturday
Evening

Suffering a heart seizure as he conversed
with friends in the business district here, Guy
M. Daniels, a native of this community where he
was born almost fifty-four years ago, fell
lifeless Saturday night shortly before nine
o'clock.

255. Indiana, Jasper County, Rensselaer
Republican, Vol 43, No. 141, Monday, 19 Jun
1939, page 1, col 8 and page 8, col 8.

GUY DANIELS

Death came without slightest warning. The
victim suddenly slumped against the city light
pole at the northeast corner of the Van
Rensselaer-Washington street intersection as he
was talking to Clay DeWeese and a Mr. Rowley.
He was dead when he was borne into a doctor's
office.

Mr. Daniel's health had not been good for
two or three years and he had been taking
medical treatment for heart trouble, but he had
suffered no severe attacks and had been able to
go about his daily duties. He apparently was in
his usual health when he came to Rensselaer
Saturday evening. Saturday forenoon he had

measured land for the soil conservation department and during the afternoon he cut some thistles. It is presumed that over-exertion and the intense heat produce the fatal attack.

A First Lieutenant with the World War forces overseas, a graduate of Rensselaer high school and prominent in farming circles here most of his lifetime. Mr. Daniels was well known and highly esteemed throughout Jasper county. His sudden death came as a keen shock to the many who knew him.

He was born in Barkley township November 8, 1885, a son of William and Sarah (Ott) Daniels, a family well known in Jasper county farming circles. His boyhood was spent on the farm. He was graduated from Rensselaer high school with the class of 1906. Following his elementary school career, he attended Marion Business college at Marion for a time. After completing that course he was employed in Marion for a time. From Marion he went to Rock Island, Illinois, where he was employed at the U.S. Arsenal. Later he was transferred to the Ordinance department at Washington, D.C., where he worked until April 1917, at which time he enlisted for World War service. He was assigned to the Ordinance department for the U.S. Army and a short time later was commissioned as a first lieutenant. He was sent overseas almost immediately and was stationed in France for the duration of the war. Following his return from overseas he was sent to Toledo, Ohio, where he acted as a dispersing officer for the Ohio Ordinance department. From there he went to Chicago and in 1921 he came back to Jasper county to engage in farming in Barkley township. Of recent years in addition to operating his 200-acre farm he did extension work for the soil conservation department.

Mr. Daniels was married to Miss Ella Denman of Toledo, Ohio, on October 11, 1922. No children were born to this union.

Beside the widow, he is survived by two foster sons, Robert and William; three sisters, Mrs. Bart Grant of Rensselaer, Mrs. Flora J. Payne of Marion and Mrs. Mellie Price of

LaPorte, and two brothers, Korah Daniels of Chicago and Elmer Daniels of Rensselaer. He was preceded in death by one sister who passed away many years ago.

Mrs. Daniels was of quiet, unassuming nature, and was extremely well liked and most highly regarded by everyone. He was progressive and public spirited and was one of the community's most able farmers. His sudden death at such a comparatively early age is deeply regretted by all. There was none who did not regard him as a deeply loyal friend. As a student of Rensselaer high school, Mr. Daniels was also one of the school's star football players. It was while he was a member of the school's football team that it won three consecutive state championships. He played halfback.

Full military rites will be accorded the deceased when services are held from the Methodist church at 2:30 o'clock Tuesday afternoon, with the Rev. Charles W. Posthill, assisted by the Rev. E.A. Bagby, and the Dewey Biggs post of the American Legion, of which he was a member, in charge. Interment will be at Weston cemetery.

261. Alice Pearl Daniels b. 25 Jan 1887 Jasper County, In d. 23 Feb 1972 in Rensselaer, In. She married[256] Bart Grant 24 Feb 1916 in Jasper County. He was the son of Shelby and Judith Caroline Israel Grant and born 22 Jul 1885 in Wabash, In and d. 31 Oct 1953 in Jasper County. Pearl and Bart are buried in the Weston Cemetery in Rensselaer, In. I have a copy of their wedding picture. Their nephew, William Daniels, remembers Bart very well. When Bill was a child his Uncle Bart drove a horse drawn school bus or "hack". He would put hot bricks on the floor of the driver's compartment to keep his feet warm. He would pick Bill up and Bill remembers riding with his feet on the bricks. The trip was five or six miles and took

---

256. Indiana, Jasper County, Marriage Book 7, page 87.

BART AND ALICE PEARL DANIELS GRANT

about an hour. Bart was hired by the county
trustee to drive the school hack. Pearl's
obituary[257] appeared in a Rensselaer
newspaper:

Mrs. Pearl Grant Dies; Rites Fri.

Mrs. Pearl Grant, 84, of 821 Grove Street,
Rensselaer, passed away at 1:55 a.m. today at
Jasper County Hospital.

---

257. Indiana, Jasper County, Rensselaer
Republican, Vol 74, No. 45, Wednesday, 23 Feb
1972, page 10, col 4.

Born in Rensselaer on January 25, 1888 she was a daughter of William and Sarah Daniels, and was married on February 23, 1916, in Delphi, to Bart Grant, who passed away October 31, 1953.

A lifetime resident of Rensselaer, she attended schools here, and was a member of the Trinity United Methodist Church, and Circle IV, Dorcas Class and WSCS of that church.

Surviving are three daughters, Mrs. Austin (Doris) McCleelan of Bedford, Indiana, and Mrs. Thane (Maxine) Shearer and Mrs. Max (Lois) Hughes both of Rensselaer; six grandchildren; and seven great grandchildren. She was preceded in death by two sisters and three brothers.

Funeral services will be held from Granlund Funeral Home at 1:30 p.m. Friday with the Rev. James Bennett officiating. Interment will follow in Weston Cemetery. Friends may call at the funeral home after 6:00 p.m. Thursday.

Pearl and Bart had:

530. Doris Lousie Grant b. 10 Jun 1918
531. Loretta Maxine Grant b. 8 Aug 1921
532. Lois Mable Grant b. 6 Nov 1923

Elmer Daniels

262. William Elmer Daniels born[258] 23 Feb 1892 in Jasper County, Indiana d. 14 Sep 1966 at Hines, Il. He married[259] Mary Leota Muster 2 Sep 1917 in Jasper County, Ind. She b. 18 Jun 1894 in Valparaiso, In and d. 26 Sep 1975 in Rensselaer. She was a daughter of Louis and Caroline Mathena Muster of Valparaiso. He worked for a plumbing contractor until WWI, when he served in the Army. After the war was

---

258. Indiana, Jasper County, Birth Book H-2, page 5.
259. Indiana, Jasper County, Marriage Book 7, page 272.

DANIEL FAMILY, LEFT TO RIGHT, SEATED: WILLIAM
LOUIS, LEOTA MUSTER AND WILLIAM ELMER.
STANDING: VIRGINIA, JEAN AND REBECCA.

over he became a general contractor and had a
business in Rensselaer, Ind. After her
husband's death she did specialty sewing and
rented rooms in her home to St. Joseph College
students. She did this as a social outlet
rather than for any need to make a living. She
was a very social woman and a member of several
clubs and other organizations in Rensellaer and
was a popular and well regarded lady as I found
on my visits there in 1994. Elmer and Leota are
buried in the Weston Cemetery, Rensselaer, Ind.
I have several pictures of them and their
family and several of him in uniform. I have a
photocopy of the original of his will. He had
an obituary in a Rensselaer newspaper:

Elmer Daniels, War I Veteran, Dies

William Elmer Daniels of 202 N. McKinley
avenue, a prominent and popular lifetime
resident of Rensselaer community and a veteran

169

of World War I, passed away in Hines Veteran's
Hospital in Hines, Illinois, at 1:15 p.m.
Wednesday. His death followed twelve years of
ill health during which time he was frequently
hospitalized here and in Lafayette and at the
Veteran's hospital. He reentered Hines Hospital
a few weeks ago following a relapse and his
condition had steadily grown worse since that
time.

Mr. Daniels was born in Barkley township
on February 23, 1892, the son of William
Daniels and Sarah (Ott) Daniels. His early
Boyhood years were spent on the farm. He
attended the Rensselaer schools after which he
engaged in carpentry here for many years until
beset by ill health. He was married to Miss
Mary Leota Daniels of Rensselaer in a ceremony
performed here on September 2, 1917. He entered
the armed service on April 27, 1918, and was
assigned to the quarter master Corps at Fort
Benjamin Harrison, Indianapolis, and from there
he was transferred to Camp Taylor, Kentucky, as
a Corporal. A few weeks later he was re-
assigned to Camp Shelby, Mississippi, for
advanced training. He was discharged from
military service January 21, 1919.

Mr. Daniels was a member of the Methodist
church and of Dewey Biggs American Legion Post
No. 29, in which he served in various offices.

Surviving him with Mrs. Daniels are a son,
Lieutenant-Colonel William L. Daniels of
Riverside, California; three daughters, Mrs.
Thomas (Virginia) Pearce of Indianapolis, Mrs.
Lowell (Jean) Light of Lake Zurich, Illinois,
and Mrs. Max (Sue) Overton of Knoxville,
Tennessee; eight grandchildren; two great
grandchildren, and sister, Mrs. Pearl Grant, of
Rensselaer. He was preceded in death by five
sisters and two brothers.

In the death of Mr. Daniels, the
Rensselaer has lost one of its most esteemed
citizens, a quiet, unassuming Christian
gentleman whose high qualities of citizenship
were recognized by all. His impeccable
character and the friendship he bestowed toward
all indeed made him a favorite among our

people. His death marks the passing of one who
was deeply admired.
Rites Saturday.
The funeral services will be held from
Jackson Funeral Chapel at 1:30 p.m. Saturday
with the Reverend James Bennett of Trinity
Methodist church officiating. Interment will be
in Weston cemetery. Friends will be received at
the Chapel after 4 p.m. Friday.

Elmer and Leota had:

533. William Louis Daniels* b. 26 Jan 1918
     d. aft 1994
534. Virginia Ruth Daniels* b. 15 Oct 1920
     d. aft 1994
535. Beulah Jean Daniels* b. 8 May 1923 d.
     aft 1994
536. Rebecca Sue Daniels* b. 3 Feb 1925 d.
     aft 1994

265. Roy Daniels b. 15 Jul 1881 in Jasper
County, In and d. 23 March 1959 at Devil's
Lake, Ramsey County, ND. He was living in Royal
Center, In when his father died in 1917, in
Devil's Lake, ND when his brother John died in
1925 and Ardmore, ND when his brother Alonzo
died in 1952.
     Roy m. Amanda Mae Hart 2 Nov 1913 at
Devil's Lake. She was born in North Dakota 6
Jun 1891, a daughter of Bill Hart, and d. 15
Dec 1972. Roy and Amanda were living in Devil's
Lake, Ramsey County, ND in 1920 during the
census[260]. Roy was a farmer and a member of
the Presbyterian church. He is buried in
Devil's Lake and Amanda in Portland, Ore. Roy's
obituary from an area newspaper follows:

ROY DANIELS DIES; Funeral Thursday

     Funeral services for Roy Daniels 77,
longtime Ramsey County resident who died Monday
evening at the Mercy Hospital, will be

---

     260. North Dakota, Ramsey County, 1920
Census, ED 114, Sht 2, Ln 87.

conducted Thursday afternoon at 2 o'clock from
the Presbyterian church in Devils Lake with Rev
Mark Witner officiating. Burial will be in the
family plot in the Devils Lake Cemetery.
    Mr. Daniels was born July 15th, at
Rensselaer, Ind, the son of the late George and
Amanda Daniels. In 1904 he came to Devil's Lake
and was employed on construction and as a taxi
driver with a local livery stable. He was
married to Amanda Mae Hart on Nov 2, 1913 in
Devils Lake and following their marriage they
farmed in Cato Township before moving to Creel
Township in 1918 and farming there until his
retirement in 1949.
    They then moved to Erdmore community where
they lived for the next five years, coming to
Devils Lake in 1951 and have resided here
since.
    Mr. Daniels was a member of the
Presbyterian Church and the I.O.O.F. Crofton
Lodge of Devils Lake.
    In addition to his wife he is survived by
three daughters, Mrs. Martin (Mae) Thomas of
Vancouver, Wash, Mrs. Charles (Vera) Campbell
of Portland, Ore and Mrs. John (Marjorie)
Pancratz of Fargo, three sons, Charles of
Minneapolis, Minn., Lyle Le Roy of Allen Park,
Mich., and Edward of Devils Lake rural. Also
surviving are 14 grandchildren and six great
grandchildren.
    He was preceded in death by four brothers
and one sister.

    Roy and Amanda had:

    537. Lyle Leroy Daniels* b. 15 Oct 1914 d.
         7 Apr 1978
    538. Mae Roseanne Daniels* b. 22 May 1917
         d. 12 May 1913
    539. Edward William Daniels* b. 13 Jul
         1918
    540. Vera Elvina Daniels* b. 11 Oct 1919
         d. 6 Jul 1977
    541. Marjorie Ann Daniels* b. 3 Mar 1931
         d. aft 1994

172

542. Charles Duane Daniels* b. 5 Dec 1933
d. 11 Dec 1990

SONS OF GEORGE AND AMANDA OTT DANIELS, LEFT TO
RIGHT: IRA MELVIN, ROY, ALONZO M., JOHN LAWSON
AND WALTER E.

266. Motty Alonzo "Lon" Daniels born[261] 2 Nov
1882 Jasper County, In died[262] 29 Mar 1952.
He married[263] first Ida Belle Walker 8 Jan
1907. She born 28 Jan 1886, a daughter of Isaac
D. Walker and Mary A. Smith, and died[264] 21
Oct 1915. Lon and his children were living with
his father-in-law in 1920 in Jasper County. He

---

261. Indiana, Jasper County, Supplemental
Records, Marriage Applications, Book 18, page
183.
262. Indiana, Jasper County, Death Book
CD-6, page 114.
263. Indiana, Jasper County, Marriage Book
4, page 391.
264. Indiana, Jasper County, Death Book D-
10, page 76.

married[265] second Anna Belle Nelson 9 Dec
1932. She b. 4 Nov 1913 and died[266] 1 Jul
1946. Anna was the daughter of Joseph and Ida
Walins Nelson. She died as a result of heart
complications that developed from childbirth.
Alonzo was a farmer. Lon, as he was called, and
both of his wives are buried in the Smith
Cemetery in Jasper County. After he died his
younger children by his second marriage were
divided among various foster parents and grew
up separately. Lon and both wives had
obituaries in Rensselaer newspapers. His
obituary[267] follows:

Alonzo Daniels Passes Away Saturday Night

Lifetime Resident Of Community Succumbs
After Several Months Of Failing Health; Funeral
Tuesday

Alonzo M. Daniels, a Jasper county farm-
figure throughout his entire lifetime, and
widely and popularly known, died at midnight
Saturday, a few hours after he was taken there
for treatment of a condition that had caused
his health to decline slowly over a period of
nine months.

Mr. Daniels was born in Jasper county
November 2, 1882, a son of George Daniels and
Amanda (Ott) Daniels, family names that occupy
important positions in the early life of this
community. His education was gained in local
schools. At a quite early age he began the
farming career he was to follow throughout his
lifetime. Eventually he purchased a tract in
Barkley township where he lived at the time of
his death.

---

265. Indiana, Jasper County, Marriage Book
13, page 71.
266. Indiana, Jasper County, Death Book
CD-5, page 158.
267. Indiana, Jasper County, Rensselaer
Republican, Vol 55, No. 77, 31 Mar 1952, page
1, col 3.

He was married to Miss Ida Walker who
preceded him in death and some years later he
was married to Anna Belle Nelson who passed
away four years ago.

Mr. Daniels was a man of quiet and
constructive ways, an excellent farmer and
progressive citizen. His life was a pattern of
exemplary living and characteristics that
endeared him to his fellow men. He did much to
promote the advancement and welfare of his
community and in all ways deported himself in a
manner that won for him the admiration of his
fellowmen.

The immediate survivors are nine children,
Mrs. Jessie DeMoss of near Gifford, Kenneth
Daniels of near Rensselaer, Lonnie Joe Daniels
at home, Thomas Daniels, at present a hospital
patient here, Nancy Daniels and Louella Daniels
of near Rensselaer, Norma Jane Daniels of
Tefft and Betty Daniels and Katherine Ann
Daniels of Kouts; two brothers, Roy Daniels of
Ardmore, North Dakota, and Walter Daniels of
Bowden, North Dakota.

The funeral services will be held from
Jackson Funeral Chapel at 2 o'clock Tuesday
with the Rev. Noah Knepp in charge. Interment
will be at Smith Cemetery.

Lon and Ida Bell had:

543. Jessie E. Daniels* b. 24 Dec 1908 d.
     30 Jun 1985
544. Kenneth Walker Daniels* b. 1 Jul
     1910 d. 27 Aug 1974
545. Mary Madeline Daniels* b. 9 May 1911
     d. 1930
546. Edna Pauline Daniels b. 16 Jun 1913
     d. 30 May 1914
547. Armanda Lucile Daniels b. 23 Mar 1915
     d. 7 Jul 1915

Lon and Anna Belle had:

548. Lon Joe Daniels* b. 17 Aug 1933 d.
     28 Oct 1986

175

549. Elizabeth Jeanette Daniels b. 7 Oct
       1934 d. 18 Nov 1934
550. Thomas Ellwood Daniels* b. 13 Oct
       1935 aft 1994
551. Nancy Ann Daniels b. 11 Sep 1936 d.
       aft 1994
552. Louellen May Daniels b. 8 Nov 1938 d.
       aft 1994
553. Betty Ann Daniels* b. 22 May 1942 d.
       aft 1994
554. Norma Jean Daniels b. 12 Oct 1943 d.
       aft 1974
555. Catherine Ann Daniels* b. 14 Oct 1944
       d. aft 1994
556. Infant b. 1 July 1946 d. 1 July 1946

267. Walter E. Daniels born[268] 27 Mar 1886
Jasper County, In d. abt 1960 at Lakota, Nelson
County, ND. He married[269] Belva Frances
Gilmore 12 Jul 1908 in Jasper County. She b. 31
Aug 1888 in Indiana and d. aft 1920. I have
seen her name spelled Velva several times. She
was the daughter of Charles W. and Mary M.
Hurley Gilmore. I think they may have left
Jasper County shortly after the birth of their
daughter. They were in Ramsey County, North
Dakota in 1920 during the census[270], Devil's
Lake, Ramsey County in 1925 and Bowden, ND in
1952. He was living with the family of his
daughter when he died. Walter and Belva had:

     557. Mary Amanda Daniels* b. 4 Feb 1909 d.
            20 Aug 1951
     558. Harry Melvin Daniels* b. 3 Apr 1911
            d. 11 Aug 1993
     559. George Gilmore Daniels* b. 10 Sep
            1924 d. 1 May 1985

     268. Indiana, Jasper County, Supplemental
Records, Marriage Applications, Book 19, page
44.
     269. Indiana, Jasper County, Marriage Book
4, page 468. Also Supplemental Marriage
Applications, Book 19, page 44.
     270. North Dakota, Ramsey County, 1920
census, ED 108, Sht 9, Ln 23.

268. John Lawson Daniels b. 7 Jul 1889 Barkley Twp., Jasper County, In and died[271] there 11 Feb 1925. He married[272] Marguerite Josephine Hurley 28 Jan 1914. She b. 20 Sep 1894 in Jasper County, In d. 3 Jun 1981 at South Bend, In, the daughter of Theodore Alexander and Mary Elizabeth Durant Hurley. After John's death she married William Beauregard. According to notes of John's children he was a bridge engineer. He had an obituary[273] in a Jasper County newspaper:

JOHN DANIELS, BARKLEY FARMER, PASSES AWAY

Well Known Agriculturist Dies From Diabetes; Leaves Wife and Seven Small Children

John Daniels, who had been in very poor health for the past couple of years, died at his home in Barkley township Wednesday night at 11 o'clock. The cause was diabetes from which he had been a sufferer for some time.

He is survived by his wife and seven small children, two of the latter being sick at this time and one of whom is being cared for at the county hospital. He is also survived by four brothers, Alonzo and Ira Daniels of Barkley township, and Roy and Walter Daniels, of Devils Lake, N.D.

Deceased was a son of George and Amanda Daniels, both deceased, but former well-known residents of this county. He was born July 7, 1889, his age at the time of his death being 35 years, 7 months and 4 days.

The funeral will be held at the Aix church Saturday morning at 10:30 o'clock, services to

---

271. Indiana, Jasper County, Death Book D-10, page 254.
272. Indiana, Jasper County, Marriage Book 6, page 98.
273. Indiana, Jasper County, Rensselaer, The Evening Republican, Vol XXVII, No. 37, Thursday, 12 Feb 1925, page 1, col 2.

be in charge of Rev. O'Riley, and burial made
in Weston cemetery in this city.

John and Marguerite had:

    560. Clarence Lawson Daniels* b. 1 Sep
        1914 d. 22 Sep 1981
    561. Mary Florence Daniels* b. 9 Apr 1916
        d. 1943
    562. Mildred Jane Daniels* b. 19 Mar 1918
        d. 1992
    563. Frances Latona Daniels* b. 1 Feb 1920
        d. aft 1939
    564. Margaret Anne Daniels* b. 26 Jan 1922
        d. 16 Mar 1925
    565. Audrey Jean Daniels* b. 27 Sep 1923
        d. aft 1994
    566. John Daniels* b. 14 Nov 1924 d. 10
        Jul 1969

269. Ira Melvin Daniels born[274] 18 Jan 1898
Jasper County, In d. 17 May 1943 in Pulaski
County, In. He married[275] Dora Alice Brouhard
15 Mar 1919 in Jasper County. She b. 21 Dec
1895 in Boone County, In, the daughter of
Charles and Jennie Shanahan Brouhard, and d. 9
Sep 1986 in Rensselaer, In. They lived in
Rensselaer and are buried in the Weston
Cemetery there. They both had obituaries in
Rensselaer, In newspapers. Ira's follows:

IRA DANIELS, EX-RESIDENT OF CITY A SUICIDE

Fear of Cancer Believed to Have Prompted Recent
Resident to Take Life With Bullet

Ira Daniels, 45, until a few months ago a
lifelong resident of Rensselaer community,
committed suicide at 8 o'clock Monday night in
a bedroom of his Francesville home by shooting
himself in the head with a bullet from a .32-

---

    274. Indiana, Jasper County, Birth Book H-
2, page 90.
    275. Indiana, Jasper County, Marriage Book
8, page 139.

calibre revolver. The bullet entered behind the right ear and caused instant death.

It is thought despondency arising from the belief that he was a cancer victim led to the act.

Only a minute before he ended his life, Mr. Daniels had requested Mrs. Daniels to go into the yard and get some water. It was during that interval that he drove the fatal bullet into his head.

Coroner Querry of Pulaski county investigated and indicated he would return a suicide verdict. The official finding has not been entered.

Mr. Daniels lived on a farm near Rensselaer until last October when he purchased a Francesville tavern and lunch room. He had been in ill health for some time according to the information forthcoming shortly after the deed was committed he had been worrying because of fear that he was suffering from a cancer.

Born Near Here

Mr. Daniels was born near Rensselaer January 18, 1898, the son of the late Mr. and Mrs. George Daniels. His mother's maiden name was Amanda Ott. He attended the county schools and until recent months his business life was devoted entirely to farming. He was married to Alice Brouhard on March 15, 1919. To this union were born two sons, Chester, who is in the U.S. Armed forces in Panama, and Virgil, an employee of the Kingsbury Ordinance plant. Other immediate survivors are three brothers, Lon of Gifford and Roy and Walter of North Dakota.

Mr. Daniels was an industrious and highly regarded citizen. It was ill health that caused him to forsake farm work for lighter duties. He was well liked and a man of exemplary habits who entered heartily into projects that brought about the betterment of the community. His death came as a great shock to the hundreds of Jasper county citizens who had known him throughout his boyhood and manhood.

The remains were brought to the W.J. Wright Chapel from where services will be held

at 2 o'clock Friday afternoon. Interment will
be at Weston cemetery.

Ira and Alice had:

567. Chester Melvin Daniels b. 27 Feb 1920
     d. 15 Jan 1947
568. Virgil Ivan Daniels* b. 18 Dec 1922
     d. 12 Apr 1985
569. Infant b. 12 May 1927

275. Mary Daniels b. Apr 1890 in Barkley
Township, Jasper County, In d. 1916. She was
living with her grandfather, John J. Pullins,
in Barkley Township during the 1900 census. Her
half sister, Dora Fern Daniels Schroyer, gave
her age at death in a Jasper County history.
According to the biography of her father she
married but I did not find a record of her
marriage in Jasper County records.

276. Dora Fern Daniels born[276] 8 Apr 1896 in
Jasper County, In and died[277] there 4 Apr
1989. She married[278] Elmer Vance Shroyer 23
Dec 1919 in Jasper County. He b. 25 Aug 1896 in
Jasper County and d. there 14 Nov 1981. He was
the son of Charles F. and Margaret E. Hinkle
Shroyer. She had an obituary[279] in a
Rensselaer newspaper:

Dora Shroyer

Dora Fern Shroyer, 92, of Rt. 2, Box 18,
Rensselaer, passed away Tuesday, April 4 at

_____

        276. Indiana, Jasper County, Birth Book H-
2, page 60.
        277. Funeral Home Records of Rensselaer,
In and surrounding areas, November 1917 - May
15, 1990, Joyce I. Lane, 1990, Rensselaer, In
Public Library.
        278. Indiana, Jasper County, Marriage Book
8, page 226.
        279. Indiana, Jasper County, Rensselaer
Republican, Vol 67, No. 60, Wednesday, 5 Apr
1989, page 2, col 1.

DORA FERN DANIELS SHROYER

2:35 a.m. at her home. She had been ill for two
months.
    The daughter of Horace Greely Daniels and
Margaret (Ginn) Daniels, both deceased, she was
born April 8, 1896 in Jasper County. She was a
lifetime resident of Jasper County.
    She married Elmer V. Shroyer Dec. 23,
1919. He died Nov. 14, 1981.
    She was educated at Rensselaer public
schools.
    She had worked as a secretary for Charlie
Sands for many years. She had also worked as a
nurse at Jasper County Hospital.
    She was a member of the United Methodist
Church of Rensselaer and a member of the
Rebekah Lodge for over 70 years.

She is survived by two sons, Elmer Harold Shroyer of Niles, Mich., and Merle Delos Shroyer of Glendale, Ariz.; a daughter, Margaret Ellen Ellis of Rensselaer; 14 grandchildren and 21 great grandchildren.

She was preceded in death by one brother, two sisters and a son.

Funeral services will be held at 10:30 a.m. Thursday, April 6 at the Steinke Funeral Home with Rev. Greg Enstrom officiating. Burial will follow at the Smith Cemetery.

Visitation will be held from 2 to 8 p.m. Wednesday, April 5, in the Steinke Funeral Home. A Rebekah Lodge service will be held 7 p.m. Wednesday at the funeral home.

Dora and Elmer had:

570. Elmer Harold Schroyer b. bef 1922 d. aft 1994
571. Charles Daniels Schroyer b. 19 Jul 1922 d. 22 Jul 1986.
572. Merle Delos Schroyer b. aft 1922 d. aft 1994
573. Margaret Ellen Schroyer d. aft 1922 d. aft 1994

Omar H Daniels

277. Omar Horace Daniels b. 6 Oct 1897 in Jasper County, In died[280] 1 Mar 1955. He married[281] Mabel Gertrude "Gertie" Faylor 24 Feb 1918 in Jasper County. She b. 3 May 1895 in Jasper County died in Rensselaer, In 21 Dec 1976. She was the daughter of John Wesly and Effie Mae Watson Faylor. Omar and Mabel are buried in the Smith Cemetery in Barkley Township, Jasper County. Both had wills

---

280. Indiana, Jasper County, Death Book C-6, page 7.
281. Indiana, Jasper County, Marriage Book 8, page 35.

probated in Rensselaer, Jasper County, In. Her
will named all of her grandchildren then

OMAR H. AND GERTRUDE FAYLOR DANIELS

living. I have copies of the originals of both
of these wills. Omar and Gertie had obituaries
in Rensselaer, In newspapers. Omar's
obituary[282] follows:

Omar H. Daniels, Lifetime Area Resident, Dies

Prominent Farmer Passes Away At Hospital
Early Today; Rites Set for Thursday

Omar H. Daniels of Barkley township, long
identified with farming pursuits and a lifetime
resident of Jasper county, died at Jasper
county hospital at 4:30 o'clock this morning.
He had been failing gradually for a five-year
period as a result of a series of
complications. His condition became critical a

282. Indiana, Jasper County, Rensselaer
Republican, Vol 58, No. 50, Tuesday, 1 Mar
1955, page 1, col 3.

few days ago and since his life ebbed swiftly. The Daniels home is on RFD 6, Rensselaer.

Mr. Daniels was born in the Rensselaer area of Jasper County on October 6, 1897, a son of Horace and Cerilda (Ginn) Daniels. He was educated in the township schools and soon following his school days he entered upon the farming career that he was to follow throughout his active life. His marriage to Miss Gertrude Faylor took place in Union township February 24, 1918.

He was a member of Aix United Brethren church and the Odd Fellows and Rebekah lodges of Gifford.

Surviving with the widow are two children, Edward Daniels of near Rensselaer and Mrs. Cerilda York of Hammond, eight grandchildren and a sister, Mrs. Elmer Shroyer, of Rensselaer.

Mr. Daniels was a citizen who enjoyed the respect and admiration of all. He was an excellent farmer and a public spirited, progressive man who participated in community projects that had as their goals the general advancement of community life.

The funeral services will be held from Jackson Funeral Chapel at 2 o'clock Thursday with the Rev. Noah Knepp officiating. Interment will be at Smith cemetery. Friends may call at the chapel after 1 o'clock Wednesday.

Omar and Gertie had:

574. Omar Edward Daniels* b. 13 Dec 1918
      d. Feb 1978
575. Cerillda May Daniels b. 27 Apr 1924
      d. 30 Jun 1986

298. Stella Ann Daniel born[283] 1 Nov 1880 in Blount Township, Vermilion County, Il and d. there 18 Nov 1972. She m. Coy Van Vickle 30 Sep 1902. Her obituary was in the Danville Commercial News, Danville, Il:

---

283. Illinois, Vermilion County, Birth Book 24, page 333.

Mrs. Stella Van Vickle, 92, died 18 November 1972, born 1 November 1880 in Blount Township. She married Coy Van Vickle 30 Sep 1902. She is survived by two sons, Ralph H. and R. Jerome; brothers, Roy of Glendale, Ca. and Everett of Gary, Indiana: one sister Mrs. Jenny Henry.

Stella and Cora had:

576. Cora Van Vickle b. aft 1902
577. Ralph H. Van Vickle b. 3 Nov 1909 d. Jul 1994
578. R. Jerome Van Vickle b. aft 1909

299. Jennie May Daniel b. 28 Jan 1882 Vermilion County, Il d. there 3 Jan 1974. She is buried in the Gundy Cemetery, Bismarck, Vermilion County. Her brief obituary appeared in the Danville, Il Commercial News. She married[284] Francis A. Watson 6 Sep 1904. He died and she m. next Ernest Henry. She lived at Bismarck, Il. Her last two children were twins, but one died young after being burned. Her obituary:

Mrs. Jenny Henry, 90, died 3 Jan 1974, born 28 Jan 1883. She married Francis Watson who died in 1920. She married second Ernest Henry who died in 1955. She is survived by one daughter, Mrs. Leora Taylor; two sons Paul L. Watson and Harold Watson. Burial at Gundy Cemetery at Bismarck, Il.

Jennie and Francis had:

579. Leora Opal Watson b. 8 Feb 1903 d. aft 1974
580. Lola Watson b. bef 1906 d. bef 1974
581. Paul L. Watson b. 9 Sep 1906 d. aft 1974
582. Harold Watson b. 1915 d. aft 1974
583. Harlan Watson b. 1915 d. 4 Mar 1922

---

284. Illinois, Vermilion County, Marriage Book 4, page 58.

William M Daniels

300. William Marion "Bill" Daniels born[285] 14
Oct 1884 in Vermilion County, Il d. Jun 1971 in
Lake County, In. He first married[286] Ardilla
A. "Dilla" Watson 30 Jun 1903 in Vermilion
County, Il. They were divorced[287] on 9 Nov
1918. Records of their divorce indicate that
she deserted her family. In 1920 she was
boarding with a Moore family in Danville,
Vermilion County. Her occupation then was
seamstress working in an overall factory. She
was born in Illinois in 1888. A copy of
William's signature is included in their case
file. In 1922 Bill was married to a woman named
Pearl. He next m. Ruth Alice Edmonds bef 1946.
He moved to Gary, Indiana and worked for U.S.
Steel there. Bill was a talented carpenter so
he and his brother Everett helped each other to
build homes for their families. He was stricken
with Alzheimer's disease in his later years as
was his grandfather, Napoleon Daniel. I have
pictures of William, Ardilla and Ruth. William
and Ardilla had:

584. Ruth Daniels* b. bef 1907 d. aft 1922
585. Opal Daniels* b. 24 Jun 1907

William and Ruth had:

586. Marilyn Joyce Daniels* b. 14 Dec 1939
d. aft 1994
587. Melvin J. Daniels* b. 2 Sep 1941 d.
aft 1994
588. Marvin Dale Daniels* b. 6 Jan 1943 d.
aft 1994

---

285. Illinois, Vermilion County, Birth
Book 24, page 333.
286. Illinois, Vermilion County, Marriage
Book 4, page 177.
287. Illinois, Vermilion County, Divorce
File #13857.

589. Mildred Joan Daniels* b. Dec 1944 d.
aft 1994
590. Margie Mae Daniels* b. 26 May 1946 d.
aft 1994

WILLIAM M. DANIELS AND DAUGHTERS RUTH AND OPAL

301. Everett Edward Daniel born 30 Aug 1891 in
Vermilion County, Il d. Dec 1973 in Porter
County, In. He married[288] Nora Bell Huffman
12 Feb 1913. She b. 1894 in Illinois d. 1963.
They are buried in the Johnson Cemetery,
Vermilion County, Il. He lived in Vermilion

---

288. Illinois, Vermilion County, Marriage
Book 6, page 126.

County in 1920 and Gary, Indiana in 1972.
Everett worked as a telegrapher for the C. &
E.I. Railroad and later, beginning in April
1922, worked for U.S. Steel in Gary. He was an
able carpenter and he and his brother Bill
helped each other to build homes for their
families. Everett and Nora had:

591. Edith Daniels* b. 1914 d. aft 1994
592. Harold F. Daniels* b. 2 Jan 1915
     d. aft 1994
593. Hazel Daniels* b. 1917 d. aft 1994
594. Ruby Daniels* b. 1919
595. Vernon Daniels* b. 26 Jul 1921 d. aft
     1994

302. Nellie Daniels b. Sep 1894 in Vermilion
County, Il and d. abt 1972. She married[289]
first Clarence Johnson 19 Oct 1913. Her name is
given as Nella Daniels in Vermilion County
marriage records. Clarence died[290] 30 Oct
1920. According to her first cousin, John
Henry Atwood, she next married Wilbur Phillips.
This is supported by her father's obituary.
They were living in Plymouth, Ind in 1939 when
her father died. According to family members in
Vermilion County they had two children, a son
and a daughter. It is thought that they moved
to Reno, Nv where Nellie died. Their daughter
moved to California where she became a
Jehovah's Witness. This seems to have caused a
rift in the family and the members in Vermilion
County lost contact with her.

Clarence and Nellie had:

596. Earl Johnson b. bef 1922

Wilbur and Nellie had:

597. Evelyn Phillips b. aft 1920

---

289. Illinois, Vermilion County, Marriage
Book 6, page 273.
290. Illinois, Vermilion County, Death
Record #6364.

CHILDREN OF NAPOLEON AND LAURA GRITTON DANIEL,
LEFT TO RIGHT: EVERETT, STELLA, JENNIE, NELLIE
AND ROY.

303. Roy E. Daniel born[291] 15 Dec 1900 in
Vermilion County, Il d. 8 Mar 1989 at New
Castle, Lawrence County, Pa. He married[292]
Bess Rose Herrin 10 Jun 1922 in Urbana,
Champaign County, Il. Their marriage record
contains copies of both of their signatures.
She was b. 15 Dec 1894 at Bristol, Va and d. 4
July 1979 at New Castle, Pa and is buried next
to her husband. After her death he married
Julie Cwynar Mruk. He was living in Glendale,
Ca when his sister Stella died in 1972. He
worked for a while for U.S. Steel in Gary but
did not care for this type of work and instead
became an auto mechanic. He was a skilled

---

291. Illinois, Vermilion County, Birth
Book 21, page 147.
292. Illinois, Champaign County, Marriage
Book 9 Jul 1921 - 12 Sep 1922, #8019 - # 8669,
marriage #8498.

carpenter. I have pictures of him and a copy
of his obituary from a New Castle, Pa
newspaper.

Roy Daniels

Roy Daniels, 88, of 520 Friendship St.
died at 12:36 a.m. on March 8, 1989, in Jameson
Memorial Hospital after suffering an apparent
heart attack.

He was born in Danville, Ill on Dec. 15,
1900, to Napoleon and Laura Britten Daniels.

His first wife, the former Bess Herren,
died in 1979. He later married the former Julie
Cwynar Mruk, and she survives.

Mr. Daniels had been employed by the
Welker Lincoln Mercury car dealership in
Hammond, Ind., where he was a mechanic for 10
years.

He belonged to First Church of the
Nazarene.

Other survivors include a son, L. E.
Daniels of New Wilmington, one grandchild and
two great-grandchildren.

He was also preceded in death by his
parents; a grandson, Rodney Daniels; and two
brothers and three sisters.

Calling hours are 7 to 9 p.m. tomorrow at
the R. Cunningham Funeral Home, 2429 Wilmington
Road. A service will be conducted at 10 a.m. on
Friday at the funeral home by the Rev. G.A.
Small, pastor of First Church of the Nazarene.

Interment will be in Castle View Memorial
Gardens.

Roy and Bess had:

599. Linden Eugene Daniels* b. 13 May 1929
     d. aft 1994

317. Raymond Safford Daniels b. Dec 1879 in New
York d. aft 1903. He was living in Oakland, Ca

when his grandmother's estate was settled in 1904 in Champaign County, Oh. There is a stone[293] with no dates for him in the Nordhoff Cemetery, Ojai, Ca but I do not know if he is buried there or not. I do not know if he married. He may be the Raymond S. Daniel in the 1920 Spokane County, Wa census. This man had a wife named Myrtle born 1889 in Iowa and a daughter named Dorothy b. 1915 in Washington.

600. RESERVED

Mary Playter Daniels

318. Mary Playter Daniels b. 18 Aug 1884 in New York d. 3 Jan 1972 probably in Ojai, Ca. She was living in Ventura, Ca when her grandmother's estate was settled in 1904 in Champaign County, Oh. There is a stone[294] for her in the Nordhoff Cemetery, Ojai, Ca. She apparently did not marry.

319. Harold Daniels b. Apr 1889 in Ventura County, Ca d. aft 1904. He was living in Ventura, Ca in 1904 when his grandmother's estate was settled. His guardian, Margaret Daniels, signed for his share as he was a minor. He was living with his mother in Ojai, Ventura County, Ca in 1900 during the census. I do not know if he married.

601. RESERVED

327. Rollo Wilson Daniels b. 4 Nov 1881 Champaign County, Ohio d. 1946 in Los Angeles,

293. California, Ventura County, Ojai, Nordhoff Cemetery, Tombstone. Also Ventura Genealogical Society Quarterly, June 1992, pp. 43-44.
294. California, Ventura County, Ojai, Nordhoff Cemetery, Tombstone. Also Ventura Genealogical Society Quarterly, June 1992, pp. 43-44.

Ca. He is the Rollo W. Daniels in the 1910 and 1920 Los Angeles, Los Angeles County, Ca censuses. His wife's name was Lavina or Vinnie. She was born 1881 in Nebraska. There were no children in their home in either census and cousins report that they had none. I am told that he lived in Hollywood, Ca.

328. John M. Daniel b. 22 May 1883 in Champaign County, Oh d. 1913. His nephews living in 1994 know only his date of death. It is not known where he died or if he married.

602. RESERVED

330. Harry Ernest "Dan" Daniel b. 14 Jan 1888 in Champaign County, Oh d. 15 Dec 1951. He married[295] Edith Wigmore 21 Nov 1932. They lived in Champaign, Champaign County, Il where he died. His relations called him Uncle Dan. He owned a Dodge automobile dealership and was later in the real estate business in Champaign, Il. After he died Edith married his brother, Fred Daniel. He had obituaries[296] in two Champaign, Il newspapers. I include one of them:

H. E. DANIELS, 62, DIES OF SECOND HEART ATTACK

Harry E. Daniels, 916 West William street, died early Sunday morning, after an illness of several weeks. He was 62 years old.

Mr. Daniels had suffered a heart attack in early fall and was hospitalized for several weeks. He returned to his home a few weeks ago but suffered another attack Saturday evening which proved fatal.

The deceased is survived by his wife, a son Thomas, who is a cadet at Sampson air base,

---

295. Notes of William Kenyon Daniel, Columbus, Ind.

296. Illinois, Champaign County, The News Gazette, Vol LVII, No. 141, Monday, 17 Dec 1951, page 3, col 8. Also Champaign-Urbana Courier, 17 Dec 1951, page 3, col 4.

Geneva, N. Y. and two brothers, Fred, Columbus, Ind., and Perry, West Liberty, Ohio.

Funeral services will be conducted at 2 p.m. Tuesday from the Mittnedorf chapel with Reverend A. Ray Cartlidge pastor of the First Presbyterian church, in charge. Burial will be in Roselawn cemetery.

Pallbearers will be: Giles Sullivan, Douglas R. Mills, W. S. Redhed, Doctor V. Thomas Austin, Rune Clark and D. S. Noel.

Mr. Daniels was in the real estate business at the time of his death. For many years he owned and operated the Dodge automobile agency in Champaign.

The deceased was born Jan. 14, 1889 in Urbana, Ohio, the son of William and Emma Daniels. Three brothers preceded him in death. He attended grade school in Urbana, Ohio and the high school at Winona, Lake County, Ind. He attended Wabash college, Crawfordsville, Ind.

Mr. Daniels first entered the automobile business in Monticello, In., 1919. He moved to Lafayette, Ind., two years later and entered into an automobile agency partnership.

He was married to Edith Wigmore of Monticello, Ind., on November 21, 1923.

Mr. Daniels moved to Champaign in 1928, purchasing the Dodge agency. He sold this business in 1940. He was a member of the First Presbyterian church of Champaign. The deceased was a member of the Champaign County Country club, the Champaign Elks lodge and was for many years a member of the Champaign Rotary club.

Dan and Edith had:

603. Thomas Harding Daniel* b. 18 Dec 1926 d. abt 1985

331. Perry Louis Daniel b. 12 Mar 1890 in Urbana, Champaign County, Oh d. Oct 1953. An article from a local newspaper describes how over fifty of his neighbors gathered to aid his widow by harvesting his corn crop after his death. This article also mentions that he died in his automobile but does not say what the

PERRY LOUIS AND LIZZIE YODER DANIELS

circumstances were. He was living in Logan
County, Oh with his wife and child in 1920.
There was a Dwight Hostetter in their home who
may have been her relative. Perry married[297]
Elizabeth Mae Yoder 24 Aug 1912 in Logan
County, Oh. She was b. 8 Aug 1888 in West
Liberty, Logan County, Oh, the daughter of
Elzra J. and Lizzie Kurtz Yoder. She died 17
Sep 1965 in Bellefontaine, Logan County, Oh.
Perry and Lizzie are buried in the Fairview

---

297. Notes of William Kenyon Daniel,
Columbus, Ind.

Cemetery, West Liberty, Oh. They were members
of the Mennonite church. Perry and Lizzie had:

604. Wilma Elizabeth Daniels* b. 27 Mar
1919 d. abt 1962
605. D. Dwight Daniels* b. 14 Apr 1921 d.
aft 1994

332. Fred Elden Daniel b. 14 Oct 1893 in
Champaign County, Oh and d. 2 Oct 1983 at
Columbus, Bartholomew County, In. He
married[298] Martha Kenyon 1 Sep 1920 in
Indianapolis, In. When Fred was two years old
his mother died and he was taken to live with
his grandmother Wilson. She died in 1901 when
he was 8 years old and his older brother, Harry
Ernest, took him to California to live with
relatives there. He spent time with several
different relatives while there and returned to
the east when he was 14. He joined the Army Air
Force and served in Texas during WWI attaining
the rank of sergeant major. He moved to
Indianapolis, In where he married and in 1932
he moved his family to Columbus, In. Fred later
became the Vice-President of Arvin Industries,
a Columbus based Fortune 500 Company. In 1960,
after his wife died, he married[299] Edith
Wigmore Daniels, widow of his brother Harry.
She died in 1970. He had obituaries in Columbus
and Indianapolis newspapers. I include one[300]
here:

---

298. Notes of William Kenyon Daniel,
Columbus, Ind.
299. Illinois, Champaign County, Marriage
License Applications, Book July 1960-July 1961,
#38645, 29 Nov 1960.
300. Indiana, Marion County, Indianapolis
Star, Monday, 3 Oct 1983.

Fred E. Daniel

Fred E. Daniel, 89, Columbus, a former
Indianapolis resident, died Sunday in
Bartholomew County Hospital in Columbus. A
native of Urbana, Ohio, he lived here about 13
years. He was employed at Arvin Industries Inc.
in Columbus for 42 years, retiring in 1974. He
was a member of First United Methodist Church,
St. John Masonic Lodge and High 12 Club, all in
Columbus, and a past president of the Columbus
Chamber of Commerce, Foundation for Youth and
Kiwanis Club. He was an Army Air Force veteran
of World War I. Services will be held at 10:30
a.m. Tuesday in Hathaway-Meyers Funeral Chapel
in Columbus, where friends may call from 3:30
p.m. to 8:30 p.m. today. Survivors include a

son, William K. Daniel, and a step-son, Thomas
Daniels. Memorial contributions may be made to
the First United Methodist Church Memorial Fund
and the Foundation for Youth.

Fred and Martha had:

606. Mary Elizabeth Daniel b. 13 Mar 1925
     d. 15 Oct 1976
607. William Kenyon Daniel b. 8 Jan 1931
     d. aft 1994

SECOND FAMILY OF WILLIAM T. DANIEL, LEFT TO
RIGHT: OPAL, HAROLD, GEORGEANA VAN KIRK, WALTER
AND OPAL.

333. Myrtle Daniel b. 1898/9 in Ohio and d.
about 1930, possibly in Spiro, Ok. She m. Jim
Strain. They had:

608. Vada Strain b. bef 1930
609. Verna Strain b. bef 1930

334. Walter Thurman Daniel b. 12 Jan 1904 at
Dayton, Montgomery County, Oh and d. 11 Jan
1948 Halstead, Harvey County, Ks. He m. Lula F.
Claar 17 May 1928 at Hays, Ellis County, Ks.
She was the daughter of Samuel Dove Claar and
Mary Margaret Hoyle. Lula was a school teacher
and a Methodist. Thurman had an obituary in an
area newspaper:

OBITUARY - Thurman Daniel

Walter Thurman Daniel, eldest son of
William T. and Georgana Daniel, was born in
Dayton, O., Jan. 12, 1904, and departed this
life at Halstead, Kan., aged 43 years, 11
months, and 30 days. In early childhood he
united with the Methodist church in Coldwater,
Kan., where he grew to manhood.
May 17, 1928, he was united in marriage to
Lula Claar, to which union four children were
born. Since 1932, the family has made their
home near Rexford, where they engaged in
farming.
He was preceded in death by his father,
William T. Daniel, and by one sister, Mrs.
Myrtle Strain.
He leaves to mourn his passing, his wife,
Lula,; his four children, Walter, Jay, Jo Ann
and Marjorie Lea; his mother, Mrs. Georgana
Daniel, of Wichita; one sister, Mrs. Robert
Innis of Wichita; one brother, Harold, of
Coldwater, besides many other relatives and a
host of friends.
Thurman will be greatly missed. His genial
disposition, his unfailing optimism, and his
willingness to lend a helping hand endeared him
to everyone he knew.
Funeral services were held Jan. 14, from
the Rexford Community church, conducted by the
Rev. Burt, pastor. Interment was in the Hawkeye
cemetery.
Relatives who attended from a distance
were Mrs. Georgana Daniel, Wichita; Mr. and

Mrs. Robert L. Innis, Wichita; Mr. and Mrs. Harold Daniel and son, Robert, Coldwater; Mr. and Mrs. James Sharrah, Hereford, Colo,; Mr. and Mrs. Evart Claar, Greely, Colo.; and from Denver Mr. and Mrs. Roe Claar and son, Mr. and Mrs. Isaac Carson, and Mrs. Pearl Graves and children.

Walter and Lula had:

610. Walter Gerald Daniel* b. 9 Jul 1930
611. Alvin Jay Daniel* b. 27 Jan 1934
612. Jo Ann Daniel* b. 13 Dec 1936
613. Marjorie Lea Daniel* b. 10 Oct 1938

335. Harold Robert Daniel b. 2 Sep 1906 at Comanche County, Ks d. 20 May 1964 at Wichita, Ks. He m. Mary Ann Schenk in 1925. He had an obituary[301] in a Wichita newspaper:

HAROLD R. DANIEL

Services for Harold R. Daniel, 57, of 2722 W. Central, who died Thursday, will be at 10 a. m. Saturday at Broadway Mortuary. Burial will be in Wichita Park Cemetery.

He was born Sept. 2, 1906, in Comanche County, Kan., and had lived in Wichita since 1951. He was a retired barber and a member of the Methodist church.

Survivors include two daughters, Mrs. Donald R. Burnett, 3215 E. Euclid, and Mrs. Claire Thompson, Coldwater, Kan.; two sons, Robert Daniel, Penrose, Colo., and Jerrold Daniel, San Francisco, Calif.; a sister Mrs. Herman Harrison, 4721 Oxford; and 12 grandchildren.

Harold and Mary had:

614. Robert Lee Daniel* b. 17 Oct 1925
615. Gwendolyn Ann Daniel* b. 27 Oct 1927
616. Shirley J. Daniel* b. 31 Oct 1931

---

301. Kansas, Sedgwick County, The Wichita Eagle, Saturday, 23 May 1964, page 48.

617. Gerald Ray Daniel* b. 18 Aug 1935

336. Opal A. Daniel b. 22 Apr 1908 at Comanche County, Ks d. of cancer 7 July 1978 at Hutchinson, Reno County, Ks. She m. Robert L. Innis. He d. 26 Dec 1956 and after his death she m. 2nd Herman Harrison. She is buried in the Burton Cemetery, Burton, Ks. Opal and Robert had:

    618. Kathleen Innis
    619. Wanda Innis
    620. Robert Dean Innis d. 23 Nov 1951

358. Cynthia Ann Daniel b. 14 Mar 1857 d. 12 Feb 1901. She lived her whole life in Platte County, Mo. and the vicinity. She married[302] Charles A. Marshall 22 Mar 1876. He d. 6 Jun 1947. They are buried in the Ridgely Community Cemetery in Platte County. They had:

    621. Edward Homer Marshall b. 20 Jan 1877 d. 18 Sep 1966
    622. Jesse B. Marshall b. 15 Jun 1880 d. 28 Aug 1961
    623. Louis Marshall b. 4 Sep 1886 d. aft 1951
    624. Connie G. Marshall b. 4 May 1895 d. 4 Dec 1963

359. Mariam Boone Daniel b. 27 Feb 1859 d. 4 July 1929 in Platte County, Mo. She m. Hiram McComas 18 Dec 1877. He d. 30 Oct 1931. They are buried in the Platte City Cemetery, Platte City, Mo. They had:

    625. Claude McComas b. 29 Nov 1880

360. Armilda J. Daniel b. 7 Sep 1862 d. 1960 in Platte County, Mo. She was married four times but her only child was by her first husband.

---

302. Missouri, Platte County, Marriage Book B, page 509.

She married[303] Luther Rhinehart 1 Mar 1882.
He was b. 30 Jan 1857 d. 29 May 1922. They are
buried in the Platte City Cemetery. They had:

> 626. Myrtle May Rhinehart b. 17 Dec 1882
>   d. 24 Jul 1938

361. Mary Frances Daniel b. 8 Oct 1864 in
Platte County, Mo d. 1920 in Missouri. She m.
John William Moore 26 Nov 1884. They had:

> 627. Dora Elaine Moore b. aft 1884
> 628. Maude Moore b. 1889
> 629. Estel B. Moore b. aft 1884
> 630. Harry Moore b. aft 1884
> 631. Nell Moore b. aft 1884
> 632. William Gray Moore b. aft 1884
> 633. Delma Moore b. 1904
> 634. J. B. Moore b. aft 1884

362. William Meredith Daniel b. 22 Feb 1874
Platte County, Mo and d. 1959 in Platte County.
As far as I know he lived in the same area all
of his life. His nickname was Polly. He was a
farmer. He married[304] Anna E. Rule. She was
b. 1881 in Missouri and d. 1965. They are
buried in the Platte City Cemetery. William and
Anna had:

> 635. Ethel Frances Daniel b. 1 Mar
>   1901 d. Aug 1923
> 636. Allie Bernice Daniel* b. 16 Nov 1905
>   d. aft 1994

363. Benjamin Franklin Daniel b. 19 Sep 1869
Platte County, Mo d. 9 Dec 1963 at Kansas City,
Mo. He m. Myrtle Irea Wilkinson about 1905. I
have not found a record of their marriage. She
was b. 20 Jun 1880 in Ohio and d. 3 May 1945 at
Kansas City, Mo. They were in the 1910 Wichita,
Ks census and the 1920 Kansas City, Mo census.

---

303. IGI, Missouri, Platte County,
Marriage Records.
304. Missouri, Platte County, Marriage
Book G, page 140.

According to the notes[305] of Alicia Pearl Daniel they were living in Aubrey, Ks by 1950. Another cousin[306] who knew them confirmed that the family I found in census records was our cousin, Benjamin, and his family. Benjamin was employed as a bookkeeper for Swift & Co. in 1910 and was apparently more than just an employee of that firm according to the census. He also owned his own home then. A cousin sent me his obituary from a Kansas City, Mo newspaper:

BENJAMIN F. DANIEL

Benjamin F. Daniel, 94, formerly of 1817 Spruce, died Monday at a nursing home at 622 Benton. He was born in Platte City and lived here 50 years. He was an accountant for the Chevrolet-Kansas City division of General Motors corporation. Mr. Daniel was a member of the Jackson Avenue Christian church. Surviving are two sons, Paul W. Daniel, Webster Groves, Mo., and Frederick G. Daniel, Jackson Heights, N. Y.; two grandchildren and a great-grandchild. Services will be held at 2 o'clock Friday at the Newcomer chapel, Brush Creek and the Paseo; burial in Memorial Park cemetery. Friends may call after noon today at the chapel.

Benjamin and Myrtle had:

637. Frederick Gaylord Daniel* b. 6 Apr
     1906 d. aft 1963
638. Paul Wilkinson Daniel* b. 10 Aug 1908
     d. aft 1963

364. Issie F. Daniel b. 15 Nov 1879 in Platte County, Mo d. 1920 in Pittsburg, Pennsylvania. She was working for the government in Pittsburg

---

305. My grandfather, Estridge Daniel by Alicia Pearl Daniel Mayer. DeKalb County, Missouri Historical Society, Maysville, Mo.
306. Mrs. Donnie June Coppinger Stoekle, Kansas City, Mo., conversation of 1 Aug 1994.

according to the obituary of her father. I have
not yet tried to locate more information about
her in Pennsylvania records. She is buried in
the Platte City Cemetery.

J. SHELBY AND MAGGIE HUNN DANIEL

372. Joseph Shelby Daniel b. 28 Dec 1866 Platte
County, Mo. d. 23 Sep 1938 Kansas City, Mo. He
m. Margaret Emma "Maggie" Hunn 30 Nov 1887. She
b. 29 Jul 1868 in Missouri d. 2 Apr 1948. They
are buried in the Elmwood Cemetery, Kansas
City, Mo. She was the daughter of Housan and
Nancy E. Davis Hunn. The Hunns are buried in
the Barry Cemetery, Clay County, Mo near the
Daniel plot. Joseph went by his middle name,
Shelby or J. Shelby. He ran a clothing store
for many years in Kansas City, Mo. I have two
sheets of stationary with his store letterhead
and several pictures of him and his wife. A
cousin told me that their first child was a
daughter who died as an infant and is buried at
the Barry Cemetery, Clay County, Mo. Another
cousin's notes also mention this child. His
obituary:

JOSEPH SHELBY DANIEL- The End to Retired Clothier is at 3516 Summit-Joseph Shelby Daniel, 71 years old, 3109 Washington Street, died early today at 3516 Summit Street. He was a retired clothier. He leaves his wife, Mrs. Maggie E. Daniel; his mother, Mrs. Susan E. Daniel, both of the home; a daughter, Mrs. D.A. Coppinger, 3118 Washington Street; a son, J. Shelby Daniel Jr., Chico, Calif.; a brother, Manza Daniel, Los Angeles, and two sisters, Mrs. Marjorie Fellows Scott, 3516 Summit Street, and Mrs. Katherine E. Doane, 3626 Brooklyn Ave. Funeral services will be held at 3:30 o'clock at the Stine & McClure chapel, 3235 Gillham Plaza.

Shelby and Maggie had:

639. Donnie A. Daniel* b. 24 Jun 1889 d. 18 Dec 1975
640. Margaret Lena Daniel b. 1901 d. Mar 1910
641. Joseph Shelby Daniel Jr.* b. 27 Nov 1903 d. 9 July 1986

373. Ermina Katherine Daniel b. 3 Apr 1869 in Platte County, Mo d. 1965. She m. Charles H. Doane 9 Mar 1892. He was b. abt 1862. I think they lived in the Kansas City, Mo area all of their lives. Her mother was living with them in 1920.

642. RESERVED

374. Mary Ellen Daniel b. 27 Jun 1873 d. aft 1938. She m. Augustus G. Walker 30 Aug 1891. I think they located in the Kansas City, Mo area. They reportedly had two children but I have the name of only one. They had:

643. Clarence Walker b. aft 1891

375. Almanza B. Daniel b. 18 Sep 1878 Platte County, Mo d. 18 Oct 1960 Los Angeles, Ca. He m. Ida May Dutcher 24 Oct 1900. She b. 5 Sep

1879 Fulton, Il the daughter of John E. and
Annie Elizabeth Zook Dutcher. He was a postman.
He went by the nickname "Manza". He was in the
1910 Los Angeles County, Ca census. Judging by
the birthplaces listed for their children they
moved to California between 1905 and 1908. They
had:

> 644. Thelma F. Daniel* b. 20 Oct 1901 d.
> 26 Jan 1961
> 645. Charles Edwin Daniel* b. 9 Aug 1904
> d. 23 May 1978
> 646. Kathryn Mae Daniel* b. 24 Mar 1907
> 647. Almanza Martin Daniel* b. 19 Jan 1910
> d. aft 1994

380. Arthur Franklin Daniel b. 4 Sep 1892
Montgomery County, Ky d. there 30 Jun 1958. He
m. Minnie Lee Ensor 27 Apr 1931. He had an
obituary[307] in a Kentucky newspaper:

Arthur F. Daniel Passes At Camargo After
Long Illness

Arthur F. Daniel, 65, watchmaker, died at
5:08 a. m. Monday at his home on the McCormick
road near Camargo following an extended
illness.
A native of this county, he was a son of
the late Pleasant and Mary Ellen Cockerham
Daniel, a member of the Christian church and a
veteran of World War I. Mr. Daniel was widely
known throughout this section, was devoted to
his family and church and was admired and
respected by all who knew him.
Survivors include his wife, Mrs. Minnie
Ensor Daniel; two sons, Charles and Edgar
Daniel; a sister, Mrs. Will Ricketts, all of
Montgomery county; three brothers, Alger and
Bradley Daniel of Mt. Sterling, and Leonard
Daniel, this county, and several nieces and
nephews.

---

307. Kentucky, Montgomery County, Mt.
Sterling Advocate, 3 Jul 1958.

Services were held at 2 p. m. Wednesday at the Eastin-Richey funeral home by the Rev. W. F. Chappel and the Rev. Franklin Wade. Burial was in Macpelah cemetery. Military services were held at the grave.

Active bearers were Charles Conley, Herbert Blevins, Ernest Greer, Walker Greer, Elmer Keath and Charles Stevenson. Honorary bearers were Holy Poynter, William Keath, Mason Young, Walter Shubert and Robert Amburgey.

Arthur and Minnie had:

648. Pleasant Edgar Daniel* b. 13 Jun 1940
     d. 1971
649. Charles Wilford Daniel* b. 4 Nov 1941
     d. aft 1994

381. William Leonard Daniel b. 16 Feb 1895 in Montgomery County, Ky d. there 13 Mar 1985. He m. Mary Ricketts Mayes 16 Jun 1926. He had no children. His obituary[308] appeared in a Kentucky newspaper:

William Leonard Daniel

William Leonard Daniel, 90, of Windsor Care Center, of Camargo, died Wednesday, March 13.

A native of Montgomery County, he was the son of the late Pleasant Jamison and Mary Ellen Cockraham Daniels, a retired farmer and a member of the Camargo United Methodist Church.

Survivors include a step son, Fred Marston Mayes of Pennsylvania; a brother, Bradley Daniel of Mt. Sterling; a sister, Gillian Ricketts of Mt. Sterling and two step-grandchildren, Fred Marston Mayes Jr., of Washington and Milinda Susan Mayes of Colorado.

Funeral services were held Saturday at 10:30 a. m. at the Eastin-Taul Funeral Home Chapel with Rev. Doug Marksberry officiating. Burial was in the Machpelah Cemetery.

---

308. Kentucky, Montgomery County, Mt. Sterling Advocate, 21 Mar 1985.

206

Casket bearers were William D. Ricketts, Arthur Ricketts, Charles Daniel, Tommie Ricketts, Victor Ricketts, Fred Mayes Jr. and Mark Greer. Honorary bearers were Kenneth Cockrell, Omar Cockrell, Robert Donaldson, Kendall Pelfrey, Kendall Keath, Glenn Stafford and Eddie Lockridge.

382. Alger Wheeler Daniel b. 5 Mar 1897 in Montgomery County, Ky d. 4 Apr 1979. He m. Mattie Turner Myers 11 Nov 1921. He m. 2nd Mae McCormick Brucker 28 Aug 1938. He had no children.

384. Gillian Frances Daniel b. 20 Oct 1903 in Montgomery County, Ky d. aft 1994. She m. William Lervis Ricketts 17 Sep 1938. I met her a couple of times and have had some correspondence and telephone conversations with her. I have a picture of her at about the age of six. Wm and Gillian had:

650. Mary Lee Ricketts b. 20 Aug 1940
651. William Lervis Ricketts b. 21 Nov 1942
652. Arthur McClure Ricketts b. 26 Apr 1944

385. Bradley Lee Daniel b. 23 Oct 1906 Montgomery County, Ky d. there 11 Mar 1993. He m. Jessie Davis Wyatt 23 Nov 1928. His obituary appeared in a Mt. Sterling, Ky newspaper:

Bradley Lee Daniel

Bradley Lee Daniel, 85, of Mt. Sterling, died March 11 at the St. Joseph Hospital in Lexington.
Born Oct. 23, 1906, in Montgomery County, he was the son of the late Pleasant Jameson and Mary Ellen Cockrane Daniel. He was preceded in death by his wife, Jesse Wyatt Daniel.
He was a retired builder and a member of the First United Methodist Church. He was also a member of the Watson Lodge, Independent Order

of Odd Fellows and a 50-year member of the
Machpelah Cemetery Board.
He is survived by one son, Tom Daniel of
Clawson, Mich.; one daughter, Dorothy Jones of
Mt. Sterling; one sister, Gilley Ricketts of
Mt. Sterling; four grandchildren, Chris Daniel,
Charlene Patrick, Diane Johnson and Donna
Jones; and one great-grandson, Mikael Johnson.
Funeral services were conducted March 14
at the Eastin-Taul Funeral Home by the Rev. Sam
Knox. Burial was in the Machpelah Cemetery.
Active pallbearers were W.D. Ricketts,
Charles Daniel, Buddy Chappel, Ronnie Agee and
F.M. Sponcil.
Honorary pallbearers were Dan Ware, L.D.
Goodpaster, Kerry Pelfry, Bob Donaldson, Wick
Davis, Eddie Lockridge, Gatewood Sorrell and
Bush Hudson.

They had:

653. Dorothy Lee Daniel* b. 21 Aug 1931 d.
aft 1994
654. Alger Thompson Daniel* b. 19 Aug 1943
d. aft 1994

388. Sarah "Sallie" Daniel b. May 1884 in
Bourbon or Montgomery County, Ky d. aft 1910.
It is thought that she had children according
to Gillian Daniel Ricketts (#384). This family
may have moved to Indiana and settled near
Crawfordsville.

655. RESERVED

389. Woodford C. Daniel b. Oct 1889 in Bourbon
or Montgomery County, Ky d. aft 1912. He
married[309] Edith Lousie Myall 3 Jan 1912 in
Bourbon County, Ky. It is thought that he had
children according to Gillian Daniel Ricketts
(#384). He was at home with his parents and
siblings in the 1910 census of Bourbon County,
Ky. This family is thought to have moved to

---

309. Kentucky, Bourbon County, Marriage
Book 1895-1930, page 187.

Indiana, possibly settling near Crawfordsville, but may have been confused with the family of his aunt, Armina Jameson Daniel Cox (#137). A search of soundexed census records for 1920 for the surname of Daniel and Daniels for Kentucky, Ohio, Illinois, Indiana, Nebraska, California, Washington and Missouri failed to produce any mention of this man or his brother, Holt.

656. RESERVED

390. Holt Daniel b. Oct 1891 in Montgomery or Bourbon County, Ky d. aft 1910. According to Gillian Daniel Ricketts (#384) it is thought that he married and had children. This family may have moved to Indiana and settled near Crawfordsville. See notes for his brother, Woodford.

657. RESERVED

THREE DAUGHTERS OF HARVEY J. AND LEORA GILKEY DANIEL, LEFT TO RIGHT: MARY FLORINE, GEORGIA CLAY AND MARGUERITE MAY.

391. Mary Florine Daniel b. 19 Aug 1881 in Montgomery County, Ky d. 6 Nov 1960 in Pasadena, Ca. She is buried in Forest Lawn

Memorial Park, Glendale, Ca. She married James
A. Glenn 27 Jul 1905 in South Boston, Virginia
and had two daughters. He was a farmer and they
resided on the Glenmary Farm, Halifax County,
Va. He was a member of the Episcopal Church and
she the Christian Church and later the
Methodist. He is reportedly buried in South
Boston, Va and she at Pasadena where she had
been living with a daughter. They had:

658. Florine Daniel Glenn b. 19 may 1906
659. Dorothy Lee Glenn b. 14 Dec 1907 d. 2
Nov 1993

392. Georgia Clay Daniel b. 14 Aug 1883 in
Montgomery County, Ky d. 21 Dec 1982 in South
Boston, Va where she is buried with her husband
in the Oakridge Cemetery. She married Edgar
Franklin Walker 29 Oct 1907 in South Boston, Va
and had seven children. Her husband was a
grocer and farmer and a Baptist. She was a
member of the Christian Church and then the
Baptist. Edgar was married to Sallie Coates
before his marriage to Georgia. He was the son
of Daniel Thomas Walker and Martha James
William Simpson. He was born 22 Dec 1866 in
Pittsylvania, Va and d. 6 Jul 1941 in South
Boston, Va. Georgia and Edgar had:

660. Winona Franklin Walker b. 9 Aug 1908
661. Leora Gilkey Walker b. 23 Dec 1911 d.
4 Feb 1985
662. Mary Clay Walker b. 12 Jul 1913
663. Carolyn Frances Walker b. 27 Oct 1914
664. Edgar Franklin Walker Jr. b. 13 Oct
1918 d. 14 Jul 1992
665. Helen Hope Walker b. 12 Jan 1921
666. Daniel Thomas Walker b. 6 Feb 1928

393. Marguerite May Daniel b. 23 Jul 1886 in
Montgomery County, Ky d. 10 Jan 1979 in
Culpeper County, Va and is buried there. She m.
William Mayfield Thompson 4 Jun 1912 in South
Boston, Va. He d. in Culpeper County and they
are both buried there. He was a preacher and a
Baptist. She was a member of the Christian

Church and then became a Baptist. They lived in
New Jersey for a time. They had one daughter.

> 667. Virginia Lee Thompson b. 21 Sep 1913

394. Charles Gilkey Daniel b. 7 Aug 1888 in
Montgomery County, Ky d. 15 Feb 1938 in South
Boston, Va. He m. Sue Cary Hawkins bef 1917.
She b. 16 Aug 1890 Halifax County, Va d. 15 Sep
1969 at Washington, D.C. They are buried in the
Oakridge Cemetery, South Boston, Va with their
daughter. They had two children, one of whom
died young and the other never married. Charles
Jr. is buried in Arlington National Cemetery.

> 668. Charles Gilkey Daniel Jr.* 6 Apr 1917
> 669. Cary Elizabeth Daniel b. 8 May 1919
>   d. 10 Nov 1920

396. Elizabeth Harvey Daniel b. 24 July 1898
Montgomery County, Ky d. 19 Jan 1981 at
Arlington, Va and is buried in the Arlington
County Cemetery. She married Harland Marshall
Start 27 Jun 1922 at Washington, D. C. He d. 23
Feb 1979 at Arlington. He was a member of the
Methodist Church and she the Christian and then
Methodist Church. He was a lawyer. They had one
daughter.

> 670. Barbara Lee Start b. 23 Jul 1928

399. Richie Daniel b. 29 Jan 1890 Montgomery
County, Ky d. there 21 Dec 1955. He
married[310] Maudie Edith Toliver 8 Sep 1926. I
have seen a picture of him as a young man. They
had:

> 671. Richie Leo Daniel* b. 9 Sep 1929

415. Tinsley Daniel b. Sep 1895 Bath County, Ky
d. aft 1910. From a conversation in 1994 with
Mr. Herbie Pergram, b 1899 in Bath County,
Tinsley Daniel was his cousin, Tinsley being a

---

310. Daniel Family Bible, in possession of
Leo Daniel of Jeffersonville, Ky.

grandson of his great aunt Mary Jane Pergram
Daniel. Mr. Pergram knew Tinsley well.
According to him Tinsley married Ruth Penix of
Bath County and they moved to Ashland, Ky where
he disappeared. In later years Mr. Pergram
tried to determine his fate but it has remained
a mystery and foul play is suspected as Tinsley
was "pool shark and a gambler". It is not known
if he had children. I have not located a record
of his marriage.

672. RESERVED

LEFT TO RIGHT, BEULAH MAE DANIEL, DAUGHTER OF
JOHN M. DANIEL AND FIRST COUSINS LORA AND
LINNIE DANIEL DAUGHTERS OF JAMES EDWIN DANIEL.

419. Beulah Mae Daniel b. 4 Sep 1878 near
Stoutsville, Monroe County, Mo d. 16 Dec 1957
in California. She married Charles W. Thomas 21
Dec 1898 at Shields, Ralls County near Monroe
City, Mo. He b. 22 Jun 1871 d. 8 Nov 1938.
After the death of her father Beulah was sent
to live with her aunt and uncle, James and
Sallie Daniel Martin, in Ralls County, Mo. I
have several pictures of her from the age of 16
or so until she was elderly. She was a very
attractive young woman. She became a little
eccentric in later years and one day her
daughter, Elta Mae, entered her home to find
her seated in front of a fire in a small trash
can slowly tossing her family pictures in one
at a time. Elta Mae rescued several
irreplaceable family photos and, being
childless, passed them to her sister-in-law,
Lena Rebecca Johnson Thomas, just before her
death. I started a long distance relationship
with Lena in 1991 when she was 90 and received
several copies of photographs from her in
addition to much of the information[311] I have
on Beulah and her siblings and their families.
Beulah lived around Barry, Mo in the old Thomas
family home for some time. Charles and Beulah
had:

673. Charles Garland Thomas b. 20 Nov 1901
674. Elta Mae Thomas b. 5 Apr 1906 d. 12
Jun 1988

420. Myrtle Meredith Daniel b. 6 Apr 1881 near
Stoutsville, Monroe County, Mo d. 13 Apr 1951
at Rawlins, Carbon County, Wyoming. According
to those who knew her, Myrtle married a very
pretty Canadian woman named Lillian. She was
known as Lillie and her hobby was raising dogs.
I have one picture of her but none of him.
After the death of his father Myrtle was sent
to live with his uncles, James Edwin and
Charles Daniel. He was living with my
grandfather, Charlie, during the 1900 census

311. Letters of Mrs. Lena Rebecca Thomas,
Fairfield, California, 1991-1993 (In my files).

but I think spent more time in and around
DeKalb County, Mo with his Uncle Ed Daniel. He
was injured in a fall from a horse as a young
man and as a result was hunch-backed. Unable to
do heavy labor he relied on his wits to make a
living. I have spoken with several relatives
who knew him. He was a rum runner during
prohibition and transported liquor from
Missouri to Texas. He was a gambler and either
rich or poor. He ran a taxi service in Cameron
and Kansas City in the 1940s. He and Lillie
moved to Rawlins, Wyoming in the late 1940s.
Everyone I have spoken to who knew him was
impressed by him in one way or another. One
cousin, A.J. Perry, was at his home on the day
he was selling his property in preparation for
his move to Wyoming. A.J. told me that he was
awed by Myrtle's skill as a salesman. I have
been told that Myrtle was a short man. Myrtle
and Lillie had no children.

421. Onie St. Elmo Daniel b. 9 Jul 1883 in
Monroe County, Mo d. aft 1905. He was last
heard from at Oswego, Montana in 1905. He had
gone there to claim government land. After the
death of his parents he was raised by his aunt
and uncle, Willie and Ed Daniel, and was close
to his various relatives so it is unlikely that
he would sever his ties with them. It is
thought that he may have been injured in the
wilderness and died. One relative told me that
he went to Oklahoma, not Montana. His fate is
still a matter of speculation among elderly
relatives in 1994.

422. Alicia Pearl Daniel born[312] 18 Sep 1885
near Kansas City, Mo d. 16 Mar 1978 in San
Diego, Ca. After the death of her father she
was sent to live with her mother's family and
grew up apart from her Daniel relatives and did
not know them well. She m. Sidney Edwin Mayer
26 Dec 1906 in Eureka Springs, Ark. He b. 10

---

312. Missouri, DeKalb County, Maysville,
The DeKalb County Historical Society, The
Daniel Family by Alicia Pearl Mayer.

214

ALICIA PEARL DANIEL LAFORCE MAYER, AGE 18

Aug 1882 Columbus, Ohio d. 30 May 1942 San
Diego, Ca. They are both buried in the Mt. Hope
Cemetery, San Diego. Alicia was an accomplished
poet, writer and artist in several mediums. She
was also active in the leadership of the many
organizations that she participated in. She was
organizer and first president of the San Diego
Genealogy Society. She authored several papers
on the Daniel family but her conclusions were
unsupported by any documentation and I believe
were erroneous. I have several pictures of her

from the age of 16 or so. Her obituary[313] appeared in a San Diego, Ca newspaper:

Mrs. Alicia P. Mayer

Alicia P. Mayer, 92, a poet, composer, sculptor, artist and lecturer, died Thursday in a La Mesa convalescent hospital. She was 92.
Mrs. Mayer, known professionally in her writings as Pearl LaForce Mayer, was born in Kansas City, Mo., and came to the county 61 years ago. She last resided at 4669 67th St.
She wrote poetry and was the author of a book titled "Historical Landmarks of San Diego." Listed in "Who's who in American Poetry." Mrs. Mayer was also editor of the California Gardens Magazine. Her poems and monologues were broadcast over the radio in the 1930s.
She was founder of the San Diego Cosmopolitan Club, former president of the San Diego Women Press Club, former president of the Burlingame Club, former county and state chairmen of the California Federation of Women's Clubs, former president of the San Diego Women's Club, founder and president of the San Diego Genealogical Society, and a past officer of the San Diego chapter of the American Pen Women.
Surviving are a son, George, of La Mesa; a daughter, Mrs. Marguerite Ferguson of Half Moon Bay; three grandchildren, six great grandchildren and one great-great grandchild.
Graveside services will be tomorrow in Mt. Hope Cemetery. Lewis Colonial Mortuary is in charge of arrangements.

Sidney and Alicia had:

675. Marguerite Elizabeth Mayer b. 25 Nov 1908
676. George Eberly Mayer (Adopted)

---

313. California, San Diego, The San Diego Union, 19 March 1978, Sunday, page B-9.

425. Linnie Maude Daniel b. 6 July 1881 near Kansas City, Mo d. 15 Feb 1976 DeKalb County, Mo. She married[314] Arthur L. Perry 18 Jan 1898 in DeKalb County and were residents of that county. They are buried in the Fairport Cemetery there. I have pictures of her from the time she was a small child until she was aged and have some of her husband as well. She was a collector and collected many things and was somewhat of a character. They had:

> 677. Gladys Perry b. aft 1898
> 678. Charles Perry b. aft 1898
> 679. Arthur E. Perry b. aft 1898

426. Lora Lee Daniel b. 25 Nov 1883 near Kansas City, Mo d. Feb 1975 at Lake Lowtana, Jackson County, Mo. She collected social security benefits at Lee's Summit, Jackson County, Mo. She married[315] Oliver Grant Mills 2 Dec 1900 in DeKalb County, Mo. They had one child and then divorced. She next m. Charles Moss bef 1903. He b. 1883 d. 1962. Charles and Lora are buried together in the Fairport Cemetery, DeKalb County. Oliver G. Mills is also buried in that cemetery. I have several pictures of her from childhood on. Oliver Grant Mills and Lora had:

> 680. Willie Mills 12 Sep 1901 d. aft 1994

Lora and Charles Moss had:

> 681. Pearl Moss b. 19 Jun 1903 d. 20 Jun 1903
> 682. Earl Franklin Moss b. 3 Aug 1904 d. 25 Jan 1923
> 683. Charles Homer Moss b. 9 Jul 1906
> 684. Bonnie Lee Moss b. 4 Mar 1910 d. 20 Dec 1966
> 685. John Edwin Moss b. 11 Mar 1912

---

314. Missouri, DeKalb County, Marriage Book H, page 43.
315. Missouri, DeKalb County, Marriage Book H, page 229.

686. George Garland Moss b. 9 Dec 1917
687. Norma Maude Moss b. 22 Aug 1924

GEORGE EDWIN DANIEL AND SON, COVELL MARK DANIEL

427. George Edwin Daniel b. 27 May 1897 DeKalb
County, Mo d. 22 July 1967 Glendale, Ca. He
married[316] Hazel Flora Pittzenbarger 19 Sep
1915 at Maysville, Mo. She b. 25 Apr 1898 d. 1
Feb 1985 in DeKalb County. He was a mortician.
I have several pictures of him and his wife.
Both have obituaries in DeKalb County
newspapers and the DeKalb County Historical

---

316. Missouri, DeKalb County, Marriage
Book J, page 60.

Society has copies[317] of their funeral cards and obituaries in their files. George's obituary:

George E. Daniel Dies in California - George Edwin Daniel, son of James Edwin and Willie H. Daniel, was born May 27, 1897 on a farm east of Fairport, Mo., and passed away in a hospital near his home in Glendale, Calif., July 22, 1967.

He was united in marriage Sept. 19, 1915 to Hazel Pittsenbarger. Two children were born to this union: a son Covell Mark Daniel and a daughter, Caroll Lorraine who passed away in 1933.

He is survived by his wife, his son and daughter-in-law, Ruth and two grandchildren, Robert Mark and Sandra Louise; two sisters, Mrs. Linnie Perry of Osborn and Mrs. Lora Moss of Maysville, and a niece, Mrs. Granville Thompson of Fairport who was reared in the family home as a sister and a host of nieces and nephews.

His home for many years was a farm near Fairport. He then became a mortician and was associated with the Pilcher Funeral Home in Maysville and the Meirhoffer and Fleeman Funeral Home of St. Joseph.

For the past 25 years his home was Glendale, Calif., where he retired as a supervisor at Forest Lawn Memorial Park in 1962 after 20 years of employment there.

He was a member of the Christian Church and Masonic Order.

Being of a pleasant and cheerful nature he made many friends wherever he went.

Funeral services were held Tuesday, July 25th at Forest Lawn in Glendale. His body was returned to the Bram Funeral Home in Maysville on Wednesday. Services will be held at 2 p.m., Friday, July 28th at the Fairport Methodist Church conducted by the Rev. Harold Johnson and

---

317. Missouri, Maysville, The DeKalb County Historical Society, Family Folders, Daniel.

the Masonic Order. Pallbearers are: George
Moss, Gerald Keener, Max A. Neil, A.J. Perry,
Paul Waltemath and Eldon Taylor. Interment will
be in the Fairport Methodist Cemetery.

They had:

688. Covell Mark Daniel* b. 28 Apr 1916 d.
     aft 1994
689. Caroll Lorraine Daniel* b. 30 Mar
     1921 d. 6 Sep 1933

WIFE AND CHILDREN OF CHARLES DANIEL, LEFT TO
RIGHT, SEATED: FREDERICK C., CECIL E., FRIEDA
BASTIAN DANIEL, GEORGE M. AND JOHN QUINCY.
STANDING: THELMA R., ELVA M. S., THEDA R. AND
JACQUELINE A. (A GRANDDAUGHTER)

428. Frederick Charles Daniel b. 21 Sep 1901 in
Ralls County, Mo d. 20 Dec 1968 at Columbus,
Oh. He is buried near his parents in the
Grandview Cemetery near Hannibal, Mo. He m.
Ruth Tope 22 Jan 1922 at Columbus, Oh. They
were divorced 20 Jul 1938 and he m. 2nd Mary
Castle 15 Dec 1938. She d. 6 Feb 1947 and he
did not remarry. All of his children were from

his first marriage. He was a WWI veteran. He
was a fireman in Columbus, Oh for many years. I
have many pictures of him from infancy on. My
Aunt Theda spoke with his former supervisor at
his funeral he told her that Uncle Fred was an
extremely intelligent man. I don't know that I
really remember him but have pictures taken
with him when I was a child and several
possessions of his that I think came to me from
his mother, my grandmother. He and my father
strongly resembled each other. He was an
alcoholic and died of cirrhosis of the liver. I
have a funeral home card and his obituary and
funeral service notice from a Hannibal
newspaper:

Fred C. Daniel

Fred C. Daniel, 67, passed away at his
home in Columbus, Ohio early this morning.
He was born Sept. 21, 1901 in Huntington a
son of Mrs. Frieda Bastian Daniel and the late
Charles Daniel.
His mother survives with 2 daughters, Mrs
Richard (Jo Ann) Epley and Mrs. Ray (Viola)
Fickle both of Columbus, Ohio; 2 brothers,
George A. Daniel of Harrisonville and John Q.
Daniel of Peoria, Ill.; 4 sisters, Mrs. Thelma
Collins of Milwaukee, Wis., Mrs. Harry C.
(Theda) Davis of San Francisco. Calif., Mrs.
Darrell (Elva) Conboy of Louisiana and Mrs.
Thomas (Jacqueline) Hooper of Saratoga, Calif.,
and 5 grandchildren of Columbus.
Besides his father he was preceded in
death by a son, Charles Daniel and by a
brother, Cecil Daniel.
Funeral arrangements are pending at the
Schwartz Funeral Home.

Fred C. Daniel

Services for Fred C. Daniel will be
conducted at 2 p.m. Monday at the Schwartz
Funeral Home. Rev. Deane K. Lierle, pastor of
First Christian Church, will officiate and the
organist will be Mrs. D. L. Chandler.

Interment will be in Grandview Burial Park with the following serving as casket bearers; James Alexander, William Knollhoff, Larry and Gary Daniel, Wayne Powell, John Herring, William Johnston and George Bastian Jr.

Friends may call at the funeral home after 9 a.m. Monday.

Ruth and Fred had:

690. Joann Daniel* b. 20 Mar 1925 d. aft 1994
691. Viola Ruth Daniel* b. 25 Mar 1926 d. Oct 1992
692. Charles Frederick Daniel* b. 9 Jun 1930 d. 1951

429. Cecil Earl Daniel b. 15 Apr 1905 in Ralls County, Mo d. 3 Jan 1968 at Hannibal, Mo. He m. Lorna Doone Howell 5 Dec 1936 at Hannibal, Mo. She was b. 22 Sep 1910 in Hannibal. He operated a barber shop in Hannibal, Mo for many years. I have pictures of one of these shops and many of him and Aunt Lorna. To me he is the best remembered of my father's brothers. He had an easy smile and a somewhat throaty voice. He seemed very tall to me but was probably just a little over six feet. He took after his mother's people physically, and had a good sense of humor. He died of a heart attack in his sleep. He was a member of the Masons. There were four notices of his death in the Hannibal newspaper. I have copies of his obituary[318] and other notices from The Hannibal Courier Post and a funeral home card:

Hannibal Barber dies suddenly

Cecil Daniels, well known Hannibal barber, died suddenly of a heart attack this morning at 6 o'clock at his home, 219 Magnolia Ave. He was 62 years of age.

---

318. Missouri, Hannibal, Hannibal Courier Post, 4 Jan 1968, Vol 30, No. 3, page 18, col 8.

Mr. Daniels had operated a barber shop at 511 Broadway for a number of years.
The body was taken to the Schwartz Funeral Home.

Funeral Tomorrow For Cecil Daniel, Hannibal Barber

Services for Cecil Daniel, well known Hannibal Barber, will be conducted at 2 p.m. Friday at the Schwartz Funeral Home. Rev. Deane K. Lierle, pastor of First Christian Church, will officiate and interment will be in Grandview Burial Park.
Masonic Rites will be conducted at the funeral home tonight at 7:30 by Hannibal Lodge No. 188, A.F. and A.M. Friends may call at the funeral home until the hour of services.
Mr. Daniel died suddenly at 6 a.m. Wednesday at his home, 219 Magnolia Ave. He had been a barber in Hannibal for the past 41 years, operating a shop at 511 Broadway at the time of his death.
He was born in Huntington, April 15, 1905, a son of Mrs. Frieda Bastian Daniel of Hannibal and the late Charles Daniel. He was married to Lorna Howell in Hannibal Dec 5, 1936 by the late Rev. John W. Golden.
She survives with two sons, Edwin C. Daniel of Kansas City, Kan., and Larry D. Daniel, serving with the U.S. Army at Fort Irwin, Calif.; three brothers, Fred of Columbus, Ohio, George of Harrisonville, Mo., and J.Q. of Peoria, Ill.; three sisters, Mrs. Thelma Collins of Milwaukee, Wis., Mrs. Elva Conboy of Louisiana and Mrs. Theda Davis of San Francisco; two grandsons, Bryan Mark and Aaron Dean Daniel of Kansas City and a niece, Mrs. Jackie Hooper of Saratoga, Calif.

NOTICE

All Barber Shops will be
closed Friday, Jan. 5th,
1 to 3 pm in observance
the funeral of...

BRO. CECIL DANIEL
RALPH MILLER, Pres. Local 271

Masonic Notice

All master Masons are urged to attend Funeral
services for Bro. Cecil Daniel a member of
Hannibal Lodge No. 188, Hannibal, Mo., tonight,
at 7:30 p.m. at the Schwartz Funeral Home.

HANNIBAL LODGE NO. 188 AF & AM

Cecil and Lorna had:

693. Edwin Clyde Daniel* b. 14 Apr 1941 d.
aft 1994
694. Larry Dean Daniel* b. 29 Feb 1945 d.
aft 1994

430. George Albert Daniel b. 21 Dec 1907 Ralls
County, Mo d. 8 Dec 1986 at Harrisonville, Cass
County, Mo. He m. first Juanita Green Jun 1930
at Hannibal, Marion County, Mo. They were
divorced and he m. second Mary Cohea 10 Jun
1937 at Hannibal, Mo. They were divorced and he
m. third Jane Morris 14 Feb 1947 at Hannibal,
Mo. She was b. 21 Apr 1919. I met him only
once. He served in the U.S. Army during WWII
and later he made his living working in a
hardware store. George was a heavy smoker and
died of cancer. He is buried at Emden Memorial
Gardens, Emden, Mo.

George and Juanita had:

695. Jacqueline Ann Daniel* b. 21 Dec 1933
d. aft 1994

George and Mary had:

696. Sue Laverne Daniel* b. 6 Sep 1938 d.
aft 1994

George and Jane had:

697. Brenda Kaye Daniel* b. 17 Feb 1949 d.
aft 1994
698. Kendall Ray Daniel* b. 5 Jun 1950 d.
aft 1994

431. Thelma Rita Daniel b. 23 Nov 1909 in Ralls
County, Mo d. aft 1994. She resides in
Hannibal, Mo. She m. Vincent Lappin 30 Nov 1930
at Hannibal, Mo. They were divorced and she
next m. Russell Collins 14 Dec 1950. I have
many pictures of her from childhood on and a
few pictures of her husbands. She lives in
Hannibal, Mo in 1994. Thelma and Vincent had:

699. Ethel Mae Lappin b. 11 Jun 1932 d.
aft 1994

432. Elva Mariam Sophia Daniel b. 24 Jun 1912
in Ralls County, Mo d. 3 Jul 1993 at Hannibal,
Mo and is buried in the Grandview Cemetery near
Hannibal. She m. Eldred Reed 14 Nov 1931. They
were divorced. She next m. Darrell K. Conboy at
Hannibal, Mo 27 Nov 1952. They lived on a farm
in Pike County, Mo and later made their home in
Louisiana, Mo. After her husband's death she
moved to Hannibal. Aunt Elva worked in the
income tax business. I knew Aunt Elva fairly
well and she was a wonderful, good natured
woman who seemed to always be in a cheerful
mood. She had no children. Her obituary[319]:

Elva M. Conboy

HANNIBAL - Services for Elva M. Conboy,
81, will be at 10 a.m. Wednesday at the James
O'Donnell Funeral Home. The Rev. Walter Reed
will officiate. Burial will be at Grand View
Burial Park.
Mrs. Conboy died at 8:12 p.m. July 3,
1993, at Hannibal Regional Hospital.
She was born June 24, 1912, in Ralls
County, to Charles and Frieda Bastian Daniel.

_____

319. Missouri, Hannibal, Hannibal Courier
Post, 4 July 1993.

She was married to Darrel Conboy in 1952. He died in 1978.

Survivors include one brother, John (Jay) Daniel of Peoria, Ill.; three sisters, Thelma Collins of Hannibal, Theda Davis of San Francisco, Calif., and Jacqueline Hooper of Sunnyvale, Calif.

She was preceded in death by three brothers, Fred Daniel, Cecil Daniel and George Daniel.

Mrs. Conboy was a member of first Christian Church in Hannibal.

Visitation will be from 6n p.m. to 8 p.m. Tuesday at James O'Donnell Funeral Home.

433. John Quincy "Jay" Daniel b. 24 Dec 1915 at Hydesburg, Ralls County, Mo d. aft 1994. He was born and grew up in the area where his father farmed and in 1929 moved with his family to Oakwood, Mo. He married[320] Willa Mae Hostetter 3 Nov 1933 at Oakwood, Marion County, Mo. She b. 15 Dec 1913 at Frankford, Pike County, Mo, the daughter of Enoch and Patra Ethel Henderson Hostetter both representatives of very old Pike County, Mo families. John and Willa moved from Oakwood to Peoria, Il in 1958.

In the 1940s John or Jay, as he is called, worked as a truck driver and drove a dry goods route across northern Missouri. He worked out of both Hannibal and Kansas City. He was later a truck driver for Arkansas Best Freight (ABF) for 35 years and taught driving at a community college when he retired. After he retired from teaching he operated an automotive repair and reconditioning business for about ten years, retiring again at about age 77. Willa worked as a housewife. Jay and Willa had:

700. Jimmie Lee Daniel* b. 10 Nov 1933 d. 22 Oct 1994
701. Sherry Jean Daniel* b. 15 Oct 1937 d. 5 May 1991

---

320. Missouri, Marion County, Marriage Book 28, page 243.

702. Gary Jay Daniel* b. 18 Nov 1939 d.
aft 1994
703. Kurtis Walton Daniel* b. 16 Sep 1954
d. aft 1994
704. Kevin Wayne Daniel* b. 16 Sep 1954 d.
aft 1994

434. Theda Ruth Daniel b. 6 Nov 1923 in Ralls
County, Mo d. aft 1994. She m. Harry C. Davis
14 Feb 1942. He was a Lt. Col in the U.S. Army
and served in WWII in the European Theater and
was among the first American troops to enter
Berlin. He "liberated" a German Shephard puppy
from Hitler's own kennels and later gave it to
my grandmother. He d. 12 Aug 1970. Theda worked
for the Internal Revenue Service in California
and retired there. She lives in San Francisco,
Ca in 1994. They had no children.

447. Giles David Daniel born May 1862 in De
Soto Parish, La d. 1912. He married[321]
Charlotte Rose "Lottie" Brown on 16 Feb 1887 at
Center, Shelby County, Tx. She b. Mar 1870 in
Alabama d. 1952. They are buried in the Grimes
Cemetery, Tyler County, Tx. They were in the
1900 Hardin County, Tx census where he was
employed as a laborer in a saw mill. He gave
his father's birthplace as Alabama and his
mother's as South Carolina. They were living in
Tyler County, Tx in 1910. Giles and Lottie had:

705. Ruth Daniel b. aft Feb 1887
706. Giles Charles Daniel* b. Nov 1889 d.
aft 1912
707. Ella E. Daniel* b. Aug 1891 d. aft
1912
708. Robert David Daniel* b. 12 Jun 1893
d. 22 Oct 1970
709. Linton Ira Daniel* b. Oct 1895 d. 10
Oct 1918
710. Ozianna Carmen Daniel* b. Feb 1898 d.
aft 1900

---

321. Texas, Shelby County, Marriage Book
1, page 245.

711. Lottie J. Daniel* b. aft 1901 d. aft
1910
712. Obie Lee Daniel b. 1903 d. aft 1910
713. James Edgar Daniel* b. 13 Feb 1905 d.
aft 1910
714. Henry Daniel b. abt 1908 d. aft 1910
715. Richard Elmer Daniel* b. 23 Jan 1911
d. aft 1920

448. Amos James Daniel b. 31 Dec 1863 in De
Soto Parish, La d. 7 Apr 1941, probably in
Shelby County, Tx. He m. Mary Elizabeth Johnson
abt 1884. She b. 20 Nov 1859 in Texas d. 29
July 1929. Her birth date, given to me by a
cousin, does not agree with the 1900 Shelby
County, Tx census which gives Dec 1860 as her
birth month and year. They are buried in the
Johnson Cemetery, Shelby County, Tx. Amos and
Mary had:

716. Samuel A. Daniels* b. 20 Sep 1885 d.
27 Oct 1931
717. John Johnson Daniels* 30 Jul 1888 d.
1 May 1959
718. Mary Jane Daniels* b. 17 Dec 1892 d.
aft 1911
719. Robert Emmet Daniels* b. 24 Feb 1894
d. 14 Apr 1952

449. Robert Monroe Daniel born 19 Sep 1870 in
Shelby County, Tx and died in Louisiana 7 Jul
1946. He married[322] Eliza Booker 1 Jul 1895
in De Soto Parish, La. She was born Jun 1878 in
Louisiana and died Oct 1900. Robert married
second[323] on 23 Dec 1902 Mrs. Lizzie English
Moorman. She was born 2 Sep 1875 in Texas and
died 23 Sep 1957. A child by her previous
marriage was in their home in 1910. Robert is
buried in the Mt. Olivet Cemetery in De Soto
Parish, La and Eliza in the Prude Cemetery of
the same place. He was a farmer. They had:

---

322. Louisiana, De Soto Parish, Marriage
Book 7, page 77.
323. Louisiana, De Soto Parish, Marriage
Book 8, page 350.

720. Sallie May Daniels* b. 1 Jun 1897 d.
10 May 1927
721. Johnnie Lorin Daniel* b. 9 Feb 1899
d. 30 Nov 1974
722. Jessie Edgar Daniels* b. 11 Nov 1900
d. 30 Jan 1987

450. Mary Jane "Sallie" Daniel born 1866 in
Texas died about 1895, probably in Louisiana.
She is buried in an unmarked grave in the Mt.
Olivet Cemetery, De Soto Parish, La. She
married[324] William Oliver Moseley 8 Jun 1885
in De Soto Parish, La. She was his second wife.
They had:

723. Jerry Moseley b. aft 1885
724. Chloe Jane Moseley b. 14 Jun 1887 d.
10 Apr 1975
725. Thomas Moseley b. aft 1887
726. William Moseley b. bef 1896

454. Henry Daniel was born before 1863 in
Hardin County, Tx and died after 1912. He is
mentioned in the deed record that settled his
grandparent's estate in 1901 and was living
then. He is also probably the H. Daniel
mentioned in Jefferson County deed grantee
indexes as late as 1926. He is almost certainly
the man mentioned in these indexes in 1912.

727. RESERVED

459. Benjamin Daniel born before 1878 in Hardin
or Jefferson County, Tx died after 1912. He is
mentioned in the deed record that settled his
grandparent's estate in 1901 in Jefferson
County and was living then. He is also probably
the man mentioned in the Jefferson County
grantee deed index there in 1912.

728. RESERVED

---

324. Louisiana, De Soto Parish, Marriage
Book 5, page 7.

229

460. Eva D. Daniel born May 1853 died after 1910. She married George McCarty about 1907 and was living in Austin City, Travis County, Tx. Her husband, born 1882, was occupied as a salesman. Her parents, Aaron Kinsey and Missouri Jula Runnels, were living with them. I did not find any of her siblings nearby. I have not attempted to locate them in census records after 1910. They had:

729. Gladdis McCarty b. 1910 d. aft 1910

480. Nancy Mahala Daniel b. 19 Dec 1876 Hardin County, Tx d. 14 Dec 1970. She is buried in the Daniel Cemetery in Kountze, Tx. She was in her father's home with one child in Hardin County in 1910. She m. Henry Shephard before 1902 and had at least four children, maybe more. They had:

730. James S. Shephard b. 1902 d. 1907
731. Annie L. Shephard b. 1904 d. aft 1910
732. Henry M. Shephard b. 1905 d. 1906
733. Emma Lou Shephard b. aft 1895

481. William Paschal Daniel b. 25 Feb 1878 in Hardin County, Tx and d. aft 1913 when he is mentioned in his father's obituary. He was living in Beaumont, Tx when his father died. He was employed as a salesman in 1900 and living in Hardin County with two of his siblings as boarders in the home of a lawyer named Will Couse. According to relatives he married a woman named Clara. In 1910 they were living in Beaumont where they owned a home and William was employed as a deputy sheriff. Clara's mother, Mollie Roberts was living with them. Clara was born in Texas in 1880. The census reported that Clara had been married for eight years and had given birth to two children, one of whom was deceased. The marriage for W. P. Daniel and Miss Clara A. Medlin in Jefferson County, Tx marriage books[325] may be for this

---

325. Texas, Jefferson County, Marriage Volume 4, page 224.

couple. Relatives told me in 1994 that William
and Clara had:

> 734. Guy Daniel b. aft 1903 d. bef 1994
> 735. Wayne Daniel b. aft 1910 d. bef 1994

482. George Oscar Daniel b. 29 Nov 1879 Hardin
County, Tx d. 1958 and is buried in the Daniel
Cemetery near Kountze, Tx. He m. first Ella
Chance. She was b. in 1882. He next m. Ada
Gates. There is a marriage for a George Daniels
and Miss Ada Flowers in Hardin County marriage
records[326] that may be for this couple. He
was a farmer. His property was part of the
original survey purchased by the Daniel family
around 1850. His son now owns this land. Ella
and George had:

> 736. Georgia Lee Daniel b. 1903 d. aft
> 1994
> 737. Jack Daniel (a daughter) b. 1906 d.
> aft 1994

George and Ada had:

> 738. George Edward Daniel* b. 16 Dec 1931
> d. aft 1994

483. James Littleton Daniel born 15 May 1882
in Hardin County, Tx d. 1955. He m. a woman
named Katie abt 1909. She was b. 1890. They
have a stone in the Old Hardin Cemetery in
Hardin County, Tx. There was no date of death
on her stone when this cemetery was surveyed
abt 1970. They had:

> 739. Jimmie Lou Daniel b. 1909 d. 1994
> 740. Charles Wilburn Daniel* b. 11 Aug
> 1915 d. bef 1994

486. Carl Wilburn Daniel b. 24 Nov 1890 Hardin
County, Tx d. 24 Dec 1972. He m. Martha Jane
abt 1913. She b. 31 Dec 1895 d. 24 Oct 1935.

---

326. Texas, Hardin County, Marriage Book
6, page 474.

They are buried in the Holland Cemetery in Hardin County, Tx. They had:

> 741. Kathleen Daniel* b. aft 1913 d. bef 1994
>
> 742. J. C. Daniel* (a son) b. aft 1913 d. bef 1994

487. Josie Vernice Daniels b. 19 Dec 1892 in Hardin County, Tx d. aft 1910. She probably married Henry M. Mitchel and they have a stone in the Daniel Cemetery in Hardin County.

SIXTH GENERATION

490. George Colwell Daniels b. 22 Jul 1893 in
Broken Bow, Custer County, Ne and d. 16 Sep
1968 in Santa Cruz, Ca. He married Zepha Belle
Weddel 3 Aug 1919. They were living in Gordon,
Sheridan County, Ne in 1920. She was born 29
Jan 1898 in Kempton, In and d. aft 1971. They
had:

743. Doris May Daniels* b. 20 May 1920 d.
aft 1994
744. Duane Wilbur Daniels* b. 8 May 1924
d. aft 1994

492. Velda E. "Joe" Daniels b. 11 Jul 1903 at
Ansley, Custer County, Ne and d. 15 Sep 1971 at
Portland, Or. He m. Mildred Copsey 18 Mar 1925
in Nebraska. They moved to Albany, Or in 1936.
There may be some confusion on his date of
death according to the Custer County Historical
Society, who sent me his obituary. His
obituary[327] appeared in an Ansley, Ne
newspaper:

VELDA E. "JOE" DANIELS, 68

Velda E. "Joe" Daniels, 68, Route 2, Box
122K, Lebanon, Oregon, died on Wednesday at the
Good Samaritan Hospital in Portland, Oregon, of
an apparent heart attack.
Funeral services were held Saturday,
September 25, 1971, at Aasum Funeral Home in
Albany, Oregon, with Father John Power
officiating. Mausoleum entombment followed at
Mt. Crest Abbey at Salem, Ore.
He was born on July 11, 1903 in Ansley,
Nebraska, and he was reared and educated in
Ansley, Nebraska before moving in 1936 to
Albany, Oregon. He married Mildred Copsey on
March 18, 1925 in Nebraska.

---

327. Nebraska, Custer County, Broken Bow,
The Custer County Chief, Thursday, 23 Sep 1971,
page 2.

233

Survivors include his widow, Mildred
Daniels, a daughter Ann, now Mrs. Del Hill of
Lebanon, Oregon, and two sons, Velda Daniels
Jr. and Jackie Alan Daniels, both of Salt Lake
City, Utah; 10 grandchildren and two great-
grandchildren. One brother, Edsel Daniels,
preceded him in death in 1945.

Joe and Mildred had:

745. Ann Daniels b. aft 1925
746. Velda Daniels Jr. b. aft 1925
747. Jackie Alan Daniels b. aft 1925

Bill + Ruth Daniels 1965

BILL AND RUTH WICKLINE DANIELS

494. Clifford Edmond "Bill" Daniels b. 21 Oct 1912 in Ansley, Custer County, Ne and d. 11 Nov 1981 in Tacoma, Pierce County, Wa. He preferred to be called "Bill". He m. Helene Ruth Wickline bef 1940. She was b. 23 Apr 1916 in Lincoln, Ne and d. 13 Apr 1969 in Tacoma, Wa of Hodgkin's Disease. They are buried in the Mountain View Memorial Park in Tacoma, Wa. He moved to Tacoma, Wa with his wife and father in 1940. He worked at a woodworking mill, a shipyard, as a gas station attendant and as a bartender before pursuing a career as a mechanic. He and his wife enjoyed fishing, hunting and camping. Bill and Ruth had:

> 748. Billie Joy Daniels* b. 1940 d. aft 1994

495. Thomas Jackson "Jack" Daniels b. 23 Jul 1914 in Wakefield, Dixon County, Ne d. aft 1994. He m. Dorothy Jean Riedel 1 Aug 1945. She b. 22 July 1922 at Bend, Or. She was employed as a registered nurse at Western State Hospital near Tacoma, Wa and in data processing at Tooele Army Depot. Thomas graduated from York High School, York, Ne in 1932. He is U.S. Army veteran and served in the Pacific Theatre during WWII. He was employed at Mount Rainier Ordinance Depot near Tacoma, Wa and Tooele Army Depot near Tooele, Utah. Jack and Dorothy had:

> 749. Paul Jackson Daniels* b. 22 Jun 1946 d. aft 1994
> 750. Tipton Joaquin Daniels* b. 21 Sep 1947 d. aft 1994

496. Ethel Anna Daniels b. abt 1916 in Nebraska d. aft 1994. She m. Reverend John Dowd. They were living in Ft. Collins, Co in 1994.

497. Doris Irene Daniels b. 10 Apr 1918 in South Dakota d. 6 May 1974 in Syracuse, Otoe County, Ne. She m. Russell Jacobson. He died and she remarried. She and her second husband moved to Syracuse, Ne where she died. She is

buried in Minden, Ne next to her first husband. Russell and Doris had:

751. Sharon Jacobson
752. Bryce Jacobson

498. Betty Daniels b. 10 Nov 1922 at York, York County, Ne. She m. Hugh Pursel. They were living in Colby, Ks in 1994.

499. Kenneth William Daniels b. 2 Sep 1911 in Custer County, Ne d. 6 Jan 1976 in Orlando, Orange County, Fl. He was serving in the armed forces in England when his mother died. He m. Alice G. Fauss 29 Nov 1941. She was born 18 Jan 1910 in Hooper, Ne, the daughter of Albert and Bertha Witte Fauss, and was a teacher. He was living in Orlando, Fla in 1962 when his father died and his widow was living there in 1994. He was a career Air Force officer and attained the rank of Major. He and his wife were members of the Lutheran Church. His wife sent me a copy of his obituary:

DANIELS, MR. KENNETH WILLIAM - Funeral services for Mr. Kenneth William Daniels, 64, 7225 Conway Circle who died Tuesday will be held Saturday at 2 PM in the Reformation Lutheran Church with Reverend Paul Bergstresser officiating. Interment will follow in Woodlawn Memorial Park. Mr. Daniels was a Veteran of WWII and the Korean War. He was a retired officer in the U. S. Air Force and a member of the Orlando Scottish Rite Bodies. He is survived by his wife, Mrs. Alice G. Daniels, Orlando and daughter, Mrs. Dee Ann Eastes, Nappanee, Indiana. In lieu of flowers contributions may be made to the Reformation Lutheran Church or the Heart Fund. Colonial Funeral Home, 2811 Curry Ford Road (Between Primrose & Crystal Lake) is in charge of arrangements.

Kenneth and Alice had:

753. Dee Ann Daniels b. 25 Sep 1948 d. aft
1994

520. Bertha A. Daniels b. 19 Jul 1891 in Jasper
County, In died 8 Jul 1951 in Oak Park, Il.
She m. George F. Brown in Nov 1920. She is
buried in the Weston Cemetery, Jasper County.
They were divorced. Her obituary appeared in a
Rensselaer newspaper[328]:

Native of Barkley Dies in Oak Park
Mrs. Bertha (Daniels) Brown Passes Away
After 6-Year Illness; Graduate of R.H.S.; Rites
Here Wednesday

Mrs. George F. Brown, nee Bertha Daniels,
a native of Barkley township and a graduate of
Rensselaer High school, class of 1911, died at
her home in Oak Park, Illinois, at 6 o'clock
Sunday evening. The death of Mrs. Brown came
after a six-year illness.
Mrs. Brown was born in Barkley township
July 19, 1891, a daughter of Korah and Margaret
(Abbett) Daniels. Her girlhood was spent on the
farm and after completing her grade school
education in the Barkley school she entered
Rensselaer high school, receiving a diploma in
1911. She then attended State Normal College at
Terre Haute. She was married to George F. Brown
in November, 1920.
Mrs. Brown was a member of the Methodist
church.
The survivors are the husband, a son,
George F. Brown, Jr., of Oak Park; a sister,
Mrs. Alice Engberg of Chicago; an uncle, Elmer
Daniels, of Rensselaer; an aunt, Mrs. Bart
Grant, of Rensselaer, and two grandchildren.
The funeral services will be held from
Jackson Funeral Chapel here at 2 o'clock
Wednesday afternoon with the Rev. Richard Haley
of the Methodist church officiating. Interment
will be at Weston cemetery.

---

328. Indiana, Rensselaer Republican, 9 Jul
1951, page 1, col 3.

Bertha and George had:

754. George F. Brown Jr. b. aft Nov 1920

521. Fred Douglas Daniels b. 31 May 1893 in Jasper County, In d. 6 May 1949 at Hammond, Lake County, In. He lived for many years in Butte, Montana and Chicago, Il where he was a cook. He never married. He retired to Rensselaer, In where it was a common sight to see him and his father sitting together on a bench on the courthouse lawn there. He and his father died the same year. According to cousins in Rensselaer who knew him he was stocky, five foot ten inches tall and two hundred and forty pounds. His obituary[329] was in a Rensselaer newspaper:

Fred Daniels Dies Suddenly At Hammond

Man Who Lived Here As Youth Dies Last Night; Services To Be Held Here Monday

Fred Douglas Daniels, during his youth and earlier adult life a resident of Rensselaer, died in St. Margaret's hospital in Hammond last night. The direct cause of his death was a ruptured hernia, with heart complications which had effected his health for several months as a contributing factor. He entered the hospital only two days prior to his death which was sudden and unexpected. His home for the past ten years was in East Chicago where he was preparing to open a restaurant in that city in the near future.

Mr. Daniels was born in Chicago Heights, Ill., May 31 1893, a son of Korah Daniels and Margaret (Abbott) Daniels. During his boyhood the family came to the Rensselaer community and the city continued to be his residence until his early adult life. After his school days he spent much of his time in western states where

---

329. Indiana, Rensselaer Republican, Volume 52, No. 108, Saturday, 7 May 1949, page 1, col 3.

he was employed as a cook in coastal city
restaurants and at other times as a ranch cook.
About ten years age he returned to Indiana and
since that time he was employed as a cook in
the Calumet area. He was employed periodically
in Rensselaer restaurants during his earlier
life.

Mr. Daniels was never married.

The immediate survivors are the father and
two sisters, Mrs. G.F. Brown of Oak Park, Ill.,
and Mrs. E.S. Engberg of Chicago. His mother
preceded him in death.

Mr. Daniels visited in Rensselaer about
three weeks ago, and at that time he stated his
health was not good.

Fred was much admired by everyone. He was
of quiet nature, jovial and was possessed of an
attractive personality. His qualities in
general demanded utmost respect. The news of
his sudden death was received with deep regret
by his many Rensselaer friends.

Rites Here.

The remains will arrive at W.J. Wright
Chapel here Sunday afternoon. Funeral services
will be conducted from the Chapel at 2 o'clock
Monday afternoon with the Rev. Earl Moore of
the Methodist church in charge. Interment will
be at Weston cemetery.

522. Alice Pearl Daniels b. 28 Sep 1899 in
Jasper County, In d. Apr 1979. She married[330]
Edwin Stanley Engberg 21 Jul 1921 in Jasper
County. He b. 1 Jul 1895 in Illinois d. May
1971 in Arlington Heights, Il. They resided in
Arlington Heights near Chicago, Il. They had:

    755. Robert Engberg b. aft 1921
    756. Janet Engberg b. aft 1921

533. William Louis Daniels born 26 Jun 1918
Rensselaer, Jasper County, Indiana d. aft 1994.
He married first Grace Cala 3 Oct 1942 at
Manteca, San Joaquin County, Ca. They were

---

330. Indiana, Jasper County, Marriage Book
9, page 140.

divorced and he later married[331] Jorja M.
Spicer 16 Feb 1980 in Jasper County, Ind. She
b. 28 Apr 1935 in Tennessee. Bill is a WWII
veteran and a retired career Air Force officer
having attained the rank of Lieutenant Colonel
with ratings of Command Pilot and Master
Missileer. During WWII Bill was an instructor
pilot for multi-engine advanced pilot training.
He was a designer on the Titan II ICBM project
and flew jet aircraft. He was a U.S. liaison
officer with the British Air Ministry 1951-1955
and Director of Engineering for the 9th Air
Force 1955-1960. He was Staff Engineer for the
314th Air Division in Korea in 1960. He retired
in 1969 and managed a construction company in
California 1970-1975. Bill has offered
invaluable assistance with the Jasper County
families and traveled with me to Champaign
County, Ohio to research records there. I have
been made to feel a welcome guest in Bill and
Jorja's home on several occasions. Bill and
Grace had:

> 757. Carole Lynne Daniels* b. 28 Sep 1944
>   d. aft 1994
> 758. John William Daniels* b. 9 Sep 1956
>   d. aft 1994

534. Virginia Ruth Daniels b. 15 Oct 1920 in
Rensselaer, Jasper County, In. She married[332]
Charles Henry Kryder 6 Jan 1940 in Rensselaer
but this marriage was later annulled. She next
married[333] Thomas E. Pearce 28 Sep 1945 in
Rensselaer. Virginia and Thomas live in
Indianapolis in 1994.

535. Beulah Jean Daniels b. 8 May 1923 in
Rensselaer, Jasper County, In. She m. Lowell

---

331. Indiana, Jasper County, Marriage Book
33, page 81.
332. Indiana, Jasper County, Marriage Book
17, page 10.
333. Indiana, Jasper County, Marriage Book
19, page 123.

Light Feb 1942 in Rensselaer, In. She prefers
to be called Jean. They had:

   759. Patricia Light b. aft 1942
   760. Daniel Light b. 1945

536. Rebecca Sue Daniels b. 2 Feb 1925 in
Rensselaer, Jasper County, In d. aft 1994. She
m. Max Nagel Overton 25 Jun 1949. He b. 1 Jan
1927 d. 14 Jun 1984 and is buried in the Weston
Cemetery, Rensselaer, In. The Ott and Daniel
family bible is in her possession in 1994. They
had:

   761. Susan Jane Overton b. aft 1949
   762. Max Overton Jr. b. aft 1949
   763. Thomas J. Overton b. 1 Feb 1957 d.
      aft 1994

537. Lyle Leroy Daniels b. 15 Oct 1914 at
Devil's Lake, Ramsey County, ND and d. 7 Apr
1978 at Allen Park, Wayne County, Mi and is
buried at Livonia, Wayne County, Mi. He m.
Annabelle Markle 4 Nov 1939 at Detroit, Wayne
County, Mi. She was b. 3 Sep 1922 at Grosse
Point, Mi the daughter of Frederick and Grace
Curtiss Markle. Lyle and Annabelle were members
of the Lutheran church. Lyle moved to Michigan
in 1938 where he worked as a supervisor. Lyle
and Annabelle had:

   764. Judith Ann Daniels* b. 14 Sep 1940
   765. Thomas Lyle Daniels* b. 3 Jan 1946
   766. Richard Dennis Daniels* b. 1 Nov 1953

538. Mae Roseanne Daniels b. 22 May 1917 at
Devil's Lake, Ramsey County, ND d. 12 May 1983
at Vancouver, Clark County, Wa. She m. Martin
Thomas. They had:

   767. Robert Thomas

539. Edward William "Ed" Daniels b. 13 Jul 1918
at Devil's Lake, Ramsey County, ND. He m.
Frances Mary Senger 7 July 1942 at Devil's
Lake. She b. 9 Nov 1921 the daughter of Mikeal

241

W. and Johanna Schwan Senger. He pursued the profession of farming near Devil's Lake but was retired in 1994. They are members of the Catholic church. Ed and Frances had:

    768. Carol Ann Daniels* b. 24 Sep 1943
    769. Edward Francis Daniels* b. 10 Oct
        1994
    770. Donald Mickeal Daniels* b. 13 Mar
        1947
    771. Michael Leroy Daniels* b. 31 Jul 1950
    772. Patrick Allen Daniels* b. 27 Nov 1954
    773. Amy Louise Daniels* b. 25 Oct 1958

540. Vera Elvina Daniels b. 11 Oct 1919 at Devil's Lake, Ramsey County, ND d. 6 July 1977. She m. Charles Campbell. They lived in Portland, Or. They had no children.

541. Marjorie Ann Daniels b. 3 Mar 1931 in Devil's Lake, Ramsey County, ND. She m. John Pancratz bef 1957. They were living in Federal Way, Wa in 1994.

    774. Steven Pancratz b. 27 Sep 1957
    775. Twila Pancratz b. 8 Jan 1960
    776. Jason Pancratz b. 23 Dec 1963

542. Charles Duane Daniels b. 5 Dec 1933 at Devil's Lake, Ramsey County, ND d. 11 Dec 1990 at Minneapolis, Mn. I located his son, Brian, living in Minneapolis in Oct of 1994 and sent him some forms to complete for family information for inclusion in this book but have not heard from him as yet. He told me that his siblings all lived in the Minneapolis area but I was unable to locate any of them using directory assistance and his telephone had been disconnected in Dec 1994. He and his siblings had five children between them. Charles had:

    777. David Daniels
    778. Scott Daniels
    779. Brian Daniels
    780. Denise Daniels

543. Jessie E. Daniels b. 24 Dec 1908 in Jasper County, In d. 30 Jun 1985. She was residing in Rensselaer, In when her brother Kenneth died in 1974 and there are probably records of her marriage to be found there. She married Louis John DeMoss before 1927. He b. 30 Jan 1895 in Wing, Il d. 10 Oct 1948 in Jasper Co., In. They are both buried in the Smith Cemetery, Jasper Co. Her obituary[334] appears in a Rensselaer, In newspaper:

Jessie E. DeMoss

Jessie E. DeMoss, 77, of Rt. 1, Rensselaer, died at 12:01 a.m. Sunday in the Jasper County Hospital.

She was born on Dec. 24, 1908, in Rensselaer, the daughter of Alonzo and Mary (Walker) Daniels, both of whom preceded her in death. She was a lifetime Jasper County resident.

She was educated in the Jasper County Public Schools. She was married to Louis J. DeMoss, who preceded her in death in 1948.

She worked in the kitchen department of Saint Joseph's College for 15 years and was a production laborer at Schumacher Electric Corporation for four years.

She belonged to the Rebecca Lodge of Wheatfield.

SURVIVORS INCLUDE two sons, John DeMoss of Wheatfield, Cecil DeMoss of Rensselaer; four daughters, Mildred Clemans of Lexington, Ky., Mrs. Alice (John) Dobson of Wheatfield, Mrs. Christine (James) Gilbert of Fair Oaks, Mrs. Janice (Charles) Sell of Goodland; two sisters, Nancy Holtz of Grand Island, Neb., Louella Osborne of Louisville, Ky.; two brothers, Lon Daniels of Almo, Ky., Tom Daniels of Kila, Mont.; and 39 grandchildren and 33 great grandchildren.

---

334. Indiana, Rensselaer Republican, Vol 83, No. 155, Monday, 1 July 1985, page 2.

She was preceded in death by one sister, one brother, four daughters, two sons, one grandson and one granddaughter.

Friends may call after 2 p.m. Monday at the Steinke Funeral Home. The funeral is at 10:30 a.m. Tuesday at the Steinke Funeral Home, with the Rev. Herbert Edwards officiating. Burial will follow in Smith Cemetery.

Jessie and Louis had:

781. Mildred DeMoss b. bef 1927
782. Louis John DeMoss b. 1 May 1927 d. 2 Sep 1930
783. Alice Patricia DeMoss b. 8 Jul 1930
784. John Lyle DeMoss b. 4 Sep 1931
785. Marjorie Ann DeMoss b. 26 Aug 1932 d. 1 Jan 1933
786. Betty Jane DeMoss b. 7 Dec 1933 d. 28 Aug 1934
787. Ethel Mae DeMoss b. 11 Feb 1935
788. Peggy Jo DeMoss b. 26 Sep 1936
789. Christine Alma DeMoss b. 6 Oct 1937
790. Janice Rae DeMoss b. 29 Jun 1939
791. Cecil George DeMoss b. 4 Oct 1940
792. William Allen DeMoss b. 5 Nov 1941 d. 8 Aug 1942
793. Larry Lee DeMoss b. 30 Nov 1942

544. Kenneth Walker Daniels born[335] 1 Jul 1910 in Gifford, Jasper County, In and died in Indianapolis, In 27 Aug 1974. He resided in Jasper County most of his life. I have found no mention of a marriage for him. He had an obituary[336] in a Rensselaer, In newspaper:

KENNETH DANIELS

Kenneth Daniels, 64, of R.R. 1. Rensselaer, passed away Tuesday morning in

---

335. Indiana, Jasper County, Birth Book H-4, page 336.
336. Indiana, Rensselaer Republican, Volume 77, No. 202, 27 Aug 1974, page 16, col 4.

Veterans Hospital, Indianapolis where he had
been a patient one month.
Born in Gifford July 1, 1910, he was the
son of Alonzo and Ida (Walker) Daniels.
A lifetime resident of Jasper County, he
attended area public schools, and was a veteran
of World War II, serving with the U.S. Army. He
was a member of American Legion Post 29 and VFW
Post 1279.
Surviving are one sister, Mrs. Jessie
DeMoss of Rensselaer, two half-brothers and
five half sisters.
Funeral services will be conducted from
Jackson Funeral Chapel at 1:30 p.m. Thursday
with the Rev. Harry McCorkel officiating.
Interment will follow in Smith Cemetery.
Friends are now being received at the chapel.

545. Mary Madeline Daniels b. 9 May 1911 in
Jasper County, In. She is probably the Mary
Daniels Sheffer buried in the Walker family
plot in Barkley Township, Jasper County. This
woman died in 1930. I do not know if she had
children.

548. Lon Joe Daniels born[337] 17 Aug 1933 in
Jasper County, In d. 28 Oct 1986 at Murray,
Calloway County, Kentucky. He m. Delores
Clemans abt 1957. They had at least one child
whose birth is recorded in Jasper County, In.
He next married Judy Jane Trimble 4 Apr 1964 at
Crown Point, In. She was b. 8 Oct 1942 at
Hammond, In, the daughter of Verl and Louanna
Jackson Trimble. Lon and Judy lived in Almo,
Ky. Lon's obituary from a Murray, Ky newspaper
follows:

Lon Joe Daniels

Services for Lon Joe Daniels will be
Friday at 2 p.m. in the chapel of Miller
Funeral Home of Murray.

---

337. Indiana, Jasper County, Birth Book H-
7, page 91.

Reed Bennett will officiate. Mrs. Oneida
White will be organist and soloist.
Burial will follow in Stewart Cemetery
with military rites at the grave site.
Friends may call at the funeral home.
Mr. Daniels, 53, Rt. 1, Almo died Tuesday
at 9:18 a.m. at Murray-Calloway County
Hospital.
He had retired after 19 years service with
Ford Motor Co. at Chicago Heights, Ill. He was
a veteran of Korean conflict.
Survivors are his wife, Mrs, Judy Trimble;
two daughters, Mrs. Charles (Lisa) Hitchcock,
Cedar Lake, Ind., and Mrs. Benny (Londa)
Harrell, Rt. 5, Murray; one son Verl Scott
Daniels, Rt. 1, Almo; two grandchildren Shasta
Harrell and Jennifer Harrell; two sisters, Mrs.
Louella Osborn, Louisville, and Mrs. Nancy
Holtz, Grand Island, Neb.; one brother, Thomas
Daniels, Kila, Mont.; parents-in-law, Mr. and
Mrs. Verl Trimble, Rt. 3, Murray.

Lon and Delores had:

794. Larry Joe Daniels b. 24 Sep 1958

Lon and Judy had:

795. Lisa Kayanna Daniels b. 15 Mar 1961
796. Londa Jo Daniels b. 19 Dec 1967
797. Verl Scott Daniels b. 14 Jun 1973

550. Thomas Ellwood Daniel born[338] 13 Oct
1935 in Jasper County, In d. aft 1994. He
married[339] Nellie Carol Messer 30 Mar 1963.
Tom works for Goodyear Tire Company in the Off-
Road Division and Nellie works with stained
glass. As a family they enjoy camping and
fishing. Tom and Nellie were living in
Forreston, Il in 1994. Their second child's

---

338. Indiana, Jasper County, Birth Book H-
7, page 118.
339. Indiana, Jasper County, Marriage Book
27, page 145.

birth is recorded in Jasper County, In. Tom and Nellie had:

    798. Beneda Kay Daniels* b. 29 Oct 1963
    799. Annette Michele Daniels* b. 2 Sep 1965
    800. Tao Lyn Daniels* b. 5 Mar 1977

LEFT TO RIGHT: THOMAS ELLWOOD DANIELS, NELLIE MESSER DANIELS, JOEL WINENKE, CELESTE MONTOYA SCHMECHEL, TERRY SCHMECHEL, TAO DANIELS WINENKE, AUDREY JEAN DANIELS MONTOYA, GUY MONTOYA, JAMES MONTOYA AND KEVIN W. DANIEL

551. Nancy Ann Daniels born[340] 11 Sep 1936 in Jasper County, In d. aft 1994. She married[341] Richard Lee Critser 6 Feb 1957 in Rensselaer, In. He b. 6 Apr 1939 in Rensselaer, In d. 8 July 1970 in South Bend, In the son of Raymond Kors and Bernice Critser. He is buried at Memory Gardens in Rensselaer. Nancy next

---

    340. Indiana, Jasper County, Birth Book H-7, page 128.
    341. Indiana, Jasper County, Marriage Book 25, page 152.

married a man named Holtz. They were residing in Grand Island, Ne in 1994.

552. Louellen May Daniels b. 8 Nov 1938 in Jasper County, In. She married[342] John William Osborn Jr. 18 Jun 1960 in Rensselaer, In. He was the son of John William and Doris Osborn. They were divorced in 1971. Louellen worked as a professional cook and is retired in 1994 and lives in Louisville, Ky. Louellen and John had:

    801. Ronald Dean Osborn b. 8 Aug 1966
    802. Joanie Lee Osborn b. 22 Jan 1977

553. Betty Ann Daniels b. 22 May 1942 in Jasper County, In d. aft 1994. She m. a man named Jasperson bef 1964. She and her siblings were separated after the death of their parents and grew up apart from one another. She was named Betty Lou by her adoptive parents. Betty had:

    803. Debra Susan Jasperson b. 1964 d. aft 1994
    804. Kenneth Harold Jasperson b. 1969 d. aft 1994

555. Catherine Ann Daniels b. 14 Oct 1944 in Jasper County, In. She married Lawrence William Depp 29 Feb 1964. He was b. 6 May 1940. They live in Las Vegas, Nv in 1994. He is an Air Force veteran and retired Poker Dealer. She is a semi-retired cashier at the Stardust Hotel and Casino in Las Vegas. She is an avid reader of mystery, romance and science fiction/fantasy novels in her spare time. They had:

    805. Lynette Depp b. 22 Sep 1968 d. aft 1994
    806. Anne Depp b. 31 Aug 1970 d. aft 1994

557. Mary Amanda Daniels b. 4 Feb 1909 in Jasper County, In and d. 20 Aug 1951 near

---

342. Indiana, Jasper County, Marriage Book 26, page 318.

Bowdon, Wells County, ND where she is buried in the Fuhrman family cemetery near the original Fuhrman homestead. She m. Gus Fuhrman 22 Dec 1934 in a Baptist church in Carrington, ND. He b. 5 Dec 1911. He remarried after Mary's death and lives in Fessenden, ND in 1994. Mary and Gus were elementary school teachers and taught in several rural schools in central North Dakota. Mary and Gus had:

807. Kenneth Fuhrman b. 21 Nov 1935 d. aft 1994
808. Clinton Fuhrman b. 24 Jun 1941 d. 13 Nov 1983

558. Harry Melvin Daniels b. 11 Apr 1911 at Hansboro, Towner County, ND d. 11 Aug 1993 at Prescott, Yavapai County, Arizona where he was cremated. He m. Leone Ellen Osborne 28 Jun 1937 at Crary, Ramsey County, ND. She was living in Issaquah, Wa in 1994. They had:

809. Linda Lee Daniels* b. 10 May 1941 d. aft 1994
810. Dean Gordon Daniels* b. 3 Aug 1946 d. aft 1994

559. George Gilmore Daniels b. 10 Sep 1924 at Devil's Lake, Ramsey County, ND d. 1 May 1985 at Columbia, Boone County, Mo. He m. Beverly Berry Jun 1951 in North Dakota. George was a civil engineer specializing in the construction of dams. He worked in Missouri. They attended the Methodist church in Columbia. George and Beverly had:

811. Steven Craig Daniels* b. 28 May 1952
812. Angela Mary Daniels* b. 6 Oct 1953
813. Christine Jane Daniels* b. 24 Jun 1956

CLARENCE LAWSON DANIELS

560. Clarence Lawson Daniels b. 1 Sep 1914 in
Jasper County, In d. 22 Sep 1981 at Dyer, Lake
County, In. He married[343] first Wandalee Ann
Smith 13 Aug 1938 in Jasper County, In. She b.
14 Sep 1921 and d. 21 Dec 1939 in Rensselaer,
In, the daughter of Robert and Flossie Hines
Smith. She died of a blood stream infection
that turned into blood poisoning as the result
of a Caesarian operation during the birth of
her daughter. She had an obituary in a
Rensselaer newspaper and is buried in the
Weston Cemetery, Rensselaer, In. Clarence
enlisted in the U.S. Navy 2 Sep 1943 and was
discharged 2 Jun 1945 at Fort Eustis Hospital.

---

343. Indiana, Jasper County, Marriage Book
16, page 22.

He served in the Atlantic Theatre. I have a picture of him from a book[344] at the Rensselaer Library. He next m. Helen C. Loetz abt 1944. His obituary[345] appeared in a Hammond, In newspaper:

DANIELS, CLARENCE L.

Daniels, Clarence L. - age 67, of Dyer, Indiana, passed away Tuesday, September 22, 1981 at Our Lady of Mercy Hospital. Survivors: wife, Helen; four sons, John (Charlotte) Daniels, George (Jo) Daniels, both of Rensselaer, Walter (Linda) Daniels of Dyer, Roger (Cathy) Daniels of Hanover Park, Illinois; three daughters, Mrs. Ruth Ann (John) Walkins of Tulsa, Oklahoma, Karen Conley of Demotte, Indiana, Mrs. Margaret (Rex) James of Rensselaer; twentyone grandchildren; four great-grandchildren; three sisters, Mrs. Jean Montoya of Riverdale, Illinois, Mrs. Mildred (Vernon) Mulvihill of Kankakee, Illinois, Mrs. Frances (Arthur) Franson of South Bend, Indiana; one brother, John (Carol) Mack of Oak Forest, Illinois; mother and father-in-law, Vernon and Catherine Loetz of Laporte, Indiana. Preceded in death by his parents, John and Margaret Daniels, a son, Dale, a brother, John and two sisters, Florence and Margaret.

Funeral arrangements are incomplete. Fagan-Miller Funeral Gardens, 1920 Hart St., Dyer, in charge. Friends may call at the funeral home Wednesday 7 to 10 p.m. and Thursday 2 to 5 and 7 to 10 p.m.

Mr. Daniels was a resident of Dyer for the past 11 years, formerly of Rensselaer; a Veteran of World War II, serving in the United States Navy; former District Commander of the V.F.W. Post #1279 of Rensselaer; member of the American Legion Post #19 of Rensselaer; former

344. Indiana, Rensselaer, Public Library, American Legion Auxiliary, Dewey Biggs Unit No. 29, R977.2977 Ser.
345. Indiana, The Times, Calumet Region, 23 Sep 1981, page C6, col 2.

Commander of Disabled Veterans Post of
Rensselaer; member of the Fathers Auxiliary
Post #1154 of Lafayette, Indiana; and retired
in 1978 from Dyer Construction Company. In lieu
of flowers, donations may be made to the
family.

Clarence and Wandalee had:

814. Ruth Ann Daniels b. 17 Dec 1939 d.
aft 1981

Clarence and Helen had:

815. John Richard Daniels* b. 30 May 1945
d. aft 1994
816. Karen Sue Daniels* b. 3 Nov 1946 d.
aft 1994
817. Margaret Yvonne Daniels* b. 11 Apr
1948
818. George William Daniels* b. 31 May
1949
819. Walter Lee Daniels* b. 23 Jan 1951
820. Roger Allen Daniels* b. 12 Feb 1953
821. Dale Gene Daniels b. 2 Apr 1954 d. 2
Apr 1954

561. Mary Florence Daniels born[346] 9 Apr 1916
in Jasper County, In d. 11 Aug 1943 at Fargo,
Cass County, ND. She married[347] Harold Vernon
Clark 13 Feb 1943 at Coeur d'Alene, Cotenai
County, Id. They did not have children. Her
obituary[348] from the Rensselaer Republican:

BRIDE OF FEW MONTHS DIES ENROUTE HERE

Mrs. Florence Clark, Nee Daniels, Stricken
on Train, Succumbs at Fargo, N. D.

---

346. Indiana, Jasper County, Birth Book
CH-13, page 66.
347. Idaho, Kootenai County, Marriage Book
44, Page 456.
348. Indiana, Jasper County, Rensselaer
Republican, Vol 46, No. 189, Thursday, 12 Aug
1943, page 1, col 4.

MARY FLORENCE DANIELS

Stricken critically ill on a train while
en route to her former home here, Mrs. Harold
V. Clark, the former Florence Daniels, died at
Fargo N. D., hospital Wednesday morning,
twenty-four hours after being stricken. Her
death was attributed to diabetes.
Mrs. Clark was the daughter of Mrs.
William Beauregard of near Rensselaer. Her late
father was John Daniels.
In company of her husband, who is an
Engineer Corps Sergeant at Fort Geiger,
Washington, Mrs. Clark left for Rensselaer
Monday night. She had not been well for some
time and decided to return here. Apparently the
train trip aggravated her illness for soon
after she boarded the train her illness became

more serious and shortly before she arrived at
Fargo her condition became critical. She was
placed in the hospital at Fargo Tuesday
morning. A wire was sent here asking that her
mother come to Fargo. However, before Mrs.
Beauregard could make arrangements to leave
another wire arrived stating that the patient
had passed away. Mrs. Clark went to Washington
last September and was married to Sgt. Clark at
Spokane on February 13. She had since lived
near his army camp.

Mrs. Clark was born in Rensselaer on April
9, 1916, the daughter of the late John Daniels
and Margaret (Hurley) Daniels. She was
graduated from the Jordan township schools and
attended Remington high school for three years,
discontinuing her high school study at the end
of that time because of ill health.

Surviving besides the husband, mother and
step-father are the following brothers and
sisters: Clarence of Decatur, Mildred, a nurse
at Kankakee, Ill., Mrs. Frances Franson of
Michigan City, Jean, a nurse at Danville, Ill.,
and John of the U.S.N.

The funeral arrangements will not be
completed pending the arrival of Mr. Clark here
with the remains Friday evening.

562. Mildred Jane Daniels born[349] 19 Mar 1918
Jasper County, In d. 16 Feb 1992 at Normal,
McLean County, Il and is buried at Kankakee,
Il. She m. Vernon Martin Mulvihill 27 May 1944.
He b. 1919 d. 16 Jan 1983. Her obituary:

Mildred Mulvihill, retired nurse

A memorial Mass for Mildred J. Mulvihill,
73, of Kankakee, will be celebrated at 11 a.m.
March 21 at St. Patrick Catholic Church in
Kankakee.
There will be no visitation.
Entombment was in the Mount Calvary
Mausoleum.

---

349. Indiana, Jasper County, Birth Book
CH-13, pp. 73-74.

254

MILDRED JANE DANIELS

Memorials may be made for the American
Lung Association.

Arrangements are by the Clancy-Gernon
Funeral Home in Kankakee.

A retired registered nurse, Mrs. Mulvihill
died Sunday (Feb. 16, 1992) at BroMenn Medical
Center in Normal.

She was born March 19, 1918 in Rensselaer,
Ind., the daughter of John and Margaret Hurley
Daniels.

She married Vernon Mulvihill on May 27,
1944 at St. Patrick Catholic Church in
Kankakee. He died Jan. 16, 1983.

Surviving are two sons and a daughter-in-law, Michael and Mary Mulvihill of Bettendorf, Iowa, and Patrick Mulvihill of Bourbonnais; a daughter, Lynn Houston, of Normal; a grandchild, Geoffrey Mulvihill; two sisters, Frances Franson of South Bend, Ind., and Audrey Montoya of Beecher; and a brother, John Beauregard of Tinley Park.

She was preceded in death by two brothers and two sisters.

Mrs. Mulvihill was a member of St. Patrick Catholic Church and the parish Council of Catholic Women.

A graduate of St. Mary's Hospital School of Nursing, Mrs. Mulvihill had been on the staff of St. Mary's Hospital in Kankakee and was employed by the Illinois Department of Public Aid.

Mildred and Vernon had:

822. Michael Vernon Mulvihill b. 11 Jun 1945
823. Lynn Marie Mulvihill b. 10 Aug 1947
824. Patrick Joseph Mulvihill b. 9 May 1952

563. Frances Latona Daniels born[350] 1 Feb 1920 in Jasper County, In d. 1 Feb 1994 at South Bend, In. She married[351] Arthur L. Franson 10 Sep 1939 in Jasper County. They had:

825. Eric John Franson b. 1940
826. Edward Charles Franson b. 14 Mar 1942
827. Karen Louise Franson b. 24 Mar 1943
828. Christine Marie Franson b. 27 Mar 1947

---

350. Indiana, Jasper County, Birth Book H-5, page 94.
351. Indiana, Jasper County, Marriage Book 16, page 242.

FRANCES LATONA DANIELS

564. Margaret Ann Daniels b. 26 Jun 1922 in
Barkley Township, Jasper County, In and d.
there 16 March 1925. She was buried in Weston
Cemetery, Rensselaer, In. Her obituary:

Margaret Ann Daniels, daughter of John and
Margaret Daniels, was born at her home in
Jasper county, June 26th, 1922, and departed
this life March 16th, 1925, at her home in
Jasper county, being 2 years, 8 months and 18
days of age.
She was a little girl of very kind and
lovable disposition, never hard to satisfy.
She leaves to mourn her departure a
mother, four sisters, two brothers, a

grandmother and grandfather, besides a host of
other relatives and friends, all of whom had
learned to love this patience little sufferer.

Another little lamb has gone
    To dwell with Him who gave
Another little darling babe
    Is sheltering in the grave,
God needed one more angel child
    Amidst his shining band,
An so He bent with loving smile
    And clasped our darling's hand.
The little crib is empty now,
    The little clothes laid by,
A mother's hope, a father's joy
    In death's cold arms doth lie.
Go little Pilgrim to thy shy home
    On yonder blissful shore,
We miss thee here but soon will come
    Where thou hast gone before.

Funeral services were held in the Brushwood
church Tuesday, March 17th, 1925, and were in
charge of Rev. Stephen O'Reilly. Interment was
made in Weston cemetery.

565. Audrey Jean Daniels b. 27 Sep 1923 in
Jasper County, In. She enlisted in the U.S.
Army Nurses Corps 15 March 1945. She served in
France and Germany and attained the rank of
lieutenant. She m. James Raymond Montoya bef
1956. He b. 7 Jun 1921 d. 1964. They had:

    829. James Craig Montoya b. 10 Dec 1956
    830. Celeste Helen Montoya b. 12 Jan 1958
    831. Guy Gregory Montoya b. 22 Oct 1959
    832. Teresa Marie Montoya b. 19 Jan 1965

566. John Daniels b. 14 Nov 1924 in Jasper
County, In d. 10 July 1969 at Tomah, Juneau
County, Wi. He enlisted in the U.S. Navy 12
June 1942. His unit received a Presidential
Citation 10 Nov 1943. He was discharged 8 Oct
1945. He married first Maxine. They were
divorced and he next m. Shirley Irene Wilson
Lowery 20 Nov 1945 at Zion, Il. His obituary:

258

John Daniels

John Daniels, 44, R. 1 Necedah, passed away on Thursday, July 10, at the VA Hospital in Tomah, after a long illness.

He was the son of John and Margaret Daniels, and was born November 14, 1924, in Rensselaer, Ind. He was united in marriage to the former Shirley Wilson on November 20, 1945 at Zion, Ill.

They lived in Zion for six years, after which they moved to a farm near Necedah, where they have lived since.

He was a Veteran of World War II.

He is survived by his wife, Shirley, three sons, John Jr., Donald and Lonne; and one daughter, Mary, all at home; one brother, Clarence, of Rensselaer, Ind.; three sisters, Mrs. Audrey Montoya of Riverdale, Ill., Mrs. Vernon Mulvihill of Kankakee, Ill., and Mrs. Arthur Franson of Moline, Ill.

Funeral services were held Saturday at 2:00 p.m. at the Hare Funeral Home in New

Lisbon. Graveside military rites were conducted by American Legion Post 277 of Necedah at Bayview Cemetery.

John and Shirley had:

833. John Daniels* Jr. b. 19 Jun 1945
834. Mary Irene Daniels* b. 5 Dec 1946
835. Donald Lee Daniels* b. 28 Aug 1954
836. Lonne Leroy Daniels* b. 14 Nov 1958

567. Chester Melvin Daniels born[352] 27 Feb 1920 in Rensselaer, Jasper County, In and died[353] there 15 Jan 1947. He was an army veteran. I have found no mention of a marriage for him. He is buried in the Weston Cemetery at Rensselaer. His obituary appeared in Rensselaer newspapers:

C..M. DANIELS WORLD WAR II VETERAN, DIES

Succumbs at Frankfort Hospital of Diabetic
Condition Wednesday A.M.

Chester M. Daniels, most of whose lifetime was spent here, passed away at the hospital in Frankfort Wednesday morning of a diabetic condition that had affected his health for several months, He was a son of Mrs. Alice Daniels of this city, who was at his bedside when death came.
A veteran of World War II, Mr. Daniels entered the service December 12, 1941, and served in the army until April 26, 1944. Following a few months of service in the States proper he was sent to the Panama Canal Zone where he remained until the conclusion of hostilities.
Since returning from the armed service he was employed in Rensselaer, Indianapolis and

---

352. Indiana, Jasper County, Birth Book CH-14, page 158.
353. Indiana, Jasper County, Rensselaer Republican, Vol 50, No. 13, Thursday, 16 Jan 1947, page 1, col 7.

Frankfort. The latter place he was employed by a Construction company.

Mr. Daniels was born in Rensselaer February 27, 1920 the son of the late Ira Daniels and Alice (Brouhard) Daniels. He was graduated from DeMotte high school. Until entering the armed service he was engaged in farm work.

Surviving besides the mother, is a brother, Virgil of this city and the maternal grandmother, Mrs. Charles Brouhard, also of Rensselaer.

Mr. Daniels was a member of the local American Legion post and also a member of the Veterans of Foreign Wars. He was a splendid young man and his death came as a great shock to his many friends here.

The funeral services will be conducted from the W.J. Wright Chapel at 2 o'clock Friday afternoon with the Rev. Earl Moore, assisted by the American Legion officiating. Interment will be at Weston Cemetery.

568. Virgil Ivan Daniels b. 18 Dec 1922 Jasper County, Ind d. 12 Apr 1989. He m. Pauline Catherine Rude 15 Apr 1946. She born[354] 15 Apr 1929 d. 29 Mar 1993 in Rensselaer, In the daughter of Howard and Anna Sullivan Rude. Her estate is administered in Jasper County and names her son and grandchildren. His obituary[355] appeared in a Rensselaer, In newspaper.

Virgil I. Daniels Sr.

Virgil I. Daniel Sr., 62, of 515 E. Vine St., Rensselaer, died at 10:45 p.m. Friday at St. Elizabeth's Hospital in Lafayette.

He was born on Dec. 18, 1922 in Rensselaer, the son of Ira Daniels and Alice

---

354. Indiana, Jasper County, Death Book HB-D3, page 125.
355. Indiana, Jasper County, Rensselaer Republican, Vol 83, No. 89, Monday, 15 Apr 1985, page 2.

(Brouhard) Daniels. He was a lifetime Rensselaer resident was educated in the Jasper County schools.

He was married on April 15, 1946 in Monticello, to Pauline C. Rude, who survives.

He was a retired bartender and had worked at the Northside Tavern for 37 years.

He belonged to the Nazarene Church and also was a member of the Eagles Lodge.

Survivors include his mother, one son, Virgil I. Daniels Jr. of Rensselaer; and three grandchildren.

He was preceded in death by his father, one daughter and one brother.

Friends may call at the Steinke Funeral Home after 2 p.m. today. The funeral is at 10:30 a.m. Tuesday at the Steinke Funeral Home with the Rev. Harold Cox officiating. Burial will follow in Weston Cemetery.

Virgil and Pauline had:

837. Virgil Ivan Daniels* Jr. b. 5 Feb 1947 d. aft 1994
838. Patricia Sue Daniels b. 30 Dec 1947 d. 1 Dec 1948

574. Omar Edward Daniels born[356] 13 Dec 1918 in Jasper County, In d. 26 Jan 1978 at Loveland, Larimer County, Co of emphysema. His will was recorded on 2 Feb 1978 at Ft. Collins, Co and on 18 Sep 1978 at Rensselaer, Ind. I have a photocopy of a copy of the original of this will. Omar enlisted in the U.S. Army 24 Sep 1941 and served in the Pacific Theatre. He was in the battles of Makin, Saipan Island and Okinawa Island. He earned the Asiatic Theatre service medal with three bronze stars, Combat Infantryman Badge and Purple Heart. He was discharged 31 Aug 1945.

Omar E. Daniels

---

356. Indiana, Jasper County, Birth Book CH-13, page 78.

OMAR E. DANIELS

Omar married[357] Colleen C. Bell 19 Jan
1947 in Jasper County. She was b. 19 Aug 1924.
Colleen was living in Loveland, Co in 1994. She
has been very helpful to me in compiling the
information on her branch of the family.

Omar and Colleen lived in Hammond, In for
almost 14 years and moved to Loveland, Co in
Jun 1977. He worked for General Motors at
Willow Springs, Il for almost 18 years. Colleen
worked for Simmons Bedding Co. for the same
amount of time. Omar and Colleen traveled
extensively in the U. S. parts of Canada. Omar
and Colleen had:

839. Roy Edward Daniels b. 28 May 1947 d.
2 Jun 1992
840. Donald Allen Daniels b. 27 Jan 1949
841. William Russell Daniels b. 19 Jul
1950
842. James Michael Daniels b. 20 Feb 1952
843. Gerald Wayne Daniels b. 30 Jan 1953

357. Indiana, Jasper County, Marriage Book
20, page 60.

844. Evelyn Kay Daniels b. 7 Dec 1956

575. Cerilda Ma Daniels b. 27 Apr 1924 in Jasper County, In and died[358] there 30 June 1986. She is buried in the Smith Cemetery, Barkley Twp, Jasper County where many of her family are buried. She married[359] Dennis F. York Jr. 29 Jun 1948 in Jasper County. Her obituary from a Rensselaer newspaper:

Cerilda York

Cerilda York, 62, of 224 North Front St. Rensselaer, died at 8:03 p.m. Monday in the Jasper County Hospital.

She was born April 27, 1924, the daughter of Omar and Mable (Faylor) Daniels, both of whom preceded her in death.

EDUCATED in the Rensselaer Public Schools, she was a lifelong resident of Rensselaer and a member of the Assembly of God.

She worked as a United Telephone operator for 10 years, and then was the head baker at St. Joseph's College for 10 years.

Survivors include two sons, Steve York of Muncie, and Lowell York of Franklin; one daughter, Sharon York; and two grandchildren.

SHE was preceded in death by one brother.

Friends may call between 6 and 9 p.m. Wednesday at the Steinke Funeral Home.

Funeral services are at 10 a.m. Thursday at the Steinke Funeral Home with the Rev. Gerald Flynn officiating. Burial will follow in the Smith Cemetery.

Cerilda and Dennis had:

845. Dennis Steven York b. 7 Apr 1949
846. Lowell Omar York b. 22 Apr 1950
847. Sharon Louise York b. 14 Aug 1953

---

358. Indiana, Jasper County, Rensselaer Republican, Tuesday, 1 July 1986.
359. Indiana, Jasper County, Marriage Book 20, page 296.

RUTH DANIELS

584. Ruth Daniels b. bef 1907, probably in
Vermilion County, Il. A family picture gives
her married name as Ruth Daniels Heist. She had
at least one child, a son, according to a
cousin. Her son is reported to have been a
police officer in northern Indiana and said to
be deceased in 1994.

848. RESERVED

585. Opal Daniels b. 24 Jun 1907, probably in
Vermilion County, Il and d. 13 Mar 1989 at West
Lebanon, Warren County, In. She m. Elbert
Benedict bef 1929. They had:

849. Eugene Benedict   b. 28 Mar 1929

OPAL DANIELS BENEDICT AND SON, EUGENE

586. Marilyn Joyce Daniels b. 14 Dec 1939 in
East Chicago, Lake County, Indiana. She m.
Robert Lloyd Elkins 29 Dec 1956. He b. 16 Dec
1937 the son of Robert R. and Mary E. Hipp
Elkins. Marilyn is a member of the Baptist
church and works as a school bus driver.
Marilyn and Robert had:

    850. Beth Ann Elkins b. 5 Jun 1962
    851. Robert Lloyd Elkins Jr. b. 6 May 1968
    852. Mary Jo Elkins b. Jun 1969
    853. Cary Sue Elkins b. Jun 1972

587. Melvin J. "Red" Daniels b. 2 Sep 1941. He married[360] Janetta Oglesby 3 Aug 1963 in Lake County, In. They were living in Hobart, In in 1994. They had one adopted child.

854. Dean Edward Daniels b. 15 Jun 1974

588. Marvin Dale Daniels b. 6 Jan 1943. He married[361] Dorisa W. Black 4 May 1963 in Lake County, In. She was b. 3 Aug 1941 at Lily, Laurel County, Ky. Marvin works as a diesel mechanic for Huber-Sod Mercury in Schnyder, Ind and Dorisa has a certificate in accounting and data processing and works as an Office Manager. They were living in Demotte, In in 1994. Marvin and Doris had:

855. Dale Marvin Daniels* b. 9 Feb 1965
856. Wayne Edward Daniels* b. 18 Jan 1967
857. Steven Edgar Daniels* b. 8 Aug 1974

589. Mildred Joan Daniels b. Dec 1944. She m. Donald Embry. They had:

858. Mary Ann Alice Embry b. Dec 1965
859. Tamitha Embry b. Jul 1972
860. Kimberly Sue Joyce Embry b. 1979

590. Margie Mae Daniels b. 26 May 1946 at Gary, Lake County, In. She is a seamstress. She m. Robert E. Hopper 3 Jul 1964. He was b. 9 Jul 1943. They are members of the Baptist Church. They moved to Cullman, Alabama where they live in 1994. Margie and Robert had:

861. Barry Lee Hopper b. 16 Jul 1965
862. Kenneth Eston Hopper b. 11 Mar 1966
863. Robert Clark Hopper b. 2 Sep 1968
864. Heath Alan Hopper b. 7 Jan 1973

---

360. Indiana State Board of Health, Marriage Index for 1963.
361. Indiana State Board of Health, Marriage Index for 1963.

591. Edith Daniels b. 1914 at Bismarck,
Vermilion County, Il. She married Martin Hess.
They did not have children. They were living in
Portage, Ind in 1994.

592. Harold Daniels b. 2 Jan 1915 at Bismarck,
Vermilion County, Il. He m. Viola Stokes. They
were later divorced. They had:

    865. Betty Jean Daniels

593. Hazel Daniels b. 1917 at Bismarck,
Vermilion County, Il. She m. Clarence Singleton
who d. bef 1994. She has given me information
on the families of her aunts and uncles. She
was living in Landing, New Jersey with her
daughter in 1994. Hazel and Clarence had:

    866. Doris Singleton
    867. Donald Singleton
    868. Beverly Singleton
    869. Virginia Singleton
    870. La Verne Singleton
    871. Darlene Singleton

594. Ruby Daniels b. 1919 at Bismarck,
Vermilion County, Il. She married Frederick
Bendt. They lived in Lake County, In. They had:

    872. James Bendt
    873. David Bendt
    874. Daniel Bendt
    875. Janet Bendt

595. Vernon Daniels b. 26 Jul 1921 at Bismarck,
Vermilion County, Il. He is an Air Force
veteran. He m. a woman named Kibler 23 Dec 1949
at Crown Point, Lake County, Indiana. Another
cousin has reported he married Marcella
Hargens. He gave me the information on his
family at a Daniels family reunion in 1993 in
DeMotte, In. They live in Gary, In. Vernon had:

    876. Kenneth Eugene Daniels* b. 31 Mar
        1953
    877. Dale Alan Daniels* b. 16 Jun 1955

878. Vernon Edward Daniels* b. 8 Nov 1956
879. Richard Alvin Daniels* b. 10 Aug 1958

599. Linden Eugene Daniels b. 13 May 1929 in Vermilion County, Il d. aft 1994. He married first Ruth Thomas bef 1954. They were divorced and he next married Lucille McClure 12 Sep 1970. They were living in New Castle, Pa in 1994. He had:

  880. Charles Thomas Daniels* b. 22 Oct 1948 d. aft 1994
  881. Rodney Lynn Daniels* b. 4 Dec 1954 d. 27 Jun 1972

603. Thomas Harding Daniel b. 18 Dec 1926, probably Lafayette, In, d. abt 1985 in Panama City, Fl. He married Phyllis Jean Roberts 21 Mar 1953. I have copies of both of their signatures from their marriage license application[362]. He reportedly became an architect and worked in Panama City, Fla. Thomas and Phyllis adopted three children.

604. Wilma Elizabeth Daniels b. 27 Mar 1919 in West Liberty, Logan County, Oh and d. there abt 1962. According to family members she developed multiple sclerosis at about the age of 19 and lived to about the age of forty. She was a member of the Mennonite church.

605. D. Dwight Daniels b. 14 Apr 1921 in West Liberty, Logan County, Oh d. aft 1994. He m. Opal A. Swartz 5 Apr 1942. Opal was b. 4 Dec 1919 at Peabody, Ks, the daughter of John Clyde and Anna Flisher Swartz. Opal d. 4 Jan 1990 at Lima, Oh and is buried in the Salem Cemetery in Elida, Allen County, Oh. Dwight and Opal both graduated from the Kitchener Bible School of Ontario, Canada. Dwight was living in Elida, Oh in 1994. Dwight and Opal had:

---

362. Illinois, Champaign County, Marriage License Applications, Book July 1952-July 1953, #31612.

882. Judith Marie Daniels b. 11 Feb 1943
883. Jay Dwight Daniels b. 6 Aug 1946
884. Infant (daughter) b. Sep 1948 d. Sep
     1948
885. Bonnie May Daniels b. 31 Mar 1950
886. Jean Anne Daniels b. 4 Jan 1953

606. Mary Elizabeth Daniel b. 13 Mar 1925, in
Indianapolis, In, d. 15 Oct 1976 in
Birmingham, Mi. She m. Wayne A. Lundy 14 Dec
1947. He b. 21 Jun 1925. They had:

     887. Carol Lundy b. 24 Jun 1954
     888. Michael Lundy b. aft 1954
     889. Jeffrey Lundy b. aft 1954

607. William Kenyon Daniel b. 8 Jan 1931, in
Indianapolis, In. He m. Lorel Ann Mohr 17 Aug
1952 in Columbus, Bartholomew County, In. She
was b. 15 Sep 1930 the daughter of Charles P.
and Mabel M. Mohr of Clifford, In. Bill and Ann
are both graduates of Columbus High School and
Indiana University. Bill received a Bachelor of
Arts degree in Business. Bill worked for the
Daniel-Hayden Electrical Company for thirty
years and was president of that company. He
works in the real estate business in 1994. Bill
and Ann had:

     890. Linda Ann Daniel* b. 15 Sep 1953
     891. Karin Leigh Daniel* b. 14 Dec 1954
     892. Susan Lynn Daniel* b. 2 May 1957
     893. Martha Ann Daniel* b. 18 May 1961
     894. William Kenyon Daniel* II b. 24 Dec
          1964

610. Walter Gerald Daniel b. 9 Jul 1930 at
Bucklin, Ford County, Ks. He m. Velma L. Trace
19 Feb 1949. He next m. Lois Vonceil Henderson.
Walter m. 3rd Alice and 4th Charlene Hanson
Burrill.

     Walter and Velma had:

     895. Jerrold Duane Daniel b. 17 Jul 1950
     896. Rhonda Lynn Daniel b. 24 Aug 1951

897. Sharon Kay Daniel b. 1 May 1956

Walter and Lois had:

898. Walter Glenn Daniel b. 30 Nov 1961

Walter and Charlene had:

899. Dennis Gerald Daniel b. 25 Dec 1971
900. Donald Gary Daniel b. 5 Aug 1973

611. Alvin Jay Daniel b. 27 Jan 1934 near Rexford, in Decatur County, Ks. He m. Deloris Mock 27 Jun 1954. They had:

901. John Thurman Daniel b. 27 Mar 1956
902. Sherry Jaye Daniel b. 7 Dec 1957
903. DeAnne Lynn Daniel b. 29 Oct 1959
904. Robin Renee Daniel b. 11 Dec 1960

612. Jo Ann Daniel b. 13 Dec 1936 near Rexford, in Decatur County, Ks. She m. Edward F. Miller 27 Dec 1955 at Oberlin, Ks in the Sacred Heart Church. They had:

905. Jane Christina Miller b. 26 May 1956
906. Paul Walter Miller b. 8 May 1957
907. John Bernard Miller b. 24 Nov 1958 d. 24 Nov 1958
908. Mary Margaret Miller b. 20 Jul 1960
909. Phillip Joseph Miller b. 9 Oct 1962
910. Gail Theresa Miller b. 5 Nov 1964
911. Mark Edward Miller b. 10 Nov 1968
912. Carole Jane Miller b. 14 May 1972
913. Gina Ann Miller b. 2 Jan 1974

613. Marjorie Lea Daniel b. 10 Oct 1938 north of Rexford, Ks in Decatur County. She m. Forrest Lynn Paddock 12 Jul 1959 at Oberlin, Ks in a Methodist church. She has given me much of the information on the descendents of William Thomas Daniel. Marjorie and Forrest had:

914. Cheryl Denise Paddock b. 13 Jun 1960
915. Terry Lynn Paddock b. 9 Oct 1962

614. Robert Lee Daniel b. 17 Oct 1925 at Coldwater, Comanche County, Ks. He m. Agnes J. Mertens 31 Jul 1948 at Scott City, Ks. She was b. 18 Jan 1929 at Willow Dale, Ks, the daughter of Henry Chris and Teresa Benchen Mertens. Robert and Agnes were divorced in Apr 1957. Robert m. second Venita Fae Allen in Kansas. She is the daughter of Mildred Cordelia Schank.

Agnes worked as a finisher for Kawasaki in Lincoln, Ne for 17 years. Robert was living in Penrose, Co when his father died. He retired after working as a lineman for Southwestern Bell in Kansas and also worked as a supervisor for the Rocket Engine Division of Estes Industries at Penrose, Co.

Robert and Agnes had:

916. Michael Lee Daniel* b. 6 Dec 1949
917. Linda Kay Daniel* b. 21 Apr 1951
918. Randal Eugene Daniel* b. 10 Dec 1953
919. Evelyn Marie Daniel* b. 23 Oct 1955
920. Jana Lynn Daniel* b. 14 Feb 1957

Robert and Venita had:

921. Diana Lee Daniel* b. 2 Jan 1966

615. Gwendolyn Ann Daniel b. 27 Oct 1927 at Coldwater, Comanche County, Ks. She m. Walter Claire Thompson 12 Jul 1946. She was living in Coldwater, Ks when her father died. Gwendolyn and Claire had:

922. Lucinda Ann Thompson b. 29 Jul 1948
923. Debra Sue Thompson b. 8 Sep 1950
924. Shari Kay Thompson b. 20 Aug 1952
925. Walter Don Thompson b. 2 Feb 1962
926. Allen Scott Thompson b. 4 Dec 1964

616. Shirley J. "Sherry" Daniel b. 31 Oct 1931 at Coldwater, Comanche County, Ks. She m. Donald Rex Burnett 30 Oct 1954. She was living in Wichita, Ks in 1994. Sherry and Don had:

927. Valerie Lynn Burnett b. 19 Nov 1955

928. Linda Down Burnett b. 10 Nov 1957
929. Randall Carey Burnett b. 30 Jan 1959

617. Gerald Ray Daniel b. 18 Aug 1935 at
Coldwater, Comanche County, Ks. He was living
in San Francisco, Ca when his father died. He
was unmarried in 1994.

636. Allie Bernice Daniel b. 16 Nov 1905 Platte
County, Mo d. aft 1994. She m. John B. Stubbs
Aug 1945. I spoke with her in 1994 but she
seems to have had little contact with her
Daniel kin during her lifetime. She has lived
in the Kansas City area all of her life. She
and John had:

930. Anna Mary Stubbs b. abt 1946
931. Marjorie Jane Stubbs b. abt 1948

637. Frederick Gaylord Daniel b. 6 Apr 1906 at
Anthony, Harper County, Ks d. aft 1963. He m.
Margaret Edmundson 10 Jan 1928. He was living
in Jackson Heights, NY in 1963 when his father
died. He may be the Frederick Daniel who died
in New York Dec 1967 and was listed in the
Social Security Death Index. Frederick and
Margaret had:

932. Carol Anne Daniel b. 31 Aug 1943 d.
aft 1963

638. Paul Wilkinson Daniel b. 10 Aug 1908 at
Wichita, Sedgwick County, Ks d. after 1963. He
m. Laura Eva Wulfert 10 July 1940. She b. 14
Sep 1905 at Seneca, Ks a daughter of Emerson
and Eva Luke Wulfert. According to cousins he
lived in St. Louis and may be the Paul Daniel
who died there 30 Nov 1988. Paul and Laura had:

933. Susan La Nelle Daniel b. 20 Mar 1948
d. aft 1963

639. Donnie A. Daniel b. 24 Jun 1889 in Kansas
City, Jackson County, Mo d. there 18 Dec 1975.
She was married twice but had no children by
her first husband and was married to him for a

273

short time. She was working for her father as a
cashier in his clothing store in 1920. She
lived her whole life in the Kansas City area. I
have several pictures of her. She lived with
her daughter when she was elderly. She is
buried in the Winchester Cemetery, Winchester,
Kansas. She m. first Homer Rybolt bef 1920. She
m. second Frank Jay Coppinger 8 Jun 1921. He
was b. 4 Nov at Winchester, Ks and d. 10 Aug
1960. Her obituary[363] appeared in two Kansas
City, Mo newspapers:

MRS. DONNIE A. COPPINGER. Mrs. Donnie A.
Coppinger, 86, of 404 W. 86th Terrace, died
Thursday at St. Mary's Hospital. She was born
here and lived here most of her life. Mrs.
Coppinger was member of Hyde Park Christian
Church. She leaves a daughter, Mrs. Donnie June
Stoeckle of the home; a brother, J. Shelby
Daniel, Jr., Phoenix; three grandchildren and a
great-granddaughter. Services will be held at
the Muehlebach Chapel; burial in Winchester,
Kan., Cemetery. Friends may call after 2 p.m.
today at the chapel.

Donnie and Frank had:

934. Donnie June Coppinger b. 1 Feb 1924

641. Joseph Shelby Daniel Jr. b. 27 Nov 1903 at
Kansas City, Mo and d. 9 Jul 1986 at Phoenix,
Az. He and his father both preferred to be
known as Shelby Daniel. He was living in Chico,
Ca when his father died in 1938. He started a
career in banking 15 Mar 1926 with the First
National Bank in Oakland, Ca, moving to their
Chico branch in 1936 as assistant manager. In
Oct 1952 he joined the Farmers and Stockmens
Bank of Phoenix as vice president and manager
of their home office. This bank was later part
of The Arizona Bank and Shelby served with them
as cashier, vice president and home office
manager at various times. He retired 31 Dec

363. Missouri, Kansas City, Kansas City
Times, 19 Dec 1975, page 9C.

1968 when he became involved in a special
historical research project for The Arizona
Bank. He m. Agnes Francesca Turner in 1924 at
Minneapolis, Hennepin County, Mn. Agnes was b.
1 Jun 1901 and is living in 1994.

J. SHELBY DANIEL JR. AND WIFE, AGNES

Shelby was an accomplished photographer
and skilled woodworker, crafting many pieces of
fine furniture for his family. He also invented
and installed a security system in his family
home. Shelby was a man of great integrity and a
devoted husband and father. Shelby and Agnes
had:

935. Patricia Ann Daniel* b. 31 Jan 1925
936. Virginia Lee Daniel* b. 12 Nov 1930

644. Thelma F. Daniel b. 20 Oct 1901 Kansas City, Jackson County, Mo d. 26 Jan 1961 at Los Angeles, Ca. She m. Wallace Titzell in 1936.

645. Charles Edwin Daniel b. 9 Aug 1904 Kansas City, Jackson County, Mo d. 23 May 1978 at San Diego, Ca. He m. Velma Maitland Morrison 15 Jun 1925. She b. 9 Oct 1906 at Somerville, Mass d. 5 May 1983 at San Diego, Ca. Charles and Velma had:

937. David Everett Daniel* b. 27 Feb 1926

646. Kathryn Mae Daniel b. 24 Mar 1907 Los Angeles, Los Angeles County, Ca. She m. Clarence Herman Lewis in 1929. She may be the Kathryn Lewis I found in the Social Security Death Index, who died Feb 1981 in Garden Grove or Huntington Beach, Orange County, Ca. They had:

938. Gordon Lewis b. aft 1929
939. Louise Lewis b. aft 1929

647. Almanza Martin Daniel b. 19 Jan 1910 Los Angeles, Los Angeles County, Ca d. aft 1994. He m. Elizabeth Stoebener in 1950. They had no children. I spoke with him in 1993 and 1994. He goes by the name "Marty". He is close to his nephew David Everett and his children.

648. Pleasant Edgar Daniel b. 13 Jun 1940 in Montgomery County, Ky. He m. Betty Hartgrove 3 Oct 1971. They had:

940. Kevin Lee Daniel b. 9 Oct 1975

649. Charles Wilford Daniel b. 4 Nov 1941 in Montgomery Co., Ky. He m. Brenda Rudd 3 Oct 1971. She b. 16 July 1950 in Winchester, Ky. He was a Kentucky State Policeman and is retired and lives in Montgomery County in 1994. They had:

941. Charles Wilford Daniel Jr. b. 9 Jan 1974

653. Dorothy Lee Daniel b. 21 Aug 1931 in Montgomery County, Ky. She m. Charles William Jones 8 Aug 1953. She has provided help to me on the Montgomery County Daniels. They live in Mt. Sterling, Ky in 1994. Dorothy and Charles had:

> 942. Katherine Charlene Jones b. 6 Oct 1954
> 943. Elizabeth Diane Jones b. 16 Aug 1958
> 944. Donna Lee Jones b. 9 Apr 1960

654. Alger Thompson "Tom" Daniel b. 19 Aug 1943 in Montgomery County, Ky. He m. Jean Sponcil 1 May 1966. He graduated from Eastern Kentucky University with a Bachelor of Science Degree in Industrial Arts in 1966 and a Master of Industrial Education in 1971. He was employed in various education and industry positions for the next twenty years and in 1994 works farming tobacco and raising pure bred cattle. They had:

> 945. Christopher Thompson Daniel* b. 31 Aug 1967

668. Charles Gilkey Daniel Jr. b. 6 Apr 1917 at South Boston, Halifax County, Va. He did not marry. He was a soldier at some time in his life and is buried at Arlington National Cemetery.

671. Richie Leo Daniel b. 9 Sep 1929 in Montgomery County, Ky. He m. Goldie Compton 14 May 1952. She b. 6 Nov 1927 d. 12 Apr 1985. He is a life long resident of Montgomery County and an enterprising businessman in Jeffersonville, Ky. Along with his sons he operates several business in that small town. He has been a great help in researching the Daniels in this county and in a visit there in 1989 took me to the old Daniel cemetery where our common ancestor, Estridge Daniel, is buried. Leo and Goldie had:

> 946. David Lee Daniel* b. 10 Feb 1953

947. Bruce Wayne Daniel* b. 14 Oct 1956
948. William Richie Daniel* b. 9 Aug 1959
949. John Morton Daniel* b. aft 1959

LEFT TO RIGHT: JOHN QUINCY DANIEL AND LEO DANIEL. (AT GRAVE OF ESTRIDGE DANIEL)

688. Covell Mark Daniel b. 28 Apr 1916 in DeKalb County, Mo. He m. Ruth Louise Redman 7 Jul 1940. She b. 15 Jan 1918 d. 15 Sep 1993 in DeKalb County, Mo. She is buried in the Shambaugh-Cope Cemetery near Weatherby, Mo. He and his wife lived outside DeKalb County for many years while he was engaged in the aerospace industry. He worked in research and development and was involved in developing autonavigators for submarines, worked on the Apollo moon shot and the space shuttle. Covell and Ruth later returned to DeKalb County, where they farmed. Ruth was killed in an accident between the farm vehicle on which they were riding and a pickup truck. They had two adopted children.

950. Robert Mark Daniel (adopted) b. 14 Dec 1949

951. Sandra Louise Daniel (adopted) b. 25 Dec 1951

690. Joann Daniel b. 20 Mar 1924 Columbus, Ohio. She m. Richard Daniel Epley 17 Aug 1945. They live in Columbus, Oh in 1994. Joann and Dick had:

952. Richard Daniel Epley Jr. b. 13 Jul 1950
953. Sunni Gay Epley b. 5 Jun 1953

691. Viola Ruth Daniel b. 23 Mar 1925 d. Oct 1992 at Columbus, Ohio. She m. Ramon Fickel 12 May 1950. He b. 2 Nov 1927. They lived in Columbus. Ray and Vi had:

954. Randall Lee Fickel b. 20 Feb 1953
955. Terrence Lynn Fickel b. 24 May 1957
956. Tami Rae Fickel b. 1 Apr 1964

692. Charles Frederick Daniel b. 9 Jun 1930 in Columbus, Oh d. 1951. He enlisted in the U.S. Navy and died in an automobile accident on his way home while on leave. He did not marry. I have a couple of pictures of him.

693. Edwin Clyde Daniel b. 14 Apr 1941 in Hannibal, Marion County, Mo. He m. Sandra Kay Skinner 5 Dec 1961 at Hannibal, Mo. She b. 9 Feb 1941 in Hannibal. They were later divorced. He next married a woman named Christine but was later divorced. He m. Christine Newsome about 1993. As a young man he piloted a tour boat in Hannibal. He lives in Ft. Lauderdale, Fl in 1994 where he pilots a pleasure boat between that place and Hollywood, Fl. Edwin and Sandra had:

957. Brian Mark Daniel* b. 9 Oct 1964
958. Aaron Dean Daniel* b. 24 Feb 1967
959. Andrea Leigh Daniel* b. 4 Sep 1971

694. Larry Dean Daniel b. 24 Feb 1945 in Hannibal, Marion County, Mo. He m. Debbie Arbuckle in Hannibal abt 1976. They were

279

divorced. He followed in his father's occupation as a barber in Hannibal and is a graduate of St. Louis Barber College. His shop in 1993 was located in the same building in which his great grandfather, Friedrich Wilhelm August Bastian, operated a furniture store in the 1880s. Larry and Debbie had one son who died at birth.

      960. Michael Daniel b. 1 Jul 1976 d. 1 Jul 1976

695. Jacqueline Ann "Jackie" Daniel b. 21 Dec 1933 in Hannibal, Marion County, Mo. She m. Thomas Albert Hooper 14 Apr 1957 at Hannibal, Mo. She worked as a Cabin Attendant for Trans-World Airlines. They live in California in 1994. Tom and Jackie had:

      961. Danielle Hooper b. 8 Dec 1959
      962. Dirk David Hooper b. 22 Jan 1963

696. Sue Laverne Daniel b. 6 Sep 1938 in Missouri. She m. Jackie Carr. They live in Eolia, Mo in 1994. They had:

      963. Belinda Carr
      964. Kathy Carr
      965. Eddie Carr
      966. Stacy Carr
      967. Kevin Carr

697. Brenda Kaye Daniel b. 17 Feb 1948 at Hannibal, Marion County, Mo. She m. Ernest Paul Flowerree 25 Feb 1967 at Quincy, Adams County, Il. He b. 15 Jan 1943. They live in Quincy in 1994. She was named "Woman of the Year" in 1981 by the Quincy Chapter of the American Business Women's Association. At that time she was a member of that association and served on its publicity committee. She was assistant to the administrator of the Quincy Clinic then. Since then she has received certification to act as Risk Manager for the clinic. She is pursuing a Bachelor Degree in Business Administration in 1994. They had no children.

698. Kendall Ray "Ken" Daniel b. 5 Jun 1950 at
Hannibal, Marion County, Mo. He m. Sandi Jean
Kenny 15 Sep 1972 at Miami, Ok. She b. 1 July
1943 at Walla Walla, Wa. Ken served in the US
Army infantry 1967-1970 and 1972-1976 and
attained the rank of Sergeant. He served in
Korea and Germany. They live in Woodburn, Or in
1994. Ken works as a driver for Rollins DCS and
Sandi works in retail sales. Ken and Sandy had:

    968. Kimberly Ray-Jean Daniel* b. 18 Dec
        1973
    969. Kandy Kaye Daniel* b. 11 Nov 1975

FAMILY OF JOHN Q. AND WILLA MAE DANIEL, LEFT TO
RIGHT: SHERRY JEAN, WILLA MAE, JOHN QUINCY,
KURTIS WALTON, GARY JAY, JIMMIE LEE AND KEVIN
WAYNE

700. Jimmie Lee Daniel b. 10 Nov 1933 at
Spalding, Ralls Co., Mo. and d. 22 Oct 1994 at
Kewanee, Henry County, Il of cancer. He m.
Geraldine L. Wilsey 12 Nov 1955 at Galesburg,
Il. She b. 5 Nov 1937 at Kewanee, Il. He was a
U.S. Army veteran and served during the Korean

War. Jim was employed as a factory worker at
the Kewanee Boiler Corporation for many years
and later as an industrial X-Ray technician. He
was a leader of the Boilermaker's Union in his
locality and served several terms as president
of his union local. Jim was genuinely good man,
well liked, well loved and well respected by
his family and a wide circle of friends. Jim's
obituary appeared in newspapers in Kewanee and
Peoria, Il and Hannibal, Mo. The Kewanee
article follows:

Jimmie Lee Daniel

KEWANEE - Jimmie Lee Daniel, 60, of 419 N.
Grove St., Kewanee, died at 4:25 p.m. Saturday,
Oct. 22, 1994, at Kewanee Hospital of cancer
after a short illness.
He was born Nov. 10, 1933, in Spalding,
Ralls County, Missouri, the son of John Quincy
and Willa Mae [Hostetter] Daniel. He was reared
and educated in Hannibal, graduating from
Hannibal High School in 1951. He joined the
Army and served during the Korean Conflict,
stationed in Alaska. He married Geraldine Lee
Wilsey, Nov. 12, 1955, in Galesburg.
She survives, as well as a daughter,
Cynthia Lee [Daniel] Troutwine of Kewanee; two
sons, Jeffrey Lee Daniel and his wife Lori and
Jay Lee Daniel, all of Kewanee, two
grandchildren, Monica Mae Daniel and Erich
James Daniel, both of Kewanee; his parents John
and Willa Mae Daniel of Peoria; three brothers,
Gary J. Daniel and Kevin Wayne Daniel, both of
Peoria and Kurtis Walton Daniel of Kent, Wash.;
six nieces and six nephews, great-nieces and
great-nephews.
He was preceded in death by one sister,
Sherry Jean Hall of Rockford and a
granddaughter, Courtney Troutwine.
He had been employed by Kewanee Boiler
Corporation since July 6, 1970. He was
currently working there as an x-ray technician
for welders. He was active in the Boilermaker's
Union Local No. 195 for the past 20 years and
was currently serving his third term as its

282

president. He was a member of the Eagles Aerie
No. 982, Kewanee, The National Rifle
Association. He enjoyed fishing and sports and
was an avid Raiders fan.

Funeral services will be at 1:30 p.m.
Wednesday, Oct. 26 at Cavanagh and Schueneman
Funeral Home, Kewanee, the Rev. Barry Lovett of
the First Baptist Church officiating. Burial
will be in the Pleasant View Cemetery where
military rites will be conducted by the Kewanee
Veteran's Council. Visitation is from 7 to 9
p.m. Tuesday at Cavanagh and Schueneman Funeral
Home, Kewanee. A memorial has been established.
Contributions may be left at the funeral home.

Jim and Gerry had:

970. Cynthia Lee Daniel* b. 24 Nov 1957
971. Jeffery Lee Daniel* b. 3 Oct 1961
972. Jay Lee Daniel b. 30 Nov 1962

701. Sherry Jean Daniel b. 15 Oct 1937 at
Hannibal, Marion County, Mo d. 5 May 1991 at
Rockford, Winnebago County, Il of cancer. She
married[364] Jerry Wayne Hall 27 Mar 1960 at
Hannibal, Mo. He b. 28 May 1937 at Hannibal,
Mo. She was a medical transcriptionist. Her
husband was a Baptist minister and she was
active in his church, ministering to children
of all ages. Sherry was a cheerful, positive
woman. She is buried in the Willwood Cemetery
in Rockford, Il. She received a tribute in The
Register Star, a Rockford, Il newspaper:

Pastor's wife also shared God's word.

Cancer victim: She never let her spirits
get down during her five year illness, her son
says.

Sherry Hall was so enthusiastic about God
that she even loved to tell people about Him
when she was shopping.

---

364. Missouri, Marion County, Marriage
Book 47, page 43.

It was nothing for her to stop in a grocery store and begin to tell someone how they, too, could become a Christian, her husband the Rev. Jerry Hall recalled.

"She never gave up on people," he said. "She'd stay with it and stay with it. In the beginning she didn't think she'd make a very good pastor's wife. She didn't think she deserved to be."

She even stopped two women in a bookstore at CherryVale Mall once to tell them about God. She saw the women buying self-help books, and told them that faith in the Lord would do more for them than any book.

Sherry Hall, who didn't decide to dedicate her life to Christ until she was 30, told the women that she had tried self-help books, but they didn't solve much.

"She said she couldn't go to the checkout line until it was taken care of," recalled Patti Loven, one of her best friends. "She was the most unique person I ever met."

Sherry Hall's friends and family say that faith in God played a primary role in sustaining her through a five-year bout with cancer and the surgery and chemotherapy she underwent to treat it.

She died in her home May 5. She was 53.

"She said she wasn't afraid to die, but she had too much to live for." her son Gregory said.

As a Pastor's wife, Sherry Hall found many other opportunities to share her faith with others. She worked in the children's church school at Pelley Road Christian's Fellowship Church, where her husband is pastor.

She helped teach young adults to perform spiritual puppet shows for younger children. The puppeteers sometimes traveled to other churches to share their talents with other children.

Jerry Hall thinks his wife honed her skills for working with children in her home. When the four Hall children were growing up, Sherry Hall would conduct a Bible study for them and their friends.

Throughout her illness, she tried to help her son Andrew deal with the pain of seeing her suffer.

"She really brought me through," he said, "I never saw her spirit down. She never said one bad thing about God."

Sherry's obituary from a Rockford, Il newspaper:

HALL - Sherry Jean Hall, 53, 3425 Pontiac Place, died at 5 p.m. Sunday, May 5, 1991, in her home following an extended illness. Born Oct. 15, 1937, in Oakwood, Mo., daughter of John Q. and Willa Mae Hostetter Daniel. Rockford resident since 1968, coming here from Chicago area. Married Rev. Jerry W. Hall in Hannibal, Mo., on March 27, 1960. Self-employed medical transcriptionist. Member Pelley Road Christian Church, where she worked extensively in Children's Ministries. Survivors include her husband Jerry; three sons, Gregory (Mary) Hall, Louisville, Ky., and Andrew and David, both Rockford; one daughter, Deborah Hall, Rockford; one granddaughter, Aimee; four brothers, Jim Daniel, Kewanee, Gary Daniel, Peoria, and Kevin and Curtis Daniel, both Seattle, Wash.; parents John and Willa Daniel, Peoria, mother-in-law, Mary Hall, Hannibal; several nieces and nephews. Predeceased by father-in-law, Cecil Hall.

Services will be at 2 p.m. Friday, May 10, in Pelley Road Christian Fellowship Church, with the Rev. Ricky Pearson, pastor of First Baptist Church, New Milford, officiating. Burial in Willwood Burial Park. Friends may call from 6 to 8:30 p.m. Thursday, at FRED C. OLSON MORTUARY, 1001 2nd Ave. In lieu of flowers, memorials to Pelley Road Christian Fellowship Church. 5-7-3

Sherry and Jerry had:

973. Gregory Wayne Hall b. 28 Aug 1962
974. Andrew Jay Hall b. 23 Aug 1969

975. Debra Jean Hall b. 19 Dec 1973
(adopted)
976. David Daniel Hall b. 19 Dec 1973
(adopted)

702. Gary Jay Daniel b. 18 Nov 1939 at
Hannibal, Marion County, Mo. He married[365]
first Donna Jean Fletcher 21 Aug 1959 at
Hannibal, Mo. She b. 25 Jan 1942 at Hannibal,
Mo. He was married twice more but his only
child was by his first wife. Gary and Donna
had:

977. Angela Gay Daniel b. 19 Aug 1962

703. Kurtis Walton Daniel b. 16 Sep 1954 at
Hannibal, Marion County, Mo. He m. Carole Ann
Maas abt 1977. She b. 28 Sep 1958 in Illinois.
They had:

978. Jon Kurtis Daniel b. 14 Jan 1982

704. Kevin Wayne Daniel b. 16 Sep 1954 at
Hannibal, Marion County, Mo. My family
relocated to Peoria, Il in 1958, where I grew
up. After graduating from high school, I
enlisted in the U.S. Army 17 August 1972 and
was a member of the U.S. Army Security Agency
serving in Okinawa and Thailand from 1973 to
1976. I attained the rank of staff sergeant,
holding a top secret security clearance. On 10
Nov 1975 I was married[366] to Nittaya
Saensenaer in Bangkok, Thailand. We were
divorced 22 Sep 1978 in Peoria, Il. There were
no children from this marriage.
After returning to the Peoria, Illinois
area in late 1976, I attended Illinois Central
College and worked as a sound technician at the
Illinois Central College Performing Arts
Center. I later worked for Caterpillar Tractor

---

365. Missouri, Marion County, Marriage
Book 46, page 466.
366. Thailand, Dusit Area, Bangkok
Metropolis, Reg. No. NG.1764/9577, 10 Nov 2518
(1975 A.D.).

Company as a factory worker. In 1979 I moved to
Seattle, Wa where I worked as a biomedical
electronic technician, completed my associate
degree in 1987, and was last employed as a
Senior Engineering Technician for Sundstrand
Aerospace. Returning to West Peoria, Il in 1992
I worked part time as a Customer Engineer for
IBM while attending Illinois State University.
I will receive a Bachelor of Science Degree in
Industrial Technology, Energy and Power Systems
Management, in July of 1995 and will enter the
graduate school of Applied Computer Science. I
am an avid motorcyclist and a Motorcycle Safety
Foundation instructor for the State of
Illinois. My interests include bicycle touring,
backpacking, fishing and genealogy.

706. Giles Charles Daniel b. Nov 1889 at
Logansport, De Soto Parish, La d. aft 1912 in
Tyler County, Tx. He m. Roxie Dean in 1912. I
do not know if they had children.

979. RESERVED

707. Ella E. Daniel b. Aug 1891 Logansport, De
Soto Parish, La d. aft 1912. She m. Scott Horn
abt 1912.

980. Howard Horn b. aft 1912

708. Robert David Daniel b. 12 Jun 1893 at
Joaquin, Shelby County, Tx and d. 22 Oct 1970
at Silsbee, Hardin County, Tx. He is buried in
the Mount Carmel Cemetery, Tyler County, Tx. He
m. Lura Mae Bacon 16 July 1919 at Jasper,
Jasper County, Tx. She was born 28 May 1902 at
Mt. Carmel, Tyler County, Tx and died 17 Feb
1960 at Port Arthur, Jefferson County, Tx.
Robert and Lura Mae had:

981. Infant b. aft 1919
982. Infant b. aft 1919
983. Olga Jeanice Daniel b. 1 Aug 1923
984. Gerald David Daniel* b. 10 Apr 1925
985. George Wesley "Dub" Daniel b. 25 Nov
1927

986. James LaWayne Daniel* b. 14 Nov 1930
987. Robert Melvin Daniel* b. 30 Nov 1938

709. Linton Ira Daniel b. Oct 1895 Logansport, De Soto Parish, La d. 10 Oct 1918 in France. He was probably a U.S. soldier. He did not marry.

710. Ozianna Carmen Daniel b. Feb 1898 Joaquin, Shelby County, Tx. She m. Ralph Dean.

988. RESERVED

711. Lottie J. Daniel b. abt 1900 probably in Tyler County, Tx d. aft 1920. She m. Ira Fowler. She may be the Charlotte Fowler I found in the Social Security Death Index. This woman was born 3 Aug 1901 and died Apr 1986 at Spurger, Tyler county, Tx.

989. RESERVED

712. Obie Lee Daniel b. abt 1903, probably in Tyler County, Tx, d. aft 1910. I do not know if he married. He may be the Obie Daniel I found in the Social Security Death Index. This man was b. 13 Oct 1902 and was issued his SSAN in Texas. He d. Apr 1979 at Pasadena, Harris County, Tx and his death benefits were paid to Woodville, Tyler County, Tx.

990. RESERVED

713. James Edgar Daniel b. 13 Feb 1905 Shelby or Tyler County, Tx. He m. a woman named Myrtle.

991. RESERVED

714. Henry Matthew Daniel b. abt 1907 at Shelby or Tyler County, Tx. I do not know if he married. He was living with his family in Tyler County in 1910.

992. RESERVED

715. Richard Elmer Daniel b. 23 Jan 1911 at Shelby County, Tx. He m. a McLeod.

993. RESERVED

716. Samuel A. Daniels b. 20 Sep 1885, probably in Shelby County, Tx and d. 27 Oct 1931. He married but I do not know the name of his wife. They had:

    994. Clarence Daniels b. bef 1931
    995. Lavon Daniels b. bef 1931
    996. Leona Daniels b. bef 1931
    997. Irene Daniels b. bef 1931
    998. Alice Daniels b. bef 1931

717. John Johnson Daniels b. 30 Jul 1888 in De Soto Parish, La d. 1 May 1959. He is buried in the Johnson Cemetery, Shelby County, Tx. He was a farmer and a member of the Church of Christ. He married[367] Jeneva Jane Bass 27 Nov 1910 at De Soto Parish, La. She b. 18 May 1895 d. 25 July 1963. She is also buried in the Johnson Cemetery. They had:

    999. Rita Ozella Daniels* b. 19 Aug 1912
         d. 5 Jun 1990
    1000. Lilly Onell Daniels* b. 7 Mar 1922
    1001. Huey Amos Daniels* b. 6 Feb 1924 d.
          12 Sep 1981

718. Mary Jane Daniels b. 17 Dec 1892. She married[368] James C. Taylor 22 Mar 1911 at Fellowship, Shelby County, Tx. They had:

    1002. Clifter Taylor b. aft 1911
    1003. Chester Taylor b. aft 1911
    1004. Arlin Taylor b. aft 1911
    1005. Rosalin Taylor b. aft 1911
    1006. Amy Taylor b. aft 1911
    1007. Lela Taylor b. aft 1911

---

    367. Louisiana, De Soto Parish, Marriage Book 9, page 501.
    368. Texas, Shelby County, Marriage Volume 7, page 168.

1008. Colonel Taylor b. aft 1911
1009. Fay Taylor b. aft 1911
1010. Ray Taylor b. aft 1911
1011. James C. Taylor b. aft 1911

719. Robert Emmet Daniels b. 24 Feb 1894 d. 14
Apr 1952. He is buried in the Lone Cedar
Cemetery, Shelby County, Tx. He had only one
arm, whether by birth or due to an accident I
do not know. He m. Mayon Wilson. They had:

1012. James Glen Daniels b. bef 1952
1013. Mary Grace Daniels b. bef 1952
1014. Robert Daniels b. bef 1952

720. Sallie May Daniels b. 1 Jun 1897 De Soto
Parish, La d. 10 May 1927. She married[369]
Homer Little 28 Jun 1918 in De Soto Parish, La.
He b. 8 Jun 1897 d. Dec 1962. They are both
buried in Mt. Olivet Cemetery, De Soto Parish,
La. They had:

1015. Elois Little

721. Johnnie Lorin Daniels b. 9 Feb 1899 De
Soto Parish, La d. 30 Nov 1974 Shreveport,
Caddo Parish, La. He m. Mamie Whitlock 27 Jul
1920 at Weatherford, Tx. She b. 27 Aug 1903
Cisco, Tx d. 4 Jun 1992. They were Baptists.
They are buried in the Mt. Olivet Cemetery, De
Soto Parish, La. They had:

1016. Roy Ennis Daniels* b. 8 Jan 1923
1017. Mildred Lucille Daniels* b. 21 Aug
      1924
1018. Doris Pauline Daniels* b. 28 Oct 1927
1019. John Lorin Daniels Jr.* 13 Jun 1935
      d. 2 Sep 1983

722. Jessie Edgar Daniels b. 11 Nov 1900 at De
Soto Parish, La d. 26 Jan 1987. He is buried in
the Mt. Olivet Cemetery, De Soto Parish, La. He
m. Janie Mae Caston 4 Nov 1928 at De Soto

---

369. Louisiana, De Soto Parish, Marriage
Book 14, page 498.

290

Parish, La. She b. 5 Aug 1911 in Mississippi.
They had:

    1020. Infant daughter b. abt 1930 d. abt
    1930
    1021. Jessie Edgar Daniel* b. 7 Apr 1932 d.
    30 Jan 1987
    1022. Robert Forest Daniels* b. 22 Feb 1934

738. George Edward Daniel b. 16 Dec 1931 Hardin
County, Tx. He m. Vaudene Walters 5 Jan 1952.
She b. 18 Apr 1934. He is a farmer and farms
land entered by his great grandfather, James
Daniel, in Hardin County. They live in Kountze,
Tx. They had:

    1023. Sandra Marie Daniel* b. aft 1952
    1024. George Edward Daniel Jr.* b. aft 1952

740. Charles Wilburn Daniel b. 11 Aug 1915 in
Hardin County, Tx d. bef 1994. He m. June bef
1943. They had:

    1025. Cathleen Daniel* b 1 Nov 1943

741. Kathleen Daniels b. aft 1913 in Hardin
County, Tx d. bef 1994. She may be the Kathleen
Daniels who married[370] Lee Walcott in Hardin
County, Tx.

742. J. C. Daniels b. aft 1913 in Hardin
County, Tx d. bef 1994. He is probably the J.
C. Daniels who married[371] Maxine Hulan in
Hardin County. She is probably the Maxine H.
Daniels buried near his parents in the Holland
Cemetery, Hardin County. She was b. 11 Feb 1914
and d. 1 Mar 1957. I do not know if they had
children.

    1026. RESERVED

---

    370. Texas, Hardin County, Marriage Book
8, page 114.
    371. Texas, Hardin County, Marriage Book
8, page 6.

743. Doris May Daniels b. 20 May 1920 in Nebraska. She m. Stanley Charles Plowright. They had:

> 1027. Nancy Lee Plowright
> 1028. Beverly Jean Plowright

744. Duane Wilbur Daniels b. 8 May 1924 in Springview, Keya Pana County, Ne. He m. Lula Margaret Starkie 26 Jul 1945. She was born 28 Jun 1924 in Merced, Ca. They were divorced about 1951 and Duane next married Shirley Ann Mannen bef 1954. She was b. 27 Aug 1929 at Mt. Vernon, Il.

> Duane and Lula had:

> 1029. Kathleen Lula Daniels* b. 28 Feb 1947
> 1030. Stephen Paul Daniels b. 25 Jan 1949
>   d. 25 Jan 1949

> Duane and Shirley had:

> 1031. Melody Ann Daniels* b. 23 Oct 1954
> 1032. Glenn Calwell Daniels* b. 16 Jul 1959
> 1033. Gary Earl Daniels* b. 10 Nov 1961

745. Ann Daniels b. aft 1925 d. aft 1971. According to the obituary of her father she m. Del Hill and was living in Lebanon, Or in Sep 1971. There is a good chance that she had children as her father's obituary says he had 10 grandchildren and two great grandchildren.

> 1034. RESERVED

746. Velda Daniels Jr. b. aft 1925 d. aft 1971. He was living in Salt Lake City, Ut in 1971 according to his father's obituary. He may have married and had children.

> 1035. RESERVED

747. Jackie Alan Daniels b. aft 1925 d. aft
1971. He was living in Salt Lake City, Ut in
1971 according to his father's obituary. He may
have married and had children.

1036. RESERVED

748. Billie Joy Daniels b. 1940 in Tacoma,
Pierce County, Wa. She m. Charles Loukes
McNiven 26 Jan 1957. Charles worked as a truck
driver for 34 years and Billie as a city
transit bus driver and school bus driver for
the handicapped. They were living in Tacoma, Wa
in 1994. Billie and Charles had:

    1037. Deborah Renee McNiven b. 31 May 1958
    1038. Elizabeth Roseanne McNiven b. 2 Mar
        1961
    1039. Michael Charles Loukes McNiven III b.
        8 Aug 1962

749. Paul Jackson Daniels b. 27 Jun 1946 at
Tacoma, Pierce County, Wa d. aft 1994. He m.
Shirleen Lunt 2 Jun 1971 at the LDS Temple,
Mesa, Az. He graduated from Brigham Young
University with Bachelor of Science Degree in
Electrical Engineering and from Arizona State
University with a Masters of Science Degree in
Electrical Engineering. He has been employed by
Motorola in Mesa, Az as an electrical engineer
since 1972. He is active in The Church of Jesus
Christ of Latter Day Saints of which he and his
family are members. Shirleen was b. 2 Jul 1950
in Stafford, Az. She was Valedictorian of her
high school class and graduated from Brigham
Young University in 1973 with a Bachelor of
Science Degree in Home Economics Education.
They had:

    1040. Sarah Daniels b. 16 July 1974
        (Adopted)
    1041. Stephen Paul Daniels b. 9 Nov 1975 d.
        9 Nov 1975
    1042. Michael Paul Daniels 13 July 1977
    1043. Amelia Elizabeth Daniels b. 17 Jul
        1981

750. Tipton Joaquin Daniels b. 21 Sep 1947. He married and had two children but was later divorced. He was living in Portland, Ore in 1994 where he was attending school.

    1044. Heather Daniels
    1045. Scott Daniels

753. Dee Ann Daniels b. 25 Sep 1948 at El Paso, El Paso County, Texas. She m. a man named Eastes before 1976 and was living in Logansport, In in 1994. They had no children.

757. Carole Lynne Daniels b. 28 Sep 1944 at Douglas, Cochise County, Az. She m. Dr. Paul Thomas Davis. Their two oldest children are pursuing medical degrees. They had:

    1046. Grace Pauline Davis b. 19 Jan 1971
    1047. Paul Thomas Davis Jr. b. 8 Sep 1973
    1048. Katherine Davis b. 1 Jun 1983

758. John William Daniels b. 9 Sep 1956 at Sumpter, Sumpter County, SC on Shaw AFB. He m. Rebecca Mechefski bef 1988. John works as a contractor and supervises construction in California in 1994. John and Rebecca had:

    1049. Morgan Daniels b. 17 Feb 1988

764. Judith Ann Daniels b. 14 Sep 1940 at Detroit, Wayne County, Mi. She m. Philip David McGaw 13 Mar 1963 at Allen Park, Wayne County, Mi. He b. 16 Sep 1939 in Detroit, the son of James and Cora Baker McGaw. Judy is a member of the Lutheran church. Judy and Philip had:

    1050. Jill Lynn McGaw b. 11 Dec 1963
    1051. Jodi Ann McGaw b. 11 Dec 1965

765. Thomas Lyle Daniels b. 3 Jan 1946 at Detroit, Wayne County, Mi. He m. Veronica Luran 31 Aug 1978 at Subic Bay, the Philippines. She was b. 19 Oct 1952 at Cebu Island, the Philippines, the daughter of Ramone Luran.

Thomas served twenty years in the U.S. Navy and
now works in the refrigeration and air
conditioning industry. He is a member of the
Lutheran church and Veronica, the Catholic
church. Thomas and Veronica had:

1052. Michelle Lynn Daniels b. 1 Oct 1982
1053. Rochelle Tiffany Daniels b. 3 Aug
      1984

766. Richard Dennis Daniels b. 1 Nov 1953 at
Dearborn, Wayne County, Mi. He m. Sompit Sakor
10 Sep 1983 at Allen Park, Wayne County, Mi.
She was b. 29 May 1947 in Thailand, the
daughter of Husian Sakor. Rick is a member of
the Lutheran church and Sompit, the Buddhist
church. Rick served in the U.S. Navy and now
works as a computer programmer. Rick and Sompit
had:

1054. Sarah S. Daniels b. 18 Sep 1990

768. Carol Ann Daniels b. 24 Sep 1942 at
Devil's Lake, ND. She m. Bernard Alban Deplazes
19 Aug 1963 at Devil's Lake. He is the son of
Bernard A. and Violet Verke Deplazes. They are
members of the Catholic church. She works as a
cook and he as an automobile dealer. Carol and
Bernie had:

1055. Troy Alan Deplazes b. 16 Apr 1964
1056. Jacqueline Deplazes b. 27 Jun 1965
1057. Janet Lee Deplazes b. 8 Jul 1966

769. Edward Francis Daniels b. 10 Oct 1945 at
Devil's Lake, Ramsey County, ND. He m. Beverly
Dockter. He works as a tax assessor. Eddie and
Beverly had:

1058. Christy Daniels*
1059. Lisa Daniels*

770. Donald Mickeal Daniels b. 12 Mar 1947 at
Devils' Lake, Ramsey County, ND. He m. Colleen
Engelhart 23 Oct 1969 and they live in Devil's
Lake in 1994. She b. 27 Jul 1950 at Devil's

Lake the daughter of Lawrence and Cecelia Meier
Engelhart. He works as a farmer and a CPA. They
are members of the Catholic church. He is a
U.S. Army veteran. Don and Colleen had:

    1060. Michele Daniels* b. 15 Jun 1971
    1061. Jamie Daniels b. 22 Ded 1974
    1062. Jody Daniels b. 19 Nov 1980
    1063. Sarah Daniels b. 15 Oct 1982

771. Michael Leroy Daniels b. 31 July 1950 at
Devil's Lake, Ramsey County, ND. He first m.
Paula Louise Stephens 9 May 1970. She b. 1 Oct
1951 at Devil's Lake the daughter of James
William and Laura Eng Stephens. He next m.
Marlene Bonita Bale. She b. 11 Feb 1949 at
Rigby, Pierce County, ND the daughter of Bennie
George and Martha C. Mork Bale. Michael works
for UPS, Paula works as a bookkeeper and
Marlene as an accountant. Michael and Paula
had:

    1064. Laurie Daniels b. 15 Mar 1971
    1065. Jennifer Daniels b. 20 Jan 1974
    1066. Steven Daniels b. 25 Aug 1979

772. Patrick Allen Daniels b. 27 Nov 1954 at
Devil's Lake, Ramsey County, ND. He married
Lory Jo Deseth bef 1981. Patrick and Lory had:

    1067. Jenny Daniels b. 16 Jul 1981
    1068. Craig Daniels b. 15 Aug 1986

773. Amy Louise Daniels b. 25 Oct 1958 at
Devil's Lake, Ramsey County, ND. She lives at
Priest River, Idaho where she works as a
painter and wood finisher. She was not married
in 1994.

795. Lisa Kayanna Daniels b. 15 Mar 1961 at
Lakeland, Polk County, Fl. She m. Charles
Timothy Hitchcock 28 Dec 1985 at Almo, Murray
County, Ky. He is the son of Neil and Anna Jean
Hitchcock. Lisa is a certified Emergency
Medical Technician and registered Phlebotomist.
She works as a medical assistant for an

Obstetrician/Gynecologist. They were residing in Cedar Lake, In in 1994. Lisa and Charles had:

1069. Kaylyn Noell Hitchcock b. 3 Dec 1991

796. Londa Jo Daniels b. 19 Dec 1967 at Gary, Lake County, In. She m. Benny Harrell bef 1987. They were living in Murray, Ky in 1987. They had:

1070. Shasta Nicole Harrell b. bef 1987
1071. Jennifer Marie Harrell b. bef 1987

797. Verl Scott Daniels b. 14 Jun 1973 at Gary, Lake County, In. He was living in Almo, Ky in 1994 where he is a construction worker. He is not married at this time.

798. Beneda Kay Daniels b. 29 Oct 1963 at Valparaiso, Porter County, In. She m. Jeff Eddington. They live near Tucson, Az in 1994. Beneda and Jeff had:

1072. Brenda Eddington b. 24 Sep 1982
1073. Tammy Eddington b. 22 Sep 1986
1074. Christopher Eddington b. 31 Mar 1989

799. Annette Michele Daniels b. 2 Sep 1965 at DeMotte, Jasper County, In. She m. Carl Shultz. They had:

1075. Joyce Shultz b. 22 Jul 1984
1076. Billy Shultz b. 30 Aug 1986
1077. Johnny Shultz b. 3 Sep 1990
1078. Dutch Shultz b. 18 Jan 1992

800. Tao Lyn Daniels b. 5 Mar 1977. She m. Joel Winenke. They did not have children in 1994.

809. Linda Lee Daniels b. 10 May 1941 at Devil's Lake, Ramsey County, ND. She m. Joel Dennis Babic 6 Oct 1962. He b. 29 Nov 1939 at St. Paul, Mn the son of Joe and Evelyn Waldo Babic. Linda and Joel had:

1079. Bonita Lynn Babic b. 22 Feb 1966
1080. Brian Joel Babic b. 22 Oct 1973

810. Dean Gordon Daniels b. 3 Aug 1946 at Devil's Lake, Ramsey County, ND. He was unmarried and living in Issaquah, Wa in 1994.

811. Steven Craig Daniels b. 28 May 1952 at Jamestown, Stutsman County, N.D. He m. Margaret Mary Wiegand bef 1979. She b. 27 May 1959 in Indianapolis, In, the daughter of Jack Richard and Janice Margaret Schopper Wiegand. Steven is a career Air Force officer, a Lieutenant Colonel in 1994. He is currently stationed at the Pentagon. He has also earned two master's degrees and a Ph.D. Margaret is a seamstress, carrying on a five generation tradition in her family. Steven and Margaret had:

1081. Stephanie Kay Daniels b. 5 Jul 1979
1082. Steven Adam Daniels b. 19 Sep 1982

812. Angela Mary Daniels b. 6 Oct 1953 in N.D. She m. Steven Weithman and they live in Columbia, Mo in 1994. Steve and Angie had:

1083. Michael Weithman
1084. Scott Weithman

813. Christine Jane Daniels b. 24 Jun 1956 at Warrensburg, Johnson County, Mo. She m. Kevin Leavy 26 Apr 1986. They own a wholesale meat distribution business and reside in San Diego, Ca in 1994. Christine and Kevin had:

1085. Jonathan Daniel Leavy b. 16 Oct 1987
1086. Sue Ann Leavy b. 6 Jun 1989

815. John Richard Daniels b. 1945. He m. first Judith Maple. They were divorced and he next married[372] Charlotte Cooper 2 Jun 1971. They were later divorced. John and Judith had:

---

372. Indiana, Jasper County, Marriage Book 29, page 479.

1087. Frank Daniels b. bef 1971

John and Charlotte Cooper had:

1088. John Richard Daniels Jr.* b. 22 Apr
1971
1089. Melissa Sue Daniels* b. 25 Dec 1974
1090. Christopher Allen Daniels b. 1978

816. Karen Sue Daniels born[373] 3 Nov 1946 in
Jasper County, Indiana. She married[374] first
Curley Conley 10 Sep 1966. They were divorced
and she next m. David Galbreath. They were
later divorced. Karen and Curley had:

1091. Billy Ray Conley b. 1967
1092. Bobby Edward Conley b. 1969
1093. Kathy Marie Conley b. 1968
1094. Bonnie Jean Conley b. 1972

817. Margaret Yvonne Daniels born[375] 11 Apr
1948 in Jasper County, In. She married[376] Rex
Dale James 30 Nov 1968 in Jasper County, In. He
is a building contractor. They live in Jasper
County, Indiana in 1994. They had:

1095. Shannon Renee James b. 26 Dec 1970
1096. Tracy Allen James b. 16 Oct 1974

818. George William Daniels born[377] 31 May
1949 in Jasper County, Indiana. He married[378]
first Darinka Zivko Knezevic 3 Apr 1971. She b.
1952. They were divorced. George next

---

373. Indiana, Jasper County, Birth Book
CH-17, page 92.
374. Indiana, Jasper County, Marriage Book
28, page 166.
375. Indiana, Jasper County, Birth Book
CH-17, page 124.
376. Indiana, Jasper County, Marriage Book
28, page 577.
377. Indiana, Jasper County, Birth Book
CH-17, page 148.
378. Indiana, Jasper County, Marriage Book
29, page 448.

married[379] Theresa Jo Cooper 2 Jul 1977. She
was born in Jasper County 17 Dec 1958. George
and his family live in Jasper County, Indiana.
He works for a company in Rensselaer, Ind.
George and Theresa had:

1097. Bert Allan Daniels b. 16 Jun 1978
1098. Brad Allan Daniels b. 28 Jun 1980

819. Walter Lee Daniels born[380] 23 Jan 1951
in Jasper County, Indiana. He m. Linda Marie
Skoczen bef 1980. She b. 1949. They had:

1099. Courtney Lynn Daniels b. 29 May 1980
1100. Lindsay Erin Daniels b. 27 Jul 1982

820. Roger Allen Daniels born[381] 12 Feb 1953
in Jasper County, Indiana. He m. Catherine
Downs bef 1975. She b. 1956. He m. second Mary
Callahan. Roger and Catherine had:

1101. Tammy Denise Daniels b. 1975
1102. Roger Allen Daniels b. 1978
1103. Richard Michael Daniels b. 1982

833. John Daniels Jr. m. Sue Becker. They live
in Osh Kosh, Wi in 1994. They had:

1104. James Daniels b. 1989

834. Mary Irene Daniel b. 1946. She m. Calvin
Bikadi. They had:

1105. Cindy Bikadi

835. Donald Lee Daniels b. 1954. He m. Julie
Wilson. They had:

1106. Donald Daniels Jr.

---

379. Indiana, Jasper County, Marriage Book
32, page 34.
380. Indiana, Jasper County, Birth Book
CH-18, page 15.
381. Indiana, Jasper County, Birth Book
CH-18, page 39.

1107. Carrie Daniels

836. Lonne Leroy Daniels b. 1958 at Racine, Wi.
They have lived in Tacoma, Wa and Phoenix, Az.
He m. Paula Maureen Kirkland. She was b. 5 Feb
1963 at Duluth, Mn. They had:

 1108. Joshua Lee Daniel b. 22 Oct 1983
 1109. Brenna Kathleen Daniels b. 27 Feb
 1988

837. Virgil Ivan Daniels Jr. born[382] 5 Feb
1947 in Jasper County, Ind. The estate
record[383] of his mother in Jasper County
names him and his children. Virgil m. Dana
Marlene White 9 Feb 1971 at Bedford, In. She
was b. 19 Jan 1949 at Bedford. He served in the
U. S. Navy in the late 1960s and in the U. S.
Army in the early 1970s. He was a police
officer in Rensselaer and Medaryville, In and
relocated to Odon, Indiana before 1994. He and
his wife had:

 1110. Kristi Marlene Daniels b. 11 Aug 1973
 1111. Eric Lee Daniels b. 16 Feb 1979
 1112. Terry Joe Daniels b. 16 Feb 1979

839. Roy Edward Daniels b. 28 May 1947 at
Rensselaer, In d. 2 Jun 1992 of a bleeding
ulcer. He did not marry. He graduated from high
school in Hammond, In. He served two tours of
duty in Vietnam in the U. S. Air Force. He
later worked about 15 years for Jones &
Laughlin Steel. He is buried in Loveland, Co.

840. Donald Allen Daniels b. 27 Jan 1949 at
Rensselaer, In. Don served in the U. S. Army in
Vietnam and also in Germany. He m. twice. His
first wife was named Dawn. He next m. Virginia
"Ginger" Huggins in Jun 1983. She b. 25 May

---

382. Indiana, Jasper County, Birth Book
CH-17, page 98.
 383. Indiana, Jasper County, Will Records,
Will of Pauline Catherine Daniels, proved 16
Apr 1993.

1950. They were divorced in Sep 1989. He works
for a heating and air conditioning company and
lives in Portland, Or in 1994. Don and Ginger
had:

    1113. Donald Daniels b. 9 Jan 1983
    1114. Paxton Daniels b. 1 Jan 1984
    1115. Franklin Daniels b. 1 Jan 1984

841. William Russell Daniels b. 19 Jul 1950 at
Rensselaer, In. He graduated from high school
in Hammond, In. He had not married by 1994. He
served in the U. S. Army during the Vietnam War
and was stationed in Germany. He resides in
Loveland, Co in 1994 and works for Food
Products in Denver.

842. James Michael Daniels b. 20 Feb 1952 in
Dayton, Oh. He graduated from high school in
Hammond, In. He had not married by 1994. He
lives in Loveland, Co and works as an engineer
for Longmont Foods in Longmont, Co. He served
in the U. S. Army during the Vietnam War and
was stationed in Germany.

843. Gerald Wayne Daniels b. 30 Jan 1953 at
Dayton, Oh. He graduated from high school in
Hammond, In. He had not married by 1994.
Because of a heart condition he was unable to
serve in the armed forces. He lives in
Loveland, Co where he works as a free lance
mechanic and autobody specialist.

844. Evelyn Kay Daniels b. 7 Dec 1956 at Gary,
In. She attended high school in Hammond, In and
later earned a G.E.D. She m. Steven Baker and
lives in Loveland, Co. She is employed by
MacDonald's Restaurants there. Evelyn and Steve
had:

    1116. Ida Kay Baker b. 5 Aug 1975
    1117. Dwight Steven Baker b. 21 Apr 1978

855. Dale Marvin Daniels b. 9 Feb 1965 at Gary,
Lake County, In. He m. Angela Suzanne Baughman
1 Mar 1986 at Ft. Wayne, In. She b. 10 Jun

303

1966. He graduated with an associate degree in Electrical Engineering Technology from ITT at Ft. Wayne, In. He works as a commercial electrician. Dale is also a volunteer fireman in Fremont, In and has Hazardous Material and First Responder Certificates. Dale and Angela had:

   1118. Randal Dale Daniels b. 31 Jul 1986
   1119. Kenneth Wayne Daniels b. 13 Dec 1987
   1120. Matthew Craig Daniels b. 21 Jun 1991
   1121. Rachel Suzanne Daniels b. 13 Jan 1993

856. Wayne Edward Daniels b. 18 Jan 1967 at Gary, Lake County, In. He m. Rae Ann Baldovin 9 May 1987. She b. 22 Jul 1967. They were divorced in Jan 1994. He works as a mechanic for a General Motors auto dealership near DeMotte, In. Wayne is a Keener Township volunteer fireman.

857. Steven Edgar Daniels b. 8 Aug 1974 at Hobart, In. He is unmarried in 1994 and works as an auto detailer for Snyder Auto in DeMotte, In.

876. Kenneth Eugene Daniels b. 31 Mar 1953 at Gary, Lake County, In. Information from his father lists no marriage for him.

877. Dale Allen Daniels b. 16 Jun 1955 at Gary, Lake County, Indiana. He m. Cindy Doppler 26 Jul 1974. They had:

   1122. Sheri Lynne Daniels b. aft 1974
   1123. Dale Allen Daniels Jr. b. aft 1974
   1124. Jamison Daniels b. aft 1974

878. Vernon Edward Daniels b. 8 Nov 1956 at Gary, Lake County, In. Information from his father lists no marriage for him.

879. Richard Alvin Daniels b. 10 Aug 1958 at Gary, Lake County, Indiana. He m. Diane Theresa Wojcik 14 Nov 1987 in Indiana. They had:

1125. Melanie Theresa Daniels b. 13 Jul
1988

880. Charles Thomas "Charlie" Daniels b. 22 Oct
1948 at Gary, In. He m. Joyce Elizabeth Crizer
19 Aug 1967 at Hobart, In. She b. 22 Jan 1948
at Gary, In, daughter of Daucy Clarke and
Vivian Victoria Swanson Crizer. Charlie and
Joyce were living in Berrien Springs, Michigan
in 1994. Charlie and Joyce adopted:

1126. Jill Daniels b. 31 May 1972
1127. Stacey Daniels b. 22 Jun 1975

881. Rodney Lynn Daniels b. 4 Dec 1954 in
Indiana and d. 27 Jun 1972 near Valparaiso,
Porter County, In. He drowned while swimming in
a lake when he was 17 years old. A family
member sent me a copy of his obituary from an
Indiana newspaper:

Rites set for victim of drowning

VALPARAISO - Funeral services will be held
Saturday for Rodney L. Daniels, a 17-year-old
Portage youth who drowned Tuesday in
Valparaiso's Long Lake.
The youth's body was found Wednesday
morning by state police scuba divers from the
Dunes post in 30 feet of water approximately
100 feet from the shore, police said.
Daniels's companions said he sank while
swimming from a boat rented from a nearby motel
shortly before 4 p.m. Tuesday.
The Portage boy is survived by his mother
and stepfather, Ruth and Tom Fauver, 3027
Beverly St., Portage; his father Linden
Daniels, of Glendale, Calif., and a sister
Cheryl, at home.
Services are set for Saturday at East Gary
Church of the Nazarene. Burial is at Graceland
Cemetery, Valparaiso. Friends may call after 3
p.m. Thursday at Geisen Funeral Home, Glen
Park.

882. Judith Marie Daniels b. 11 Feb 1943 at West Liberty, Logan County, Oh. She m. Calvin Schmucker Brenneman 10 Aug 1963 at Oneida, Tenn. He b. 27 Jul 1943 at Lima, Allen County, Oh the son of Ralph and Caroline Schmucker Brenneman. Judith is a Registered Nurse and Ralph works as a General Agent. They are both members of the Missionary Church. Judith and Calvin had:

    1128. Maury Calvin Brenneman b. 19 Jul 1964
    1129. C. Monte Brenneman b. 19 Jun 1966
    1130. Marcy Gail Brenneman b. 20 Jan 1969

883. Jay Dwight Daniels b. 6 Aug 1946 at Dennison, Iowa. He m. Joyce Kaylene Troyer 12 Jul 1970 at Elida, Allen County, Oh. Joyce was b. 24 Mar 1947 at Lima, Oh, the daughter of Robert E. and Mary Louise McCleary Troyer. Jay is a carpenter and Joyce an occupational therapist. They are both members of the Mennonite church. Jay and Joyce had:

    1131. David Jay Daniels b. 19 Jun 1974
    1132. Nathan Dwight Daniels b. 19 Jun 1974
    1133. Mark Robert Daniels b. 15 Jul 1977
    1134. Deborah Joyce Daniels b. 15 Nov 1979

885. Bonnie May Daniels b. 31 Mar 1950 at Lima, Allen County, Oh. She m. William Dean Harlow 7 Mar 1982 at Staunton, Augusta County, Va. William b. 11 Apr 1953 at Staunton, Va, the son of William Andrew and Maxine Harlow. Bonnie is a Social Worker and William works in the Mental Health profession. Bonnie is a member of the Mennonite church and William the Methodist church. Bonnie and William had:

    1135. Heather Nicole Harlow b. 26 Jul 1987
    1136. Zachary Scott Harlow b. 8 Nov 1988

886. Jean Anne Daniels b. 4 Jan 1953 at Lima, Allen County, Oh. She m. Ronald P. Wallerstein 22 Oct 1983. They were divorced 27 Mar 1991. They did not have children. Jean works as a Banker.

890. Linda Ann Daniel b. 15 Sep 1953, at Columbus, Bartholomew County, In. She m. Dr. Phillip C. Johnson. The reside in Houston, Tx in 1994. Linda and Phillip had:

    1137. Kara Ann Johnson b. 4 Jan 1983
    1138. Andrew Phillip Johnson b. 13 May 1985
    1139. Patrick Carl Johnson b. 21 Mar 1988

891. Karin Leigh Daniel b. 14 Dec 1954, at Columbus, Bartholomew County, Oh. She m. Lynn Frye. They reside in Ft. Wayne, In in 1994. Karin and Lynn had:

    1140. Kristin Ann Frye b. 11 Nov 1980
    1141. Derek Westin Frye b. 10 Jul 1983
    1142. Nicholas Kenyon Frye b. 24 Jun 1986

892. Susan Lynn Daniel b. 18 May 1957, at Columbus, Bartholomew County, In. She m. William Schmeissing, an Alliance minister. They reside in Orlando, Fl in 1994. Susan and William had:

    1143. Scott William Schmeissing b. 7 Jun 1984
    1144. Mark David Schmeissing b. 30 Jul 1987
    1145. Jeremy Paul Schmeissing b. 19 Apr 1989

893. Martha Ann Daniel b. 2 May 1961, at Columbus, Bartholomew County, In. She m. Trip De Maree. They reside in Scottsdale, Az in 1994. Martha and Trip had:

    1146. Jack De Maree b. 30 Jul 1987
    1147. Adam De Maree b. 25 May 1990
    1148. Samuel De Maree b. 10 Dec 1991

894. William Kenyon Daniel II b. 24 Dec 1994 at Columbus, Bartholomew County, In. He m. Robin Wieland. They live in Knoxville, Tn where William works for Arvin Industries, as his

grandfather did for nearly fifty years. William and Robin had:

1149. Ann Mohr Daniel b. 14 Mar 1990
1150. William Kenyon Daniel III b. 25 Feb 1992

916. Michael Lee Daniel b. 6 Dec 1949 at Garden City, Finney County, Ks. He served in the U.S. Navy from 1969 to 1973 and was stationed in San Diego and on the USS Ticonderoga. He attended Kearney State College. Michael operated his own electrical business for several years and later became an outside salesman for an electrical company. He is unmarried and lives in Lincoln, Ne in 1994.

917. Linda Kay Daniel b. 21 Apr 1951 at Garden City, Finney County, Ks. She m. Richard Claybaugh 18 Aug 1973 in Nelson, Nuckolls County, Ne. Richard is a pharmacist and they own and operate a drugstore in Beatrice, Ne. Linda and Richard had:

1151. Nathan Daniel Claybaugh b. 11 Oct 1977
1152. Tyler Lavern Claybaugh b. 19 Apr 1982

918. Randal Eugene Daniel b. 10 Dec 1953 at Pratt, Pratt County, Ks. He m. Bernice Leise 15 Nov 1986. He served in the U.S. Army from 1973 to 1976. Randal is a tool and die machinist and Bernice operates a day care business. They live in Ceresco, Ne in 1994. Randal and Bernice had:

1153. Chad Michael Daniel b. 8 Nov 1987
1154. Kristin Nicole Daniel b. 24 Jul 1992

919. Evelyn Marie Daniel b. 23 Oct 1955 at Pratt, Pratt County, Ks. Evelyn m. Harold Powell in Nov 1971 in Nelson, Nuckolls County, Ne. They were divorced and she next m. Lonnie Bell 25 Oct 1975 at Deshler, Thayer County, Ne. They were divorced in 1991 and Evelyn next m. Steve Corman in Aug 1994 at Lincoln, Lancaster

County, Ne. Evelyn works for Centerium in Lincoln in 1994.

Evelyn and Harold had:

1155. Travis Lynn Powell b. 9 May 1972 d. 29 Sep 1972

Evelyn and Lonnie had:

1156. Christopher Michael Bell b. 7 Aug 1976
1157. Lonna Gayle Bell b. 29 Mar 1980

920. Jana Lynn Daniel b. 14 Feb 1957 at Greensburg, Kiowa County, Ks. She m. Paul Miller 3 Sep 1976 at Lincoln, Lancaster County, Ne. They were divorced in Jul 1984. She works as an assembler for Transcript, a Lincoln electronics company. Jana and Paul had:

1158. Rebecca Lee Miller b. 5 Mar 1982
1159. Mathew Jenz Miller b. 20 Sep 1983

921. Diana Lee Daniel b. 2 Jan 1966 at Florence, Fremont County, Co. She m. Scott Glen Parnell 15 Apr 1992 at Penrose, Fremont County, Co. Diana works in security for BanTek and resides in Thornton, Co in 1994. Diana had:

1160. Marissa Lee Daniel b. 27 Oct 1985
1161. Brittney Anne Parnell b. 8 Dec 1987
1162. Chellby Nichole Parnell b. 27 May 1991

932. Carol Anne Daniel b. 31 Aug 1943 d. aft 1963. She m. a man named Puracci. I have only these few bits of information concerning her from a cousin who collected them some years ago. Dinah had:

1163. Dinah Marie Puracci b. bef 1963

935. Patricia Ann Daniel b. 21 Jan 1925. She m. first Charles Howard van Bronkhorst 30 Jan 1944 at Chico, Ca. She lived at Oxnard, Ca in 1994.

She was divorced and next m. Bruce Parks. They were divorced and she m. third Jerry Matay. Patricia and Charles had:

1164. Karen Marie van Bronkhorst 1947
1165. Karl Shelby van Bronkhorst b. 1950

936. Virginia Lee "Jinny" Daniel b. 12 Nov 1930. She m. Fred Erich Walther 27 Mar 1954. She next m. Carl Winik. Jinny was a school teacher and taught first grade until she retired in 1985. She was inducted into the Glenn County, Ca Educator's Hall of Fame in Jun 1993. Jinny and Fred had:

1166. Judith Lyn Walther b. 26 Jan 1956
1167. David Wayne Walther b. 9 Dec 1960
1168. Lelitia Rose Walther b. 8 Dec 1962

937. David Everett Daniel b. 27 Feb 1976 at Hollywood, Los Angeles County, Ca. He m. Claire Barbara Steinbaugh 20 Feb 1926 at Las Vegas, Nv. She b. 20 Feb 1926 at Los Angeles, Ca. They later divorced and he next m. Joyce bef 1964. David and Claire had:

1169. Kirk Morrison Daniel* b. 10 May 1948
1170. Cynthia Claire Daniel* b. 16 Jan 1950
1171. Carolyn Denise Daniel* b. 16 Apr 1954
1172. David Blair Daniel* b. 16 Sep 1957

David and Joyce had:

1173. Charles Owen Daniel b. 23 Apr 1964
1174. Steven Wayne Daniel b. 31 Jan 1967

945. Christopher Thompson Daniel b. 31 Aug 1966. He m. Kristen Scrivner Huntzinger 26 Mar 1994. They live in Camargo in Montgomery County, Ky in 1994. He assists his father with farming.

946. David Lee Daniel b. 10 Feb 1953 Montgomery County, Ky. He m. Ardith Rebecca Justice 31 Dec 1979. They had:

310

1175. David Lee Daniel Jr. b. aft 1979

947. Bruce Wayne Daniel b. 14 Oct 1956 in
Montgomery County, Ky. He m. Wilma Bernice Rice
5 May 1976. She b. 24 Aug 1957. They had:

1176. Nathan Wayne Daniel b. 5 Dec 1979
1177. Matthew Bruce Daniel b. 2 Aug 1983

948. William Richie Daniel b. 9 Aug 1959 in
Montgomery County, Ky. He m. first Virginia
Charlee Setters. He m. second Susan Louise
Mitchell. She b. 30 Apr 1959. William and
Virginia had:

1178. Charles Richie Daniel b. 30 Oct 1979
1179. Angela Nichole Daniel b. 6 Oct 1980

William and Susan had:

1180. Amber Dawn Daniel b. 3 Sep 1985

949. John Morton Daniel b. aft 1959 in
Montgomery County, Ky. He m. first Desiree
Smith 28 Jul 1981. He m. second Kathy Maggard
15 Apr 1985. John and Desiree had:

1181. Lashonda Daniel b. 18 Jul 1983
1182. Shelly Daniel b. 2 Jan 1985

John and Kathy had:

1183. Amy Maggard Daniel b. 12 Jun 1985
1184. Goldie Jean Daniel b. 15 Mar 1987

957. Brian Mark Daniel b. 9 Oct 1964 at Kansas
City, Mo. He m. Dyana Michelle Rose 6 Apr 1991
at Stanley, Ks. She b. 28 Feb 1967 at Carmel,
Ca. Brian and Dyana had:

1185. Austin Michael Daniel b. 29 May 1994

958. Aaron Dean Daniel b. 24 Feb 1967 at Kansas
City, Mo. He m. Michelle Lynne Burton 23 Nov
1991. She b. 28 Sep 1968 at Kansas City, Ks.
They had:

1186. Ariele Rhiane Daniel b. 13 May 1991

959. Andrea Leigh Daniel b. 4 Sep 1971 at Kansas City, Mo. She has supplied me with most of the information on her siblings. She lives in Kansas City, Ks in 1994.

968. Kimberly Ray-Jean "Kimmie" Daniel b. 18 Dec 1973 at Ft. Lewis, Wa. She m. Michael D'Antonio in July 1993 and they live in Kansas City, Mo in 1994. They expect their first child in January 1994.

969. Kandy Kaye Daniel b. 11 Nov 1975 at Kansas City, Mo. She lives in Woodburn, Or in 1994. Kandy had:

1187. George Kendall Daniel b. 16 Feb 1994

970. Cynthia Lee Daniel b. 24 Nov 1957 at Loma Linda, Ca. She m. Richard Troutwine 21 Jun 1983 at Wyoming, Il. They were divorced but she had issue from this marriage after the fact. She earned an Associate Degree in Computer Information Systems from Black Hawk Community College near Kewanee, Il. Cindy and Rich had:

1188. Erich James Daniel b. 27 Dec 1988

971. Jeffery Lee Daniel b. 3 Oct 1961 at Loma Linda, Ca. He m. first Arletta Mae Knowles abt 1981 at Kewanee, Henry County, Il. She b. 6 Jun 1965 in Illinois. They were divorced and he next m. Lori Peterson 24 Mar 1990 in Kewanee. She b. 18 Jun 1967 at Galesburg, Il the daughter of Mike and Kathy Kranz Peterson. He served in the U.S. Army Reserves. He and his brother operated an automotive repair business in Kewanee, Il for a time. He was employed as a welder for the Hyster Company in Kewanee in 1994. Jeffery and Arletta had:

1189. Monica Mae Daniel b. 2 Feb 1982

312

972. Jay Lee Daniel b. 30 Nov 1962 at Loma
Linda, Ca. He served in the U.S. Army Reserves.
He operated an automotive repair business with
his brother in Kewanee, Il. He resides in that
city in 1994 and is employed by the Hyster
Company there.

977. Angela Gay Daniel b. 19 Aug 1962 at
Hannibal, Mo. She m. Gregory John Skotniki at
Peoria, Il. They lived in West Peoria, Il.
Angela had:

 1190. Nathan Grey Daniel b. Sep 1994

983. Olga Jeanice Daniel b. 1 Aug 1923 at Mount
Carmel, Tyler County, Tx. She m. Winford
Anderson Barclay 1 Jun 1951. He was b. 26 Oct
1920 at Chester, Tyler County, Tx. She was also
m. to Philip Milford Roy but I do not know
which marriage was first. Jeanice and Winford
had:

 1191. William David Barclay b. 27 Jan 1942

984. Gerald David Daniel b. 10 Apr 1925 in
Jasper County, Tx d. 23 Aug 1979 in Port
Arthur, Jefferson County, Tx. He married[384]
Geraldine Yawn Oct 1950 in Jefferson County,
Tx. She b. 7 May 1929 in Fred, Tyler County,
Tx. They had:

 1192. Gary LaWayne Daniel* b. 28 Oct 1952
 1193. Dirk Allen Daniel* b. 10 Oct 1954
 1194. Paul Stephen Daniel* b. 1957

985. George Wesley "Dub" Daniels b. 25 Nov
1927. He married[385] Sallie Janice Hicks in
1952 in Jefferson County, Tx. They had:

 1195. George Wesley Daniels Jr. aft 1952
 1196. Debra Jeanice Daniels aft 1952

---

    384. Texas, Jefferson County, Marriage
Volume 72, page 587, #55180.
    385. Texas, Jefferson County, Marriage
Volume 80, page 496, #60209.

986. James LaWayne Daniel b. 14 Nov 1930 at Jasper, Jasper County, Tx. He m. Patilea Gilbreath 31 Oct 1953 at Amarillo, Potter County, Tx. She b. 1 Sep 1933 in Amarillo. She died 13 Aug 1984 at Keller, Tarrant County, Tx. They had:

    1197. Cynthia Renae Daniel* b. 19 Sep 1954
    1198. Mark David Daniel* b. 28 Oct 1955
    1199. Joe Bruce Daniel* b. 27 Oct 1958
    1200. James Paul Daniel* b. 7 Jan 1964

987. Robert Melvin Daniel b. 30 Nov 1938 at Kirbyville, Jasper County, Tx. He married[386] Eugenia Abel 15 Aug 1959 at Port Arthur, Jefferson County, Tx. She b. 19 Jun 1939 in Port Arthur. They had:

    1201. Dana Lee Daniel* b. 15 May 1960
    1202. Leslie Mae Daniel* b. 2 Dec 1962
    1203. Scott David Daniel* b. 28 Aug 1963

999. Rita Ozella Daniels b. 19 Aug 1912 in Louisiana d. 5 Jun 1990. She m. Rudolph David Pharis 27 Aug 1937 at De Soto Parish, La. He d. 14 Jul 1976. She was living in Montgomery, La at the time of her death. Rita and Rudolph are both buried in the New Friendship Cemetery in De Soto Parish. They had:

    1204. Beth Pharis b. aft 1937
    1205. David Pharis b. aft 1937

1000. Lilly Onell Daniels b. 7 Mar 1922 in Louisiana. She m. Mitchell Jefferson "Mickey" Ariola 13 Jan 1940. He b. 23 Jan 1920 d. 28 Mar 1985. He is buried in the Magnolia Cemetery in De Soto Parish, La. They had:

    1206. Brenda Joyce Ariola

---

386. Texas, Jefferson County, Marriage Volume 103, page 211, #74694.

314

1001. Huey Amos Daniels b. 6 Feb 1924 d. 12 Sep 1981 in De Soto Parish, La. He m Yvonne Ariola 16 Mar 1946. He is buried at the Mt. Olivet Cemetery, De Soto Parish, La. They had:

    1207. Huey Amos Daniels Jr.* b. 23 Aug 1946
    1208. Richard Conner Daniels* b. 12 Nov 1948
    1209. William Lewis Daniels* b. 1 Mar 1953
    1210. Bruce Alan Daniels* b. 10 Aug 1957
    1211. Brett Daniels* b. aft 1957

1016. Roy Ennis Daniels b. 8 Jan 1923 in De Soto Parish, La. He m. Maxine Phillips.

    1212. RESERVED

1017. Mildred Lucille Daniels b. 21 Aug 1924 in De Soto Parish, La. She m. Steve Mitchell.

    1213. RESERVED

1018. Doris Pauline "Polly" Daniels b. 28 Oct 1927 in De Soto Parish, La. She m. Ernest Norwood.

    1214. RESERVED

1019. John Lorin Daniels b. 13 Jun 1935 in De Soto Parish, La d. 2 Sep 1983. He m. Helen Sims.

    1215. RESERVED

1021. Jessie Edgar Daniels Jr. b. 7 Apr 1932 in De Soto Parish, La d. 30 Jan 1987. He is buried in the Mt. Olivet Cemetery, De Soto Parish, La. He m. Virgie Wells. She was b. at Centerville, Tx. He was a Baptist. They had:

    1216. Brenda Elaine Daniels b. Jan 1956
    1217. Sherry Lynette Daniels b. 14 Aug 1959
    1218. Darlene Daniels b. 24 Nov 1960

1022. Robert Forest Daniels b. 22 Feb 1934 in
De Soto Parish. La. He is a truckdriver. He m.
Betty Jean Pierce 24 Nov 1951 at Center, Shelby
County, Tx. She b. 4 Oct 1936 in De Soto
Parish. They are Baptists. They had:

    1219. Terry Dale Daniels* b. 23 May 1952
    1220. Catherine Diane Daniels* b. 31 Jul
        1954
    1221. Debbie Sue Daniels* b. 7 Nov 1955
    1222. Doris Irene Daniels* b. 4 Oct 1959
    1223. Robin Angela Daniels b. 5 July 1964
    1224. Robert Pierce Daniels b. 9 Sep 1967

1023. Sandra Marie Daniels b. aft 1952 in
Hardin County, Tx. She m. Jodie Crosby bef
1994. They had

    1225. Dannie Crosby
    1226. Jamie Crosby

1024. George Edward Daniel Jr. b. aft 1952 in
Hardin County, Tx. He m. Jane Marie Cherry bef
1991. They were living in Hardin County in
1994. They had:

    1227. Hannah Daniels b. 1991
    1228. Heather Daniels b. 1991

1029. Kathleen Lula Daniels b. 28 Feb 1947 at Santa Cruz, Ca. She m. David Royce Hollingsworth 15 Dec 1967 at Berkeley, Ca. He b. 3 Aug 1946 at Terre Haute, In. They were living in Sunnyvale, Ca in 1994. They had:

    1229. William Scott Hollingsworth b. 9 Mar 1971

    1230. Laura Melinda Hollingsworth b. 30 Nov 1973

    1231. Andrew Morgan Hollingsworth b. 10 Dec 1980

1031. Melody Ann Daniels b. 23 Oct 1954 in San Jose, Ca. She first m. William Lee Roth 23 Sep 1978 at Norwich, Ct. They were divorced in Jan 1984. Melody m. second William McGee Jr. 26 Sep 1990 at Warwick, RI. He was b. 1 Sep 1958 at Cranston, RI. They were living in Providence, RI in 1994 where she works as an Information Systems Manager. Melody had no children by either marriage.

1032. Glenn Calwell Daniels b. 16 Jul 1959 in Temple, Tx. He m. Veronica Ann "Vee" Van Egmond 6 Jun 1981 at Oskaloosa, Ia. She was born 2 Apr 1959 in Oskaloosa. They were living in Indianola, Ia in 1994. Glen and Vee had:

    1232. Kaleena Erin Daniels b. 19 Mar 1983
    1233. Kelsey Ann Daniels b. 9 Jan 1989

1033. Gary Earl Daniels b. 10 Nov 1960 in Santa Cruz, Ca. He m. Melissa K. Bailey 17 Jul 1982 at Lewiston, Id. She b. 12 Dec 1960 at Clarkston, Wa. They were living in Clarkston, Wa in 1994. Gary and Melissa had:

    1234. Alexander Martell Daniels 17 May 1983
    1235. Marcus Cain Daniels b. 12 Mar 1985
    1236. Bethany Nicole Daniels b. 25 Nov 1991

1058. Christy Daniels b. aft 1965. She m. Ed
Werner before 1994.

1059. Lisa Daniels b. aft 1965. She m. John
McCarthy before 1994.

1060. Michele Daniels b. 15 Jun 1971 at Devil's
Lake, Ramsey County, ND. She m. Allen Johnson
11 Jul 1992. They did not have children in
1994.

1088. John Richard Daniels Jr. born[387] 22 Apr
1971 in Jasper County, In. He m. bef 1989 and
had two children:

    1237. Zeb Andrew Daniels b. 1989
    1238. Aliza Jo Daniels b. 1990

1089. Melissa Sue Daniels born[388] 25 Dec 1974
in Jasper County, In. She m. Jason Edward
Steele bef 1992. He b. 1972. They had:

    1239. Coty Dean Steele b. 1992
    1240. Donya Ann Steele b. 1992

1169. Kirk Morrison Daniel b. 10 May 1948 at
Altadena, Los Angeles County, Ca. He m. first
Deborah Lynn Smithberg in Jun 1968. They were
divorced in 1974. He later m. Patricia Ann Burt
22 Jun 1979 at the Washington D.C. LDS Temple
in Montgomery County, Md. She was b. 3 July
1958 at Wurzburg, Germany. She is the daughter
of Clarence J. and Brunhilde Selma Krikowa
Burt. Kirk and Patricia are members of the
Church of Jesus Christ of Latter Day Saints and
reside in Huber Heights, Ohio in 1994. They
had:

    1241. Audra Jo Daniel b. 7 Apr 1980
    1242. Aaron Wesly Daniel b. 28 Dec 1981
    1243. Karl Allan Daniel b. 19 Jun 1984

---

    387. Indiana, Jasper County, Birth Book
HB-B1, page 86.
    388. Indiana, Jasper County, Birth Book
HB-B2, page 63.

1244. Kathleen Claire Daniel b. 22 Dec 1987

1170. Cynthia Claire Daniel b. 16 Jan 1950 at Pasadena, Ca. She was first m. to Richard King. She next m. Dale Davis at Laguna Beach, Orange County, Ca. Cynthia and Richard had:

    1245. Lisa Michelle King b. 3 Jan 1971
    1246. Chad Jerome King b. 3 Jan 1971

1171. Carolyn Denise Daniel b. 16 Apr 1954. She m. first a man named Brewer bef 1972. She next m. a man named Snyder. By her first husband she had:

    1247. Naomi Abra Brewer b. 11 Sep 1972

1172. David Blair Daniel b. 16 Sep 1957 at Pasadena, Ca. He m. Natalie Christy bef 1988. They had:

    1248. Megan Marie Daniel b. 14 Oct 1988

1192. Gary LaWayne Daniel b. 28 Oct 1952, probably in Jefferson County, Tx. He married[389] Rebecca Ruth Roberts in 1970 in Jefferson County, Tx. Gary and Rebecca had:

    1249. Christa Michele Daniel b. 7 Dec 1970
    1250. Andrew Paul Daniel b. 12 Jun 1977

1193. Dirk Allen Daniel b. 10 Oct 1954, probably in Jefferson County, Tx. He married but I do not know his wife's name. They were later divorced. Dirk had:

    1251. Cassie Daniel b. 31 Oct 1982
    1252. Michelle Daniel b. 13 Apr 1984

1194. Paul Stephen Daniel b. 1957, probably in Jefferson County, Tx. He m. first Rhonda. They were divorced and he next m. Shanna.

---

389. Texas, Jefferson County, Marriage Volume 147, page 259, #100612.

Paul and Rhonda had:

1253. Shannon David Daniel b. 22 May 1982

Paul and Shanna had:

1254. Mitchell Paul Daniel b. 23 Mar 1989

1197. Cynthia Renae Daniel b. 19 Sep 1954. She married Ky Wayne White 30 Mar 1975 in Bryan County, Oklahoma and in 1994 they were living in League City, Tx. Ky was born 26 Aug 1953 in Rising Star, Eastland County, Tx a son of Oscar McField and Selma Louise Whitehead White. Ky and Cindy are members of the Church of Jesus Christ of Latter Day Saints. They have sent me some of the information on this branch of the family. They had:

1255. Danielle Renae White b. 29 Sep 1975
1256. Amanda Kaye White b. 21 Mar 1977
1257. Robin Lea White b. 28 Nov 1978

1198. Mark David Daniel b. 28 Oct 1955 in Dumas, Moore County, Tx. He m. Donna Durfee 16 Sep 1978 at Virginia Beach, Princess Anne County, Va. She b. 18 Jul 1959. They had:

1258. Meredith Elaine Daniel b. 30 Apr 1982
1259. Robert David Daniel b. 26 Aug 1991

1199. Joe Bruce Daniel b. 27 Oct 1958 at Amarillo, Potter County, Tx. He m. Kathryn Parrish 21 Feb 1982 at Oklahoma City, Ok. They had:

1260. Carly Marie Daniel b. 30 Jul 1982
1261. Sean Thomas Daniel b. 23 Oct 1984
1262. Kathryn Nicole Daniel b. 25 Sep 1986

1200. James Paul Daniel b. 7 Jan 1964 at Amarillo, Potter County, Tx. He m. Vickie Lynn Grigar 4 Nov 1989 at Webster, Harris County, Tx. She was b. 23 Dec 1967 at Houston, Harris County, Tx. They had:

1263. Haley Ann Daniel b. 2 Dec 1993

1201. Dana Lee Daniel b. 15 May 1960. She m. Daniel Breaux.

1202. Leslie Mae Daniel b. 2 Dec 1962. She m. Don Charpentier.

1203. Scott David Daniel b. 28 Aug 1963. He m. a woman named Yvette.

1207. Huey Amos Daniels b. 23 Aug 1946 in Logansport, De Soto Parish, La. He is a U.S. Army veteran. He works for AT & T and is a Baptist. Huey was not married in 1994.

1208. Richard Conner Daniels Sr. b. 12 Nov 1948 in Converse, De Soto Parish, La. He first m. Carolyn Joyce Cotton bef 1971. They were divorced in 1973. He next m. Kayla Jane Parker. He m. third, Sheri Marie Still 18 Dec 1976. She was b. 19 Aug 1959 in Houston, Tx. They were divorced 16 Dec 1993. He is a U.S. Air Force veteran. He works for Louisiana Pacific Corporation and is a Baptist. He has lived in Joaquin, Tx and Logansport, La.

Richard and Carolyn had:

1264. Richard Conner Daniels Jr. b. 19 May 1971

Richard and Sheri had:

1265. Tracy Ann Daniels b. 19 May 1981

1209. William Lewis Daniels b. 1 Mar 1953 at Mansfield, De Soto Parish, La. He m. Patsy Fedila Farmer 28 Apr 1978 at Logansport, De Soto Parish, La. She was born 11 Sep 1952 in Carthage, Panola County, Tx, the daughter of R.H. and Lucille La Growe Farmer. He is employed as a roughneck. They are members of the Pentecost Church. Their children were born in Bossier City, Bossier County, La. They had:

1266. William Heath Daniels b. 1 Jun
1980
1267. Angela Nichole Daniels b. 17 Jan
1987

1210. Bruce Alan Daniels b. 10 Aug 1957 at
Mansfield, De Soto Parish, La. He first m.
Nancy Louise Gallaspy. He next m. Brenda Jo
Hawkins bef 1985. She was b. 4 Apr 1957 at
Bessemer, Al. He is an oilfield worker. Bruce
lived for a time at Albuquerque, NM. They had:

1268. Brian Alan Daniels b. 2 Dec 1985

1219. Terry Dale Daniels b. 23 May 1952 in De
Soto Parish, La. He m. Judy Lynn Bissell 9 Dec
1971 in De Soto Parish. She was born in De Soto
Parish.

1220. Catherine Diane Daniels b. 31 July 1954
in De Soto Parish, La. She m. Douglas Devon
Ammons 16 Jun 1974 in De Soto Parish.

1221. Debbie Sue Daniels b. 7 Nov 1955 in
Center, Shelby County, Tx. She m. William
Leonard Parker 14 Feb 1976 in De Soto Parish,
La. He was b. in Mansfield, De Soto Parish, La.

1222. Doris Rene Daniels b. 4 Oct 1959 in
Center, Shelby County, Tx. She m. Milton Kyle
Smith 15 May 1975 in De Soto Parish, La. They
were divorced in 1980.

Bethany Nicole 317
Betty 155, 236
Betty Ann 176, 248
Betty Jean 268
Betty Lou 248
Beulah Jean 171, 240
Beulah Mae 128, 213
Bill 235, 240
Billie Joy 235, 294
Bob 141
Bonnie May 270, 306
Brad Allan 301
Bradley Lee 118, 207
Brenda Elaine 315
Brenda Kaye 225, 280
Brenna Kathleen 302
Brett 315
Brian 242
Brian Alan 322
Brian Mark 279, 311
Bruce Alan 315, 322
Bruce Wayne 278, 311
Caldwell 58
Capitola 31
Capt. Estridge 14
Capt. William 14
Carl Wilburn 151,
  231
Carly Marie 320
Carna 18, 50
Carna Polk 52
Carney 50
Carol Ann 242, 296
Carol Anne 273, 309
Carole Lynne 240,
  295
Caroll Lorraine 219,
  220
Carolyn Denise 310,
  319
Carrie 302
Cary Elizabeth 211
Cassie 319
Catherine Ann 176,
  248

Catherine Diane 316,
  322
Cathleen 291
Cecil 136
Cecil Earl 136, 222
Cerilda Mae 264
Cerillda May 184
Chad Michael 308
Charles 49, 79, 83,
  107, 123, 133
Charles Andrew 123
Charles Duane 173,
  242
Charles Edwin 205,
  276
Charles Frederick
  222, 279
Charles Gilkey 121,
  211, 277
Charles Henry 67,
  157
Charles Owen 310
Charles Richie 311
Charles Thomas 269,
  305
Charles Wilburn 231,
  291
Charles Wilford 206,
  276
Charlie 136, 141,
  305
Chattie 84, 85
Chester Melvin 180,
  260
Christa Michele 319
Christine Jane 249,
  299
Christopher Allen
  300
Christopher Thompson
  277, 310
Christy 296, 318
Clara Emily 150
Clara Emma 67, 157
Clarence 289

Clarence Lawson 178, 250
Clifford Edmond 154, 235
Columbus Quincy 43, 119
Colwell 57, 69
Colwell T. 69
Colwell Travis 23, 58
Courtney Lynn 301
Covell 132
Covell Mark 219, 220, 278
Craig 297
Cynthia Ann 110, 200
Cynthia Claire 310, 319
Cynthia Lee 283, 312
Cynthia Renae 314, 320
D. Dwight 195, 269
Dale Alan 268
Dale Allen 304
Dale Gene 252
Dale Marvin 267, 303
Dan 192
Dana Lee 314, 321
Daniel Brother's Well Boring Company 57, 67
Daniel Cemetery 151
Darlene 315
David 242
David Blair 310, 319
David Everett 276, 310
David Jay 306
David Lee 277, 310, 311
Dean Edward 267
Dean Gordon 249, 299
DeAnne Lynn 271
Debbie Sue 316, 322
Deborah Joyce 306
Debra Jeanice 313

Dee Ann 237, 295
Dell Libbie 28, 87
Denise 242
Dennis Gerald 271
Diana Lee 272, 309
Dirk Allen 313, 319
Donald 301, 303
Donald Allen 263, 302
Donald Gary 271
Donald Lee 260, 301
Donald Mickeal 242, 296
Donnie A. 204, 273
Dora 84
Dora E. 39, 107
Dora Fern 86, 180
Doris Irene 155, 235, 316
Doris May 233, 293
Doris Pauline 290, 315
Doris Rene 322
Dorothy Lee 208, 277
Duane Wilbur 233, 293
Dub 287, 313
Earnest Jesse 66, 156
Eastridge 7, 8, 29, 92
Eastridge M. 52, 145
Ed 49, 130, 241
Edith 188, 268
Edith Pearl 70, 159
Edmond Mose 66, 154
Edna 82
Edna Pauline 175
Edsel E. 154
Edward 107
Edward Francis 242, 296
Edward William 172, 241
Edwin Clyde 224, 279
Elihu 8, 11, 22, 29

326

Margie Mae 187, 267
Margira 107
Marguerite May 121,
    210
Margueritte 37
Mariam 139
Mariam Boone 110,
    200
Mariam Boone Wright
    108, 131
Mariam Wright 136
Marilyn Joyce 186,
    266
Marion 54, 69
Marion E. 52
Marion Francis 23,
    68
Marissa Lee 309
Marjorie Ann 172,
    242
Marjorie Lea 199,
    271
Mark David 314, 320
Mark Robert 306
Marm 89
Marse 64
Martha 79, 83
Martha Ann 270, 307
Martha Jane 53, 73,
    147, 149
Marvin Dale 186, 267
Mary 51, 60, 84, 85,
    144, 146, 180
Mary (English) 79,
    83
Mary Adelia 37, 100
Mary Amanda 176, 248
Mary Ann 77, 162
Mary E. 146, 151
Mary E. E. 52
Mary Elizabeth 55,
    197, 270
Mary Ellen 26, 77,
    115, 204
Mary Florence 178,
    252

Mary Florine 121,
    209
Mary Fox 129
Mary Frances 110,
    201
Mary Grace 290
Mary Irene 260, 301
Mary Jameson 43, 121
Mary Jane 31, 90,
    97, 144, 228,
    229, 289
Mary L. 44, 124
Mary Lucretia 42,
    115
Mary Madeline 175,
    245
Mary Pergram 44
Mary Playter 99, 191
Matilda 54
Matthew Bruce 311
Matthew Craig 304
Maud 70, 158
Megan Marie 319
Melanie Theresa 305
Melissa Sue 300, 318
Mellie 162
Melody Ann 293, 317
Melvin Guy 77, 163
Melvin J. 186, 267
Meredith Elaine 320
Michael 280
Michael Lee 272, 308
Michael Leroy 242,
    297
Michael Paul 294
Michele 297, 318
Michelle 319
Michelle Lynn 296
Mildred Jane 178,
    254
Mildred Joan 187,
    267
Mildred Lucille 290,
    315
Milton 12, 36

331

Richard Alvin   269,
   304
Richard Conner   315,
   321
Richard Dennis   241,
   296
Richard Elmer   228,
   289
Richard Michael   301
Richie   121, 211
Richie Leo   211, 277
Rilla   86
Rita Ozella   289, 314
Robert   136, 290
Robert David   227,
   287, 320
Robert Emmet   228,
   290
Robert Forest   291,
   316
Robert Francis   39,
   106, 107
Robert L.   157
Robert Lee   199, 272
Robert Mark   278
Robert Melvin   288,
   314
Robert Monroe   144,
   228
Robert Pierce   316
Robert Quincy   50,
   140
Robin Angela   316
Robin Renee   271
Rochelle Tiffany   296
Rodney Lynn   269, 305
Rody   79
Roger Allen   252, 301
Rollo Wilson   103,
   191
Roy   77, 79, 81, 171
Roy E.   94, 189
Roy Edward   263, 302
Roy Ennis   290, 315
Roza   107
Rubie   82

Ruby   188, 268
Ruth   186, 227, 265
Ruth Ann   252
Sallie   120, 141,
   208, 229
Sallie May   229, 290
Sally   128
Samuel A.   228, 289
Sandra Louise   279
Sandra Marie   291,
   316
Sarah   5, 37, 51,
   120, 125, 142,
   208, 294, 297
Sarah Adaline   149
Sarah Adelaide   55
Sarah Alice   35, 37,
   99
Sarah Ann   23, 70
Sarah C.   52, 146
Sarah Eleanor Isabel
   49, 128
Sarah Elizabeth   150
Sarah S.   296
Scott   242, 295
Scott David   314, 321
Sean Thomas   320
Shannon David   320
Sharon Kay   271
Shelby   7, 8, 15, 16,
   24, 25, 32, 38,
   41, 44, 79, 83,
   203, 274
Shelly   311
Shelton   122
Sheri Lynne   304
Sherry   272
Sherry Jaye   271
Sherry Jean   226, 283
Sherry Lynette   315
Shirley J.   199, 272
Stacey   305
Stella Ann   93, 184
Stephanie Kay   299
Stephen Paul   293,
   294